Sahel Visions

Arizona Studies in Human Ecology

Sahel Visions

Planned Settlement and River Blindness Control in Burkina Faso

Della E. McMillan

THE UNIVERSITY OF ARIZONA PRESS

Tucson & London

The University of Arizona Press
Copyright © 1995
The Arizona Board of Regents

99 98 97 96 95   5 4 3 2 1

Library of Congress Cataloging-in-Publication Data
McMillan, Della E.
    Sahel visions : planned settlement and river blindness control in
Burkina Faso / Della E. McMillan.
        p.   cm.—(Arizona studies in human ecology)
    Includes bibliographical references (p.   ) and index.
    ISBN 0-8165-1487-9 (hb : acid-free, archival-quality paper)—
    ISBN 0-8165-1489-5 (pb : acid-free, archival-quality paper)
    1. Land settlement—Burkina Faso.   2. Rural development
projects—Burkina Faso.   3. Land use—Burkina Faso—Planning.
4. Autorité des aménagements des vallées des Volta.
5. Onchocerciasis Control Programme in the Volta River Basin
Area.   6. Mossi (African people)—Economic conditions.
I. Title. II. Series.
HD1018.Z63M33   1995
338.9′1′096625—dc20   94-21940
                                                           CIP

British Cataloguing-in-Publication Data
A catalogue record for this book is available from the British Library.
Publication of the paperbound edition of this book is made possible in
part by a grant from the United Nations Development Program.

This book is dedicated to the memory of
Abdoul-Kader Zampaligré, warehouse manager;
Michel Compaoré, bloc chief; and
Sommaila Sawadogo, sociologist.

All three men played a key role in reshaping the AVV vision
of development at V3 and in the other AVV villages
where they worked.

Contents

Contents

Photographs Following Page xxxi

A deserted village.

A village where onchocerciasis is now controlled.

A man blinded by onchocerciasis being led by a small boy.

The *tenga naba* of Damesma.

The household of Noaga Ouédraogo on the eve of moving.

Noaga Ouédraogo's family preparing for their departure.

The interior courtyard of an established household in the
    new village.

An example of ox-drawn animal traction.

The Muslim holy man, or marabout, Tassaré Ouédraogo.

Muslim settlers at the V3 mosque for a naming ceremony.

Boukary Ouédraogo in the stall of a used-bicycle merchant
    at Kaya.

Another man named Boukary Ouédraogo selling kola nuts.

Moustapha Ouédraogo with his new cloth display in
    Mogtedo.

Mariam Ouédraogo in front of her corral for goats and sheep.

Maps

Figures

xii

List of Figures

Tables

Foreword

In 1972 the United Nations Development Programme (UNDP) funded the feasibility study of an Onchocerciasis (river blindness) Control Programme (OCP) in West Africa. The visionary development leaders of OCP saw clear linkages between disease control, poverty alleviation, food production, and environmental protection of the vast areas affected by this dreaded disease. Operational activities commenced in 1974.

By the twentieth anniversary of OCP in 1994, the battle against river blindness had been won in the eleven participating countries thanks to the unwavering support of African governments, the Sponsoring Agencies (UNDP, the World Bank, WHO and FAO), and the donor community. Up to 25 million hectares of rich agricultural lands have been liberated from river blindness. Migration to some of these areas has been rapid, and the expanded utilization of agricultural lands is increasing production.

In 1988, UNDP funded the Land Settlement Review, which examined land settlement activities and developed policy recommendations to facilitate sustainable development practices in the OCP areas. This review provided the basis for an African Ministerial Meeting in 1994, which resulted in an agreement on a set of guiding principles for sustainable settlement to promote long-term social and economic gains from the "development dividend" of OCP.

Settlement is very much central to the UNDP's mission of forging sustainable development around human development concerns. From the UNDP perspective, the sustainable human development paradigm sees the overall success of a national economy as measured in terms of improved health conditions, employment creation, and access to productive assets. Sustainable human development is equally measured by its vision, by the regeneration of the environment for future generations, and by the empowerment of people to participate in the decisions that affect their lives. Sustainable human development is thus people centered and gender sensitive, environmentally sound and participatory.

The dynamics of settlement provide their own special challenges. Settlement, the link of people to land, the most important asset of the rural poor, lies at the heart of people's lives, involving potentially creative and disruptive tensions. Visions of progress may differ between settlers and development facilitators.

Sahel Visions provides a personal assessment of the land settlement experience in Burkina Faso over a period of fifteen years. It is an important contribution to the field of development anthropology in Africa. The UNDP is pleased to provide support to the publication of a paperback edition of this volume. While welcoming research that enhances an understanding of sustainable human development strategies, policies, and programs, the views of the author are entirely her own and do not necessarily reflect those of the UNDP or of the World Health Organization as Executing Agency of OCP.

New York,
New York

Ellen Johnson Sirleaf
UNDP Assistant Administrator
and Director, Regional Bureau
for Africa

Ouagadouguo,
Burkina Faso

Ebrahim Samba
Director, Onchocerciasis
Control Programme

Acknowledgments

I wish to thank a few of the people who influenced my thinking and without whom this study would never have been completed. The man who turned my initial intrigue with Burkina Faso into an interest in the AVV (Autorité des Aménagements des Vallées des Volta) and the much broader issue of development planning in areas covered by disease control is Professor Bill Morris of the Department of Agricultural Economics at Purdue University. It is largely because of his informed vision and the sound methodological advice of Dr. Josette Murphy, then country director of the West Africa Farming Systems Project in Burkina and now at the World Bank, that I did research in one of the traditional "home" villages as well as in the AVV project villages.

The distinctive imprint of Professor George Dalton is highly visible in every part of my early fieldwork and in the very way I think about development. Dalton's legacy has been obscured by his championing of the so-called substantivist side of the substantivist-formalist debate that divided economic anthropology in the 1960s. In the wake of this rancorous debate, some of the key and still vital insights of the substantivists were discounted by succeeding generations of development anthropologists. It is indeed ironic that the first groups to rediscover the utility of concepts like reciprocity and redistribution and the social context of economic systems in the early stages of market integration were economists, political scientists, and so-called Marxist anthropologists rather than development anthropologists. Dalton was at least twenty years ahead of his time in arguing that anthropologists should participate in multidisciplinary field research. He was also firmly committed to the concept that anthropologists specializing in development have a strong grounding in at least one related field (such as agricultural economics, soil science, animal science, public health, or nutrition). In the absence of such training, he caustically advised us to carry calling cards that read, "Have frame of reference, will travel." Dalton's emphasis on multidisciplinary training and team work was rare in most departments of social anthropology in the 1970s, when the "Lone Ranger" anthropologist setting off for exotic sunsets, taking along a portable typewriter, a bottle of gin, and lots of notepaper, was still lionized. Dalton also believed that one could not expect concrete, genuine social and economic change in periods of less than fifteen years.

Thayer Scudder, currently a codirector of the Institute for Development Anthropology and professor of anthropology at the California Institute for Technology, is the person who formalized the planning concept of resettlement stages. The genius of this simple four- or five-stage model is that it translates the complex anthropological concept of socially embedded economic systems described by Dalton and others into a meaningful policy tool. This particular tool helps explain why the painful experience of reconstituting community ties after resettlement influences how settlers respond to development policies. Scudder's model allows policy makers to anticipate the problems and opportunities that are likely to prevail at each stage of resettlement and community reconstitution. This is precisely the sort of theoretically informed policy model that anthropology needs. Good social theory should influence policy, and the evaluation of policy initiatives should provide the raw material for revising basic theory.

My field research was greatly enriched by the steadfast cooperation of the AVV. I am especially indebted to Emmanuel Nikiema, general director of the Office National d'Aménagement des Terroirs (ONAT), formerly the AVV, and Frédéric Guira, Arthur-Felix Yanogo, Benjamin Tabsoba, Michel Compaoré, Abdoul Kader Zampaligré, and Sommaila Sawadogo, who were also associated with the former AVV. In the Onchocerciasis Control Programme (OCP), I wish to express my deep appreciation to Dr. Ebrahim Samba, the general director, and Jean-Baptiste Zongo of the OCP Economic Unit, who freely shared their considerable knowledge, enthusiasm, and support. In the World Bank, I wish to thank Bruce Benton and John Elder, the coordinator and sociologist of the Oncho Unit, Scott Guggenheim, Michael Cernea, and Cynthia Cook; and in UNDP, Ben Gurman.

The 1983 and 1987 restudies could not have been completed without the generous support and friendship I received from various sympathetic staff at the United States Agency for International Development (USAID) in Ouagadougou—especially Bonaventure Traoré (from 1983 to 1987) and Al Smith (in 1983).

At different times, I benefited from the very able fieldwork assistance of Tinga Ouédraogo, who grew up at V3 and is now a student at the University of Ouagadougou, and Salifo Boena, an outstanding researcher with the Institut d'Etudes et des Recherches Agricoles (INERA) in Ouagadougou. Tinga and his comrade Lucien Ouédraogo, both sons of Damesma settlers living in the AVV, are (as far as I know) the first two children from Damesma to attend the university. This further attests to the success of the early AVV settlers and the long-term legacy of the AVV.

Kimseyinga Savadogo, associate professor of economics and dean for research at the School of Economics at the University of Ouagadougou, and David Brokensha, codirector of the Institute for Development Anthropology, were steadfast, reliable colleagues during the 1989 restudy. Jean-Baptiste Nana and Thayer Scudder helped me to look at the data in new ways. I want also to thank Anne Doizé, Christina Gladwin, Art Hansen, Martin Meltzer, Robert Netting, Mehir Saul, Thayer Scudder, Elliott Skinner, and Carol Lauriault for their detailed and careful comments on all or sections of the manuscript. I would like to thank the University of Arizona Press for its willingness to support this project through two rounds of outside review and two revisions. A special note of thanks is due to Virginia Croft, Alan Schroder, and Christine Szuter. Lonnie Harrison deserves credit for making my home a peaceful haven during the final editing and production.

I am forever indebted to my hosts, the Damesma naba and his family; his provincial chief, the Sanmatenga naba in Kaya; and Boukary Ouédraogo. All three men gave me invaluable guidance. Frédéric Guira of ONAT (formerly AVV) and Moustapha Ouédraogo have been my closest field comrades since 1977 and 1983, respectively, and the source of a great deal of the information that appears in this book. Credit for the visions concept in the title must go to Victoria Bernal, a fellow graduate student at Northwestern, who came up with the title when we shared a brisk walk through the hills of upstate New York at a reunion in 1988.

I wish to thank again my parents, who have encouraged me at every step. Neither my maternal grandfather nor my father ever shied from exposing me

Acknowledgments

to the raw side of poverty and prejudice or the role of public policy in at-tempting to reverse these trends in the rural and small-town Georgia, where I grew up. In their own way, my mother and maternal grandmother taught me the importance that a people attach to their noble vision of a vanquished past when the present is less than noble. These were valuable lessons that I had to learn once again in Burkina. Last, I want to thank my beloved hus-band, David Wilson, who has subsidized me, as well as this project, both financially and emotionally.

Introduction

This book describes the first attempt by a West African government to de-
velop a comprehensive land-use plan for its river basins covered by the
Onchocerciasis (meaning "river blindness") Control Programme (map 1).
The agency charged with the coordination of this plan was the Volta Valley
Authority (Autorité des Aménagements des Vallées des Volta), or AVV.
River blindness disease control was one of the great development visions to
emerge from the 1968–74 drought in West Africa. By controlling river
blindness, foreign donors felt they could create vast new settlement opportunities; the associated increase in food and cash crop production would
improve living standards, raise the gross national product, and reduce the
severity of future droughts. For Burkina Faso (then known as Upper Volta),
the program appeared to offer an unprecedented opportunity to resettle one-
tenth of the country's population on more productive land and at the same
time triple cotton production.

When I began this research in 1977 as a second-year graduate student,
my initial idea was to describe the impact of the AVV's planned settlements
on settlers from Burkina's densely settled Mossi plateau. I anticipated that
the study would describe the rationale behind the project's design, delineate
the project's goals, and discuss how and why the settlers' responded as they
did to the project's proposed policies. On the advice of Bill Morris and Josette Murphy of Purdue University, two of the senior researchers on the

grant that funded the initial research, I determined to compare farmers who had remained in one of the "traditional" home villages with settlers from this same village who had moved to an AVV project village.

My first one-week visit "up country" to the home villages was organized by the AVV Migration and Transfer Service. As part of this trip, the service director took me to two traditional villages with high rates of immigration to the project. One of these villages was Damesma, a village established sometime in the seventeenth or eighteenth century by Mossi immigrants spreading north out of their capital, Ouagadougou. Damesma is located outside the regional capital of Kaya (map 2). The following year I received two letters from the chief of Damesma. The chief, or *naba*, scion of a powerful old family, was quick to see the political advantage of receiving a foreign anthropologist. It was his hope that my work would direct foreign donor and national attention to the declining crop yields, low income, and impoverished soils that were causing his villagers to leave what had been a densely settled village. I succumbed to the naba's charm and chose Damesma and the settlers who immigrated from Damesma to the AVV as the focus of my dissertation research.

In May 1978, I returned to Damesma and, at the chief's urging, constructed a small house attached to his court. This arrangement made it blatantly obvious that I was his guest and therefore under his protection. I think the chief saw me as an overeducated, somewhat naive daughter. To his mind he was doing my father a great service. He was. It is a debt I still owe. Locked into daily morning tea with the chief, his seven wives, and a few others, I was ideally placed to observe the function of the chieftaincy persist despite new lands settlement and the emergence of a modern nation state. Almost daily the naba received delegations from different migrant communities and surrounding villages seeking or bringing brides to the village. From his position as village chief, as well as head of his chiefly clan, the naba was entitled to award many brides. He would also be asked to approve arranged marriages. The evenings were filled with discreet private, and occasionally public, hearings. Through this close linkage to the chief, I met several AVV settlers who were to become a part of the study before I ever moved to the project.

The chief's protection served me well when I moved to the AVV project village in 1979. He was a wise man who was well aware of the social and economic changes that were transforming his people at the project. Rather than choosing a member of his own extended family for me to live with, he selected the household of one of the three richest farmers, a family that historically had not been eligible for the chieftaincy and had never inter-

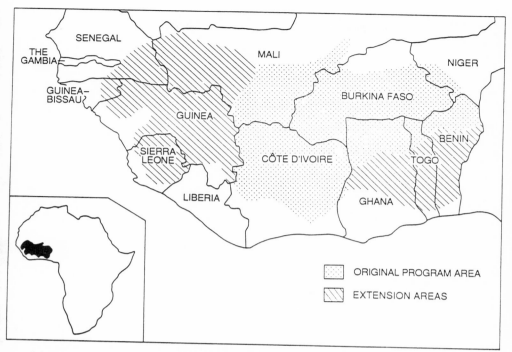

Map 1. The Onchocerciasis Control Programme. (McMillan, Painter, and Scudder 1990)

married with the chief's family. From their position of newfound wealth in the AVV, this family was now weaving a new, highly prestigious relationship with the chief. Once again I was the grateful, albeit unwitting, beneficiary of a turn of the social tables. The head of the family, Boukary, like the chief, took me under his aegis and, just as Alimata, one of the chief's daughters by his first wife, lived with me in Damesma from May 1978 to May 1979, so did Boukary's two fourteen-year-old daughters share my quarters in Village 3 in the AVV-sponsored settlements located outside Mogtedo (map 2). These people, along with my four research assistants and the elementary school teachers and extension agents posted to the villages, were the eyes through which I first saw the events described in this book.

In early April 1980, I returned to Purdue and Northwestern universities. In late June 1983, I finished the final editing of my dissertation, and the next morning I caught a flight to Burkina Faso, which was still known as Upper Volta. Because I was unwilling to face the chief and settlers alone and still unmarried, I asked one of my three younger brothers, Charles, to

Map 2. Case study research sites. (McMillan, Nana, and Savadogo 199?
appendix; reprinted courtesy of the World Bank Cartography Section
The boundaries, denominations, and any other information shown o

this map do not imply, on the part of the World Bank Group, any
judgment on the legal status of any territory, or any endorsement or
acceptance of such boundaries.)

Introduction

accompany me. By this time Boukary's family had grown, and there was no room for us in their compound at V3. We had the great fortune instead to have access to an extension worker house that had been equipped by a Peace Corps volunteer, William Gladstone.

Still allied to all of the families I had worked and lived with before—especially Boukary's—I designed a restudy of the settlers' evolving farming systems. By 1983 successful settlers like Boukary had so expanded their fields that I could no longer measure them with the simple compasses and steel tape measures I had used in 1978–79. My brother Charles, a professional civil engineer, designed a new field measurement technique that relied on a larger, more complex compass and a viewing device that could be focused on ten-foot wooden poles that we painted red and white. Because of the great distances involved, we were forced to communicate between the compass and the poles with hand signals. In 1983 many of the successful farmers—those investing in livestock and those farming much larger fields—were beginning to make plans to move at least part of their family to the regional trading center at Mogtedo to set up trading enterprises.

On August 4, 1983, Thomas Sankara took power in a military coup that stunned both the villagers and me. My single-minded commitment to the micro-level village study I was conducting had left me completely oblivious to the brewing political storm. We were kept informed of events in the capital by way of curt radio announcements that intermittently broke through the military music that had canceled out all other programming. I was immediately impressed by a new distance that suddenly separated me from the villagers. Neither they nor I knew what to expect; what we did know was that the radio messages were strongly anti-West. I soon sensed that under certain conditions, my presence in their village and the villagers' implicit obligations to me could become more of a liability than an asset to them.

Soon after, Upper Volta's name was changed to Burkina Faso. Following the 1983 coup, the United States Agency for International Development (USAID) was much less willing to fund research in what was characterized as a pro-Communist regime, and my main source of grant money disappeared. Finally, in 1987 I was able to secure two small grants from the Research Foundation of the University of Kentucky, where I was then teaching, and the National Institutes of Health (NIH). On May 17, 1987, I was married, much to the relief of the chief, the villagers, and the nuns with whom I stayed when I was in the capital city, Ouagadougou. Fearful of losing the grants, I returned to Burkina Faso in July—much to the chagrin of my parents, who feared that my bemused husband might disapprove. Using a borrowed moped, I was able to repeat my 1983 farming systems survey.

In 1987 the high levels of donor intervention that had characterized the early AVV were visibly winding down. Three extension agents now served the six-village group that in 1979 had access to twelve to fifteen agents. Many of the most prosperous farmers had abandoned the highly labor-intensive cash crop cotton, which had proven to be too risky and expensive in that particular agro-ecological zone. Instead, they were investing heavily in livestock and trade. By 1987 two Damesma farmers in the sample had acquired space in the Mogtedo market, and others planned to follow. I was also struck by the fact that, for the first time, there seemed to be someone in each family who could read and write. Although the future did not look as bright as in 1979 or in 1983, the settlers still had much higher living standards than their counterparts who remained behind in Damesma, and no one had gone home.

In May 1988, I took an unpaid leave from the University of Kentucky to write this book. I was deep into the project when I received a letter from Boukary's son, Moustapha, who had worked for many years as my research assistant. In his letter Moustapha informed me that he, along with almost half of the farm families who had been included in my baseline research and whom I had known for ten years, had left the AVV project. These families had not returned home to Damesma, nor had they moved to an adjacent nonproject site. Rather, they had moved 200 kilometers southeast to Kompienga, a new settlement that had developed next to the country's first hydroelectric dam on the Togo-Benin border (map 2). Moustapha believed this was an area where there were better opportunities to develop trade and agricultural enterprises.

My initial reaction to Moustapha's news was complete dismay. All of my tidy academic plans for returning year after year to study the continuing success of the AVV settlers and to monitor their changing economic and social patterns appeared to be gone. I was especially embarrassed that my earlier elaborate prediction that the settlers would continue their march toward ever higher levels of development now appeared to be wrong. In 1979 and 1983 the settlers' success appeared to offer a glimmer of hope for a country—and a continent—where development successes have been few and very far between. I was willing to excuse the project's failure to revolutionize the settlers' agricultural production. I was less willing to excuse the fact that I hadn't deduced their obvious, well-planned intention to move.

A later, more dispassionate analysis of the letter, grounded in my familiarity with the farmers over a ten-year period, indicated that the decisions leading toward departure were anything but random. It became increasingly clear that the final decision to leave—or remain—followed a pattern of community reconstitution and development that, if one were observant, was apparent as early as the settlers' fifth year. By and large, the successful settlers who left were the economically minded entrepreneurs, the risk takers. In contrast, the core group of V3 settlers from Damesma who continued living at the project remained heavily focused on agriculture and reinvestment in the immigration of additional members of their extended families. The settlers who left had moved not because the AVV had failed but because it had been a success. They had not moved out; they had moved on. The AVV had given them a financial start, a leg up, so to speak, and their immigration to Kompienga was a further step in their own personal economic development. In this instance, the settlers' view of "success" was markedly different from the success envisioned by the donors or by me.

In December 1988, I was able to return for a full one-year restudy of the V3 settlers. This research was funded as part of an eleven-country survey of settlement and development in the basins affected by river blindness control with funds from the United Nations Development Program (UNDP), executed by the World Bank through the Institute for Development Anthropology (IDA) (see McMillan, Nana, and Savadogo 1993; McMillan, Painter, and Scudder 1992). The funds accorded to this project gave me a unique opportunity to examine the hypotheses that had emerged from the earlier case study on a wider sample. Working with some of the village research assistants and AVV researchers I had worked with between 1977 and 1980, I conducted a revised version of the farming-systems survey I had used earlier. The new study included 20 households living at V3, some of which had been in my original survey, as well as 60 of the 120 households that had been included in the 1979 AVV Statistical Service Survey (see appendix A). This same restudy permitted me to conduct comparative research with the former AVV settlers living at Kompienga as well as at three non-AVV sites at Solenzo and Niangoloko and in the Classified Forest at Toumousseni (map 2).

This book describes the results of my fieldwork conducted at the AVV over the course of these four different time periods (1978–79, 1983, 1987, 1989–90). Because I conducted a longitudinal study and returned time and again to the same small sample of farmers, I was forced to examine the question of how development does or does not occur. I was also forced to reexamine, reevaluate, and revise my ideas or visions—as well as those held by others—of what development should be. Thus, a theme running throughout this book is the way development "visions" originate and are revised. Four distinct levels of development visions are related here: those of the foreign donors, those of the Burkinabè government, those of the settlers, and finally, those of researchers like myself. The latter "vision" is an important one for anthropologists to consider as we contemplate our future role in development research and planning.

Early planning for Burkina's AVV program was based on the most expert sociological, hydraulic, and geographical information of the time. The decision to fund river blindness control and, in conjunction, the AVV, was influenced by a vision that included specific assumptions and theories about the causes of rural underdevelopment in the West African Sahel. The design of both projects was influenced further by the funding priorities, political aspirations, and commercial interests of the foreign donors. These considerations gave planners the policy levers that they thought would best yield the desired economic, political, and environmental results. The final design of each project was indeed the "best-laid plan" of a group of international planners working within the political, financial, ideological, and theoretical context of their times.

The development theories and political exigencies that guided donor funding and national planning for the Sahel have changed dramatically in the two decades since 1973. The early (1974–81) top-down AVV planned-settlement model and agricultural program, which focused on intensive commercial cotton production, was designed under one set of planning theories and evaluated under yet another; this early model was found wanting and eventually set aside. Nonetheless, the residual effects of this older planning model—set in motion in 1974—are still evident in the 1990s. They are evident in the roads and bridges that were developed in a vast area of Burkina's relatively fertile, isolated river basins, and evident again in the design of an expensive array of new rural education and health programs. The same model left an indelible mark on the training and careers of one of the most highly trained generations of Burkina's agricultural extension service. All of these interventions continue to be important. The lives (and beliefs) of thousands of farmers, policy makers, and researchers were also changed. Such long-lasting project legacies cannot be easily dismissed.

For policy planners and researchers to dispose of one set of planning theories for another seemingly more appropriate set misses the point. There are important grains of truth in almost all of the development theories that have guided foreign aid and government investment in Africa since the Second World War. No single cause, or cure, is likely to be found for the immense problem of poverty and hunger in the West African Sahel. We are dealing with a situation that is exceedingly complex.

The brave families who voluntarily immigrated to the AVV went in pursuit of their own development visions. Like immigrants throughout the world, they aspired to a better life for themselves and their children. They were ambitious, hardworking, resilient, and most of all, courageous enough to gamble everything on the uncertainties of an uncleared, largely unknown, new land. Their visions changed as well. When the first settlers immigrated to the AVV in 1975, bringing along what they could carry, their immediate goal was simply to survive. After the difficult first year, they could begin to entertain a wider range of aspirations. Over the course of the years, certain settler households became highly successful—the first generation of what extension agents called *les millionnaires*. Others improved their living standards, but for a variety of reasons that included labor constraints, age, and that elusive something we call management skills, they did not excel. In either case, the goals of most settlers, after the initial adjustment period, were categorically different from what they had been when they first arrived. As will be shown, these goals did not always coincide with those envisioned by the project planners.

My own vision of what development is and should be has been dramatically affected by the fifteen years I've worked with the AVV settlers. When I began the research in 1977, I was convinced that the answer to economic development lay in the design of better crop and livestock technology and supporting programs. The key, I thought, was Farming Systems Research (FSR). Following contemporary models of FSR, I interpreted my role as an anthropologist to be to provide policy makers with a better understanding of the settlers' traditional farming systems and how these systems would be affected by the AVV's agricultural and social policies. These same naive visions blinded me to the political realities that burst to the surface in a series of military takeovers after 1980. Absolutely nothing I had studied or lived prepared me for the enormous psychological and policy changes set in motion by the new revolutionary government that took power in 1983.

With all these levels of rapidly changing and conflicting visions, it should not surprise us that the new struggling governments of the West African nations have not been able to bring forth economic miracles. Rural agriculturalists and pastoralists know this. They also know they cannot afford to bank too heavily on the visions of foreign donors and/or their governments for miracles to come.

Those of us who make a living exploring, constructing, and refining the development visions of the Third World can learn from the farmers' visions, as well as their perceptions of our visions. I believe that our ability to understand these issues can be aided by returning to an earlier time when social scientists like myself were less concerned with developing pat solutions to concrete problems than with understanding how the economic and social systems of Africa really worked. Some of the concepts and analytical tools we developed for this quest have real meaning for those seeking to understand the visions of local farmers and how they interact with state and foreign donor policies in situations like the AVV and OCP.

One of the key insights I hope to convey in this volume is a firm belief, based on concrete data and experience, in the tremendous resilience of the male and female agriculturalists and pastoralists in the OCP river basins in responding to the development visions and "revisions" set in motion by policy planners, scholars, and researchers like myself. These rural people will continue to respond to development planning in private, very rational, realistic ways that outsiders may not be able to predict. It is incumbent upon us to attempt to understand the reasoning behind their responses. They are not pliant software that we can reprogram at will. Why they respond in a particular manner is often very simple. In the OCP river basins, our goal should be to work with local people to enhance the environmental sustainability of the settlers' and hosts' own diversified, integrated local systems—rather than force them to adapt to our Western visions of what that sustainability should be. In doing so, we are much more likely to increase the economic rate of return of scarce development dollars, and the resulting systems are far more likely to be socially, environmentally, and economically sustainable in the long run. Most Western aid donors expect visible returns in a short three- to five-year funding cycle. For that reason, large quantities of money are funneled into a project in the very first years, not later when the beneficiaries are more likely to be able to make better use of it. In most cases, the same amount of money phased in over a much longer period of time would be better used. We must recognize that sustainable development requires not only funds but those immeasurable elements of patience, understanding, and time.

A village that has been deserted, presumably because of the high incidence of river blindness. The inhabitants of the most severely infected river basins followed a cyclical migration pattern, leaving the valleys in response to the disease, then returning when the poor inland soils could no longer support their numbers. (Reproduced with permission of the World Bank)

A village where onchocerciasis is now controlled. Large, productive communities can exist where onchocerciasis once prevented settlement. (Reproduced with permission of the World Bank)

A man blinded by onchocerciasis is led by a small boy who may already have the disease himself. This is an increasingly rare sight in the project area, but it is still very common in the parts of West Africa where the disease is not controlled. (Reproduced with permission of the World Bank)

The *tenga naba* of Damesma. The settlers who are the focus of the study emigrated from Damesma, a Mossi village. From the fifteenth to the late nineteenth century, the Mossi formed a loose confederation of tribal states in the sudano-sahelian belt of West Africa. After independence the village chief, or tenga naba, continued to be the people's most direct link with the new national government.

The household of Noaga Ouédraogo on the eve of moving to the project in 1979. Noaga Ouédraogo immigrated with his first and second wives, the two women on the far right. His nephew and younger brother remained at Damesma but "fused" their households.

Noaga Ouédraogo's family preparing for their departure.

The interior courtyard of an established household in the new village. Although the homes do not appear to be that different from those in the settlers' home area, village settlement and field structure follow a grid that is dramatically different.

In return for the use of a plot in an AVV planned settlement, a settler was required to sign a contract specifying that he would follow the project plan for intensive cultivation. After the first year, all settlers were required to adopt ox-drawn animal traction, like that shown here, and to plant a prescribed rotation of crops, including sorghum, cotton, and legumes.

The shift to a more independent transition community was signaled by the emergence of new village leaders like this Muslim holy man, or marabout, Tassaré Ouédraogo.

Muslim settlers gathered at the V3 mosque for the naming ceremony of a child. Conversion to Islam became an important mechanism for creating cross-cutting social ties between Damesma clans, and between the Damesma settlers and settlers from other zones.

Boukary Ouédraogo, a Kaya poultry merchant, in the stall of a used-bicycle merchant in the market at Kaya. Labor migrants to Côte d'Ivoire typically return after one or two years, carrying cash and owning a new bicycle or moped. After a long visit, the bicycles are usually sold to pay for the migrants' transportation back to Côte d'Ivoire.

Boukary Ouédraogo (not the man shown above) sells kola nuts in front of the V3 school, an example of the increased diversification into trade that resulted from the project. A prosperous kola trader at the AVV, Boukary now lives at Kompienga.

Many settlers, like Moustapha Ouédraogo, shown here with his new cloth display, attempted to expand into the more profitable regional market in Mogtedo. They were thwarted, however, by the indigenous peoples' animosity toward settlers.

A more successful long-term result of the project was increased investment in small livestock. Here, Mariam Ouédraogo, the project-trained V3 midwife, stands in front of the corral for part of her rapidly expanding herd of goats and sheep.

Sahel Visions

1

The Original Visions

Water is life, but in the sahelian and sudano-sahelian regions of West Africa, this scarce life-giving force is also host to some of the most debilitating diseases known to humanity. Malaria, schistosomiasis, human and bovine trypanosomiasis (sleeping sickness), and onchocerciasis (river blindness) are all endemic to the area and have an enormous economic impact.

In 1974, in an effort to at least partially address this problem, the World Health Organization launched a massive $56.2 million program as Phase One of an effort to control onchocerciasis in a seven-country area of West Africa (map 1). The decision to focus on river blindness was based largely upon foreign donors' visions of the control program's potential positive economic impact on the area. Early planners described onchocerciasis as "the most important single deterrent to human settlement and the subsequent economic development of many fertile valleys, which lie uninhabited and unproductive. This situation inhibits the development of the vast savannah belt of the Volta River Basin area, and countless thousands of families have left productive ancestral lands to crowd the adjacent areas where low-yielding poor soil predominates" (PAG 1973:1).

In 1974 nearly 700,000 square kilometers with a population of 10 million were affected by onchocerciasis in the original seven-country control zone (WHO 1980:1). Of this number, an estimated 1 million people were infected and 70,000 to 100,000 were either blind or suffering serious eye impair-

ments. The infected valleys included the majority of the area with good
potential for irrigation in the drought-ridden sudano-sahelian zone. It was
anticipated that the Onchocerciasis Control Programme, or OCP, would provide new settlement opportunities for impoverished farmers from the sahelian areas worst hit by the 1968–73 drought, and the associated increase in
rain-fed and irrigated crop production could begin to reduce trade imbalances and foster food security. In sum, what donors envisioned was a wide
range of "forward and backward development linkages" (Hirschman 1958)
resulting from a single health intervention.

Background

In Arabic the word *sahel* means "shore." The metaphor transforms the Sahara Desert into an ocean, and the caravans that pass through it into ships.
The large towns that border the northern Sahel symbolize ports of trade. As
a geographical referent, the term applies to a loosely defined "shore" of semi-
arid steppe and dry savanna (average rainfall 150 to 900 millimeters) that
lies between the Sahara Desert and the coastal forests of West Africa
(map 3). For centuries the Sahel marked the crossroads of the profitable
trans-Saharan trade routes that linked sub-Saharan Africa with Europe,
North Africa, and the Middle East. This same nexus of trade routes coincided with a band of precolonial states that stretched across the Sahel from
present-day northern Guinea to northern Nigeria (map 4). Not until the
early nineteenth century did the locus of economic activity begin to shift
from the Sahel to the coast. Despite this considerable shift, some of the old
kingdoms continued to exert considerable political power as a result of
their high population densities coupled with their linguistic and cultural
homogeneity.

Over the course of the twentieth century, the Sahel continued to recede
from the mainstream of the new world economic and political order. The
Sahel's extremely unfavorable physical location (800 to 1000 miles from
major seaports), resulting in enormously high transportation costs, made it
difficult to exploit its few commercially viable crops and minerals. Efforts to
develop cash crops like peanuts and cotton were hamstrung by the same high
transportation costs. As early as 1909, General Charles Mangin referred to
France's chief economic interest in its sahelian colonial areas as a *"reservoir
d'hommes"* (Davis 1934), a labor reservoir that the colonial governments
eagerly tapped as a source of foot soldiers and construction labor (Balesi
1979; Catrice 1931; Davis 1934; Delavignette 1970; Echenberg 1975;
Thompson and Adloff 1975). After independence this same labor reservoir

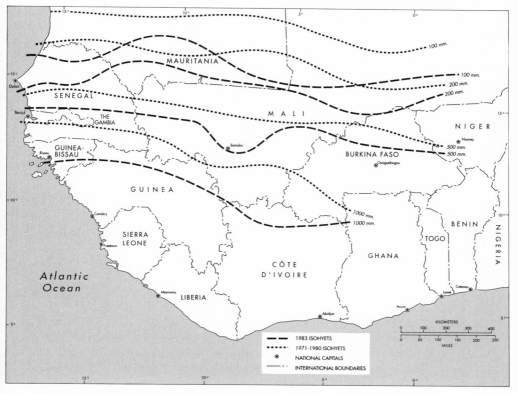

Map 3. Major agroclimatic zones of the Sahel (in average millimeters of rainfall). (McMillan, Painter, and Scudder 1992:9; reprinted courtesy of the
University of Indiana Press and the World Bank Cartography Section. The
boundaries, denominations, and any other information shown on this map
do not imply, on the part of the World Bank Group, any judgment on the
legal status of any territory, or any endorsement or acceptance of such
boundaries.)

became an important source of seasonal and short-term wage labor for the
more developed coastal countries (Amin 1974; Finnegan 1976, 1980; Gregory 1974a, 1974b; Skinner 1965) (map 5).

The name Sahel gained a more specific meaning in the mid-1970s as a
result of a new generation of donors anxious to assist the countries most
severely affected by the 1968–73 drought. All or parts of the nations of
Mauritania, Senegal, Gambia, Mali, Niger, Burkina Faso (then known as
Upper Volta), and Chad lay within the drought zone. Since independence,
at least five of these sahelian countries (Burkina Faso, Chad, Mali, Mauri-

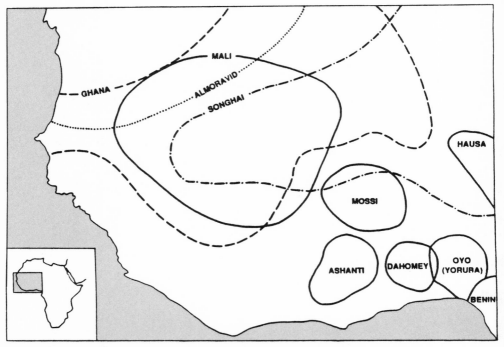

Map 4. Major African states throughout the nineteenth century. (Martin and O'Meara 1986:76; reprinted with permission of the University of Indiana Press)

tania, and Niger) had consistently been listed as among the poorest and least-developed countries in the world, measured in terms of almost all the leading indicators—literacy, school enrollment, energy consumption, life expectancy, and per-capita gross national product (Berg 1975). These same five countries also figured prominently on almost all of the mid-seventies' lists of chronically underdeveloped countries compiled by the World Bank, the United Nations, and the Rome Food Conference (Berg 1975).[1]

The drought years between 1968 and 1973 exacerbated the Sahel's already perilous economic equilibrium. Country after country reported a decrease in the total volume of rainfall (figure 1.1), irregular rainfall, and substantial variation in the total amount and spacing of rainfall between regions. At the height of the drought (1970–73), most countries showed a leveling off or a slight decline in food grain production and a much sharper decrease in the production of cash crops like cotton and rice (Berg 1975; Giri 1983). The same countries typically experienced a substantial increase

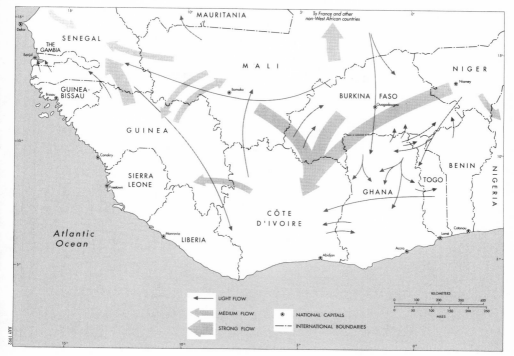

Map 5. International labor migration streams within West Africa in the mid-1970s. (LSR Site Reports and Case Studies; reprinted courtesy of the World Bank Cartography Section. The boundaries, denominations, and any other information shown on this map do not imply, on the part of the World Bank Group, any judgment on the legal status of any territory, or any endorsement or acceptance of such boundaries.)

in food imports—both in absolute terms and as a percentage of total imports. Especially alarming was an average 10 to 15 percent decrease in per-capita food production over the decade (Berg 1975; Christensen et al. 1981).

Droughts are a recurrent phenomenon in the sudano-sahelian and sahelian areas of West Africa (figure 1.1). Indeed, the 1968–73 drought was not distinguished in terms of its severity as a climatic phenomenon (Glantz 1976; Nicholson 1986), nor its toll in terms of famine and death (Berg 1975; Caldwell 1975). What distinguished this drought and the ensuing famine was its visibility in the international media. In the wake of that visibility came an unprecedented outflow of international relief and foreign development assistance (figure 1.2). This outflow could be measured both in terms

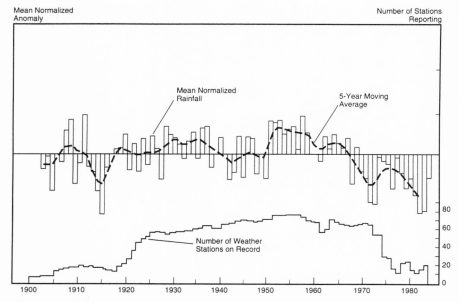

Figure 1.1. Mean normalized rainfall in selected weather stations in the West African Sahel. The ratio of annual minus long-term average rainfall to the long-term standard deviation in rainfall. Values for the mean normalized anomalies are seasonal May to October totals. (Jayne, Day, and Dregne 1989:5)

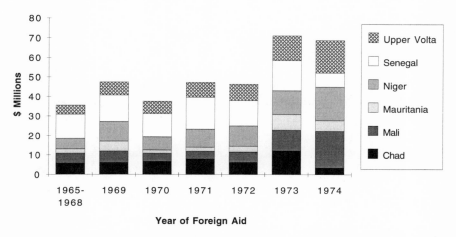

Figure 1.2. Net foreign aid disbursements to the Sahel, 1965–1974. (Berg 1975:65)

of dollar amounts expended and in the number of bilateral, multilateral, and nongovernmental organizations (NGOs) that became active in the region. Almost overnight, Ouagadougou, the capital of Burkina Faso and the most centrally placed of the region's capitals, became the centerpiece of a new sahelian aid establishment.

Earlier attempts to develop rain-fed agriculture and animal husbandry in the area had been frustrated by the sudano-sahelian area's physical isolation, its poor soils, its characteristically erratic rainfall, and the limited level of education among its population. Opportunities to develop irrigated farming also were quite limited. For Western aid donors anxious to help, disease control—specifically, controlling river blindness—seemed to offer a straightforward and long-lasting means toward reducing the impact of future droughts.

The Onchocerciasis Control Programme

The disease onchocerciasis is caused by the threadlike worm *onchocerca volvulus*. The adult worms have an estimated life of fourteen years in the human body, where they inhabit the subcutaneous tissues of the skin, causing raised nodules. Each female worm produces millions of microscopic microfilaria, which live for about two years. These microfilaria migrate in the epidermis, causing itching, skin depigmentation, and eventually, eye lesions that can result in blindness. The disease is transmitted to humans by the bites of the female blackfly of the *Simulium* genus.[2] The flies can breed only in fast-flowing streams or rivers. As a result, the highest incidence of onchocerciasis occurs among people who live in the river valleys—hence the name river blindness.

The inhabitants of the most severely infected river basins followed a cyclical migration pattern, leaving the valleys in response to the disease, then returning again when the poor inland soils could no longer support their numbers (Hervouet 1977, 1978; Hilton 1960; Marchal 1978; Remy 1968). Williams provides a graphic description of the gradual demise of a village in a badly infected area:

> One-tenth to one-half of the men may be partly or totally blind. Brides, traditionally drawn from neighboring villages, refuse to leave home. The younger men start to leave, to get out before they in turn go blind. As the population shrinks, the rate of bites per person increases. The village takes on the aspect of death. The children, rough stones in hand, listlessly scratch arms and legs that already itch with worms. As their sight is so far unimpaired, they act as human guide-dogs for the already blind. The village com-

pound of beaten earth, once well swept, is scattered with old animal bones
and corn husks. The expanse of millet and sorghum fields gradually contracts.
When the last old people die, so does the village. (1974:78)

When the OCP began in 1974, there was no acceptable mass treatment
for onchocerciasis. As a result, the early program focused on controlling
the blackfly vector by repeatedly spraying the infected river basins with bio-
degradable insecticides (the choice depending on the time period and location) to destroy the fly's larvae. The original sphere of operation covered
764,000 square kilometers in seven countries—Benin, Burkina Faso, Côte
d'Ivoire, Ghana, Mali, Niger, and Togo (map 1). In 1986 the control zone
was expanded to cover 1.3 million square kilometers, including additional
areas of Benin, Ghana, Mali, and Togo, and parts of Guinea, Guinea-
Bissau, Sierra Leone, and Senegal.

Through the years the OCP has maintained an active monitoring program
to ensure that the incidence of the disease remains below a critical level.
This entomological surveillance of the original (pre-1986) control area was
implemented through a network of six sectors and twenty-one subsectors
linked by radio transceivers. Within each of the sectors, the OCP has established approximately three hundred collection points. Entomologists examine the catches to determine infestation rates. Based on these evaluations
and other factors (such as temperature, rainfall, and river depth), the OCP
entomologists plan the weekly insecticide treatments. In addition to spraying, the OCP has actively supported and collaborated with researchers to
develop more effective methods of mass treatment and prevention. One such
collaboration culminated in the discovery in 1982 that oral doses of ivermectin, a drug commonly used in treating heartworm in dogs, could be used
effectively to prevent river blindness. The OCP is now working with national
governments to distribute ivermectin, free of charge, through the national
health services.

Training national health professionals to ensure the progressive takeover
of the OCP by the countries involved was an OCP priority from the start. By
1991, 98 percent of the OCP's staff positions, including the directorship, were
occupied by specialists from African countries. In addition, numerous scientists in national institutions have attended WHO-sponsored courses on the
entomology, cytotaxonomy, parasitology, and ophthalmology of onchocerciasis. The program has awarded 338 graduate-degree fellowships in entomology, hydrobiology, pesticide science, parasitology, epidemiology, public
health, and ophthalmology to country nationals. During the early years the
OCP's Economic Unit helped the affected countries find additional funding

for specific programs. More recently, in 1983 and 1984, the unit coordinated a ten-year assessment of the socioeconomic impact of control (OCP 1986). From 1986 to 1990 it also supported a series of studies to assist participating governments with follow-up planning (Hunting Technical Services, Ltd. 1988a; McMillan, Painter, and Scudder 1992).

Early planning documents estimated the twenty-year (1974–94) costs of the original control program at about $200 million (Caldwell 1975). In fact, the actual costs for the first ten years (1974–83) had risen to $170,682,000, in large part because of the inclusion of an additional 110,000-square-kilometer area and an increase in research spending on insecticide and early chemotherapy treatments (OCP 1985). Despite these numbers, the OCP is considered to be highly cost-effective, with annual costs estimated at less than U.S. $1.00 per beneficiary (Benton and Skinner 1990; Liese et al. 1991; OCP 1985, 1986, 1989, 1990).

Planning Issues

Opening a vast area of formerly underutilized river basin land to settlement presents a host of new opportunities and constraints. Chief among these is the fact that the majority of new lands settlement is likely to be spontaneous. By far the major criticism of unassisted, spontaneous settlement has been that unassisted settlers tend to cultivate the largest area possible, giving little attention to sound management of the new area's soil, forest, or water resources.[3] As long as immigration rates remain low, extensive cultivation and livestock practices are ecologically and socially sustainable. Invariably, however, as population densities increase, problems arise. Land constraints begin to make it more difficult to allow for periods of fallow sufficient to restore soil fertility. Increases in population density are associated as well with greater competition for potable water, grazing areas for livestock, and sources of fuel wood, and with a growing number of land-tenure disputes.

If new land that can be cleared and farmed is still available and easy to acquire, and if the economic and social costs of abandoning old land are low, then a sizable portion of the original settlers—or their offspring—may relocate at this point in the settlement cycle. Such relocation is often to an adjacent or more distant area in the same "frontier" zone. In the absence of some sort of organized planning response, the cycle is likely to repeat itself until the new resource frontier is exhausted and becomes a "dependent social periphery" (Van Raay and Hilhorst 1981:iii).

Research demonstrates that settlers require assistance if they are to adopt more sustainable, less ecologically destructive production practices. This assistance includes government and private investment to develop basic infrastructure like roads and bridges, crop and livestock extension services, schools and health facilities. Foreign donors and national governments have used a wide range of policy models for this type of follow-up assistance. At one end of the continuum are projects in which some agency is involved in almost every phase of development, including preparation of the land; transfer, installation, and initial support of the settlers; and implementation of major technical innovations such as irrigation and mechanized plowing. At the other extreme are projects that provide a minimum of basic infrastructure and social services to direct spontaneous settlers to certain areas.

Although the ultimate goal of the OCP was to facilitate economic development in the zone, the program limited its activities to control. Each affected country was responsible for the settlement and development of its own control areas. In six of the seven countries, government programs provided basic infrastructure and social services for immigrants who were expected to move into the control areas on their own, as well as for a few more specialized projects (see Akwabi-Ameyaw 1990; Buursink and Painter 1990; Hunting Technical Services, Ltd. 1988a, 1988b, 1988c, 1988d; Koenig 1990; McMillan, Painter, and Scudder 1992; OCP 1986; Painter 1990).

Burkina Faso, then known as Upper Volta, was the only country to designate development planning for the OCP river basins as a national priority. Burkina's decision to support a strong program of follow-up planning was based on the extremely large area of the country that was affected by river blindness control and on the country's pressing demographic problems. The decision was influenced as well by earlier models for development dating back to colonial times. These models emphasized the need to draw settlers from Burkina's densely settled plateau to the less populated areas in the country's higher-rainfall southwest.

Burkina's River Basins

Burkina's river basins straddle two broad climatic zones: a northern sudanian region with an average rainfall of 600 to 800 millimeters and a southern sudanian region with an average annual rainfall of 800 to 1,200 millimeters (map 6). Both agroclimatic zones are characterized by a single rainy season and a six- to eight-month dry season. Burkina's river valleys have long been important to West Africa's livestock industry—both for grazing and for transportation from the landlocked cattle-producing areas of Niger, Mali, and Burkina to the coastal countries of Ghana, Côte d'Ivoire, Benin, and Togo. The river basins have also been an important source of fuel wood and

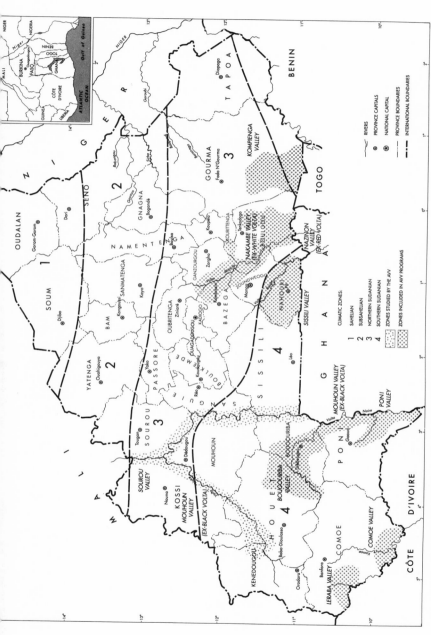

Map 6. Major river basins in relation to agroclimatic zones in Burkina Faso. (McMillan, Nana, and Savadogo 1993: appendix; reprinted courtesy of the World Bank Cartography Section. The boundaries, denominations, and any other information shown on this map do not imply, on the part of the World Bank Group, any judgment on the legal status of any territory, or any endorsement or acceptance of such boundaries.)

construction materials. In 1974—as today—the highest concentration of Burkina's protected wildlife and forest reserves was in the underpopulated river basins. The river basins also included the majority of Burkina's unprotected natural forest cover. Foreign donors and national governments determined that Burkina's uncleared river basins had greater potential for rainfed agriculture than the adjacent plateau areas. The infected valleys also included the areas most suitable for irrigation.

Some 235,000 square kilometers, or 80 percent of the territory of Burkina Faso, were included within the original river blindness control program (map 1). Of this total area, 41,000 square kilometers (Hervouet et al. 1984) or 47,000 square kilometers (AVV 1985c:6) of the river basin land were uninhabited and uncultivated before the OCP began in 1974. Exceptions to this pattern were a few large Bissa communities on the Nakambe River (formerly the White Volta) (Hervouet 1977) and Dagara villages on the Mouhoun (formerly the Black Volta) (Paris 1980, 1983). Examining these anomalies, researchers discovered that onchocerciasis does not generally pose a threat to areas with population densities above 35 to 50 per square kilometer (Hervouet et al. 1984; Remme and Zongo 1989). Outside these highly populated villages, the average population density was extremely low in 1974.

The sparse settlement of Burkina's "empty valleys" contrasted sharply with the high population densities of the central plateau (map 7). To this day the vast majority of farmers on the central plateau depend on subsistence agriculture. There are limited possibilities for irrigation, and government programs to introduce animal traction have not met with widespread success (Barrett et al. 1981; de Wilde et al. 1967; Jaeger 1983; SAED 1976; Singh 1988; Tabsoba 1973). The plateau's high population densities have forced many farmers to shorten the fallow cycle necessary to restore soil nutrients, decreasing soil fertility and increasing farmer vulnerability to periodic and more lengthy droughts (Broekhuyse 1974, 1982a, 1982b; de Wilde et al. 1967; Nagy, Sanders, and Ohm 1988; Rey 1980).

The poverty of the central plateau region led to high rates of out-migration. One emigration stream involved young men leaving to work as labor migrants in the more developed coastal countries—first Ghana (before 1969), then Côte d'Ivoire (map 5) (Conde 1978; Coulibaly et al. 1980; Deniel 1967; Finnegan 1980; Gregory 1974a, 1974b; Remy 1973; SEPIA 1990; Songre 1973). A second population movement, which gained momentum after the 1968–73 drought, was that of Mossi settlers moving off the plateau to the less populated but fertile non-Mossi regions of the southwest.[4]

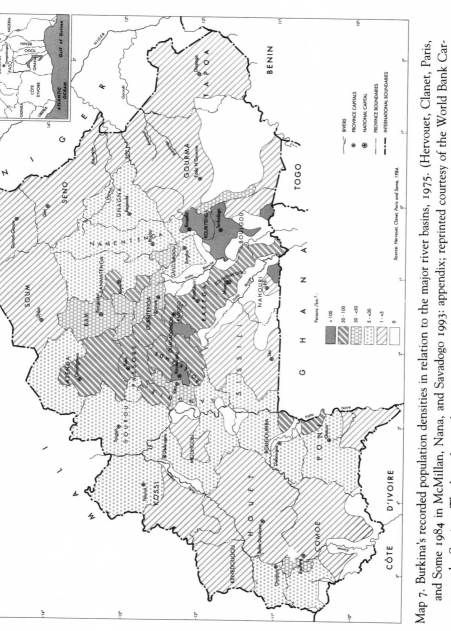

Map 7. Burkina's recorded population densities in relation to the major river basins, 1975. (Hervouet, Clanet, Paris, and Some 1984 in McMillan, Nana, and Savadogo 1993: appendix; reprinted courtesy of the World Bank Cartography Section. The boundaries, denominations, and any other information shown on this map do not imply, on the part of the World Bank Group, any judgment on the legal status of any territory, or any endorsement or acceptance of such boundaries.)

As early as the 1920s the colonial government of francophone West Africa argued that efforts to increase agricultural production and raise rural living standards on the Mossi plateau would meet with only limited success, given the area's high population densities. The result was the creation of a group of planned-settlement schemes (the Office du Niger,[5] and projects in the Vallée du Sourou,[6] Vallée du Gando, and Vallée du Kou[7]) whose stated goals were (1) to attract farmers from the densely settled plateau, thus helping to "decongest" the area, and (2) to encourage the intensification of agricultural production practices in the "new" frontier zones (Remy 1973).

Despite low population densities and relatively high-quality soil in the river basins, along with high population pressure in some of the adjacent plateau zones, almost no immigration was directed to the areas immediately adjacent to the Volta river system prior to 1974 because of the high incidence of disease near the rivers, particularly river blindness disease. Uneven soil quality and periodic flooding may also have contributed to the lack of settlement in the valleys (Berg et al. 1978; Huntings Technical Services, Ltd. 1988a). Certain basins have a Precambrian basement complex with poor aquifer qualities, making it necessary to drill deeply for reliable drinking water (Berg et al. 1978:14). Also, the heavy clay soils characteristic of much of the region are difficult to work with only a hand-held hoe.

Hervouet (1977, 1978, 1983, 1990) argues that the Nakambe and Nazinon (formerly White and Red Volta) river basins were never densely settled. Indeed, he points out that settlement patterns in 1974 were approximately the same as in precolonial times (Hervouet 1978). After 1880 the river basins were occupied by Mossi groups fleeing from the colonial conquest of the capital, Ouagadougou. During this period a number of refugee villages were established in the valleys. A second wave of refugee villages was created by people fleeing from the forced labor and taxes imposed by the French. Hervouet (1978) estimates that the refugees established 191 new villages in the Nakambe and Nazinon between 1905 and 1928.

After 1928 a large number of the refugee villages were abandoned, contributing to a massive immigration across the French colonial border into the British Gold Coast (present-day Ghana). The remaining river basin population was ravaged by a succession of trypanosomiasis and yellow fever epidemics during the first half of the century (Hervouet et al. 1984). In many cases onchocerciasis simply completed the ravages of these epidemics by further destroying the scattered, low-density settlements that were left in their wake (Hervouet 1978). The presence of these other factors, however, does not in any way diminish the importance of onchocerciasis in deterring settlement over the years. Donors anticipated, therefore, that effective control of the disease could open vast areas to settlement and make a substantial contribution to development (Berg 1975; Caldwell 1975; Christensen et al. 1981).

The Volta Valley Authority (AVV)

Armed with one of seven planning grants that the United Nations Development Program (UNDP) awarded to the OCP countries in 1973,[8] some limited assistance from the French Aid and Cooperation (FAC) for preliminary testing, and technical assistance from the French Institute for Tropical Agriculture (IRAT), the Burkina government prepared a highly detailed, comprehensive development plan for the valleys of the Nakambe and Nazinon basins. Project planners were enthusiastic about the potential economic impact of control. An estimated 44 percent of the river basin land was deemed suitable for agriculture; other land was designated as best used for forest, tourism (wildlife reserves), and pasture. Four potential dam construction sites were identified. The final project plan appeared in five volumes with separate sections describing the proposed interventions in the areas identified for planned settlement, cropping, livestock, and to a lesser extent, forestry and wildlife (tourism) (AVV 1973a, 1973b, 1973c, 1973d, 1973e). Planners anticipated that the execution of these plans would provide the country with a continuously fertile, drought-resistant cultivation band.

In 1974 the financing and execution of this comprehensive development plan was vested in an independent agency of the Burkina government—the Volta Valley Authority (Autorité des Aménagements des Vallées des Volta), or AVV. By presidential decree the AVV was given complete control over 30,000 square kilometers of river basin land—one-tenth of the total land area of the country—where the control program was expected to increase immigration (map 6). The AVV's official mandate was to study, promote, coordinate, and execute (or control the execution of) the operations necessary for the economic and social development of the areas placed under its administration. The ultimate goal was the sound development and management of all the natural resources in the lands adjacent to the Volta rivers and their major tributaries. This official mandate was declared valid for a twenty-year period, after which the AVV was scheduled to dissolve as a separate government agency. Its activities would then be placed under the already established regional and national development agencies under different ministries, such as Education, Rural Development, and Health.

The early AVV program was a deliberate attempt to offset some of the deleterious land-use practices commonly associated with spontaneous new lands settlement in southwest Burkina. The first step involved the use of aerial photography and soil and water surveys to classify each river basin into land-use zones. The plan also elaborated a series of special projects for live-stock, forestry, and rain-fed agriculture (map 8). No special planning was made for the Mouhoun (then known as the Black Volta), which had already benefited from substantial donor investment in agricultural research and ex-tension to promote cotton.[9]

In theory, the project plan and the presidential mandate restricted settle-ment to groups, or blocs, of six to seven sponsored villages. The settlement blocs were created in areas that were deemed to have the highest and best potential for rain-fed agriculture. The AVV was responsible for the selection of sites, the installation of basic infrastructure such as roads, wells, and bridges, and such basic social services as health care and schools. In return for cultivation rights to a 10- or 20-hectare project farm in one of the im-proved project villages, the settlers were required to adopt the proposed model for intensive rain-fed farming. To promote this model, the AVV em-ployed a dense network of trained extension agents. The AVV land-use plan-ning, planned-settlement, livestock,[10] and forestry[11] programs were coordi-nated through a centralized administrative structure in Ouagadougou. The administration was divided into five directorates (figure 1.3): General, Fi-nance and Administration, Planning, Construction, and Agricultural De-velopment. Each directorate was broken into divisions and subdivisions. At the top was a board of directors composed of high-level government admin-istrators and chaired by the Minister of Plan. The general director of the AVV was appointed by cabinet decree.

Planners foresaw the evolution of the AVV program in terms of a gradual increase in the number of sponsored settlers, basic infrastructure and ser-vices, and livestock and forestry projects. By 1979 the project included 1,700 families living in forty-seven planned villages in nine different blocs consisting of six to seven villages each. This was only the first stage. Over the next fifteen years the AVV planned to settle another 63,000 families, at a cost of approximately 828,571 CFAF (U.S. $3,300) per household, in the Nakambe and Nazinon valleys (appendix B, tables B-1, B-2, and B-3). Higher costs were projected for the entire project, which was expected one day to include irrigated areas and the Mouhoun basins as well.

The Burkina government and its donors predicted that the high cost of the planned-settlement program would be offset by the associated increase in food production, export crop sales, and regional development. In addi-tion, they expected that the successful AVV settlers would provide a model

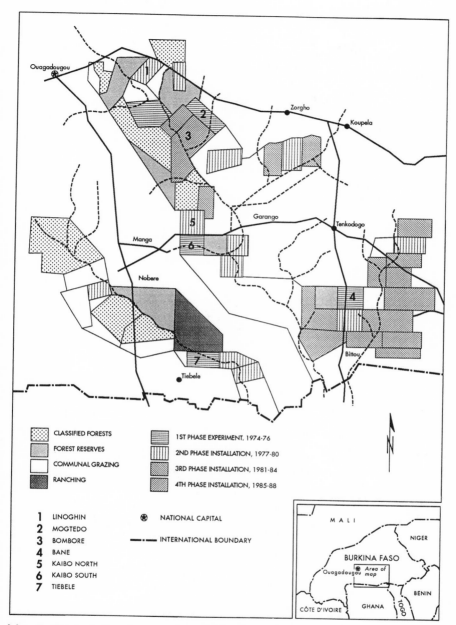

Map 8. Original classification of the Nakambe and Nazinon (formerly White and Red Volta) river basins by suitability to broad categories of land use, 1974. (AVV in McMillan, Nana, and Savadogo 1993:97; reprinted with permission of the World Bank. The boundaries, denominations, and any other information shown on this map do not imply, on the part of the World Bank Group, any judgment on the legal status of any territory, or any endorsement or acceptance of such boundaries.)

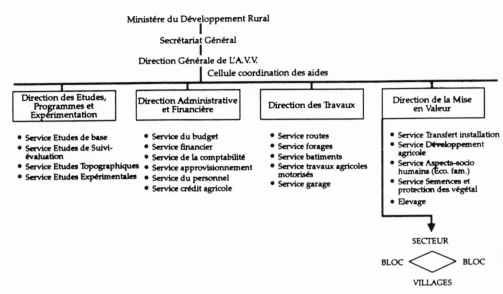

Figure 1.3. Early AVV administrative structure, 1979. (AVV 1985c in McMillan, Nana, and Savadogo 1993:108)

for sustainable rain-fed agriculture in the surrounding areas. The high up-front costs of basic infrastructure and services were justified by arguing that the AVV planned settlements could provide stable, centrally placed administrative and market centers once the valleys were being actively resettled. In 1978 approximately 3 percent of the AVV budget came from the Burkina government; 12 percent represented funds that the AVV generated through its own commercial activities; and the remaining 85 percent was met through grants from foreign donors—France, the Netherlands, and the European Economic Community (FED).

Some of the projected benefits of the proposed development program over a twenty-year period were

1. to settle an estimated 650,000 persons in planned villages—290,0000 persons in areas supported by rain-fed agriculture and another 360,000 in areas served by irrigation near proposed dams;
2. to reduce population pressure in some of the more densely settled areas of the plateau;
3. to control settlement and development in the valleys in order to mini-mize the negative consequences of higher population densities through the introduction of a system of intensive cultivation;

4. to provide a regional grain surplus to allow the country to offset a large part of its projected food deficit;
5. to triple Burkina's production of cotton as an export crop;
6. to improve the standard of living of the 15 to 20 percent of the country's population who would be living in the AVV villages (AVV 1974; Nikyema 1977; F. Ouédraogo 1976).

Although no one considered the "new lands" being released by the OCP to be a panacea for Burkina's many economic problems, they appeared to offer "a vitally needed breathing space, time to address the fundamental problems: improvement and eventual transformation of farming practices in the direction of permanent intensive cultivation" (Berg et al. 1978:iv).

2

Damesma: The Social Context of Immigration to the AVV, 1978–1979

In 1978, when this study began, I was struck by the fact that the farmers living in Damesma referred to their absentee brethren at the AVV project villages as living at "Bitto." I would seek clarification: "You mean they are at the AVV at Mogtedo?" They would nod yes but then continue to refer to the settlers as living at "Bitto." Bitto is in fact a town. The problem was that it is located several hundred kilometers away, near the Ghana border. It soon became clear that the farmers were not referring to the actual town of Bitto; rather, in their world view, "Bitto" referred to agricultural new lands settlement in the south-central part of the country. Immigration to "Bitto" (south-central Burkina) was to be compared with immigration to "Bobo," in the extreme southwest. Both the area around Bitto and the area around Bobo had experienced massive Mossi in-migration prior to river blindness control.

This confusion over precise geographical locations points to a deeper issue. If you were to ask any of the Mossi settlers why they immigrated to the AVV, the inevitable response would be "land." The search for new, uncleared agricultural land is an important underlying theme in Mossi history, one that is deeply embedded in almost every aspect of their traditional social, economic, and political structure. Indeed, ethnographers argue that various Mossi social institutions have evolved in direct response to the need to facilitate new lands settlement (Finnegan 1976, 1978; Hammond 1966;

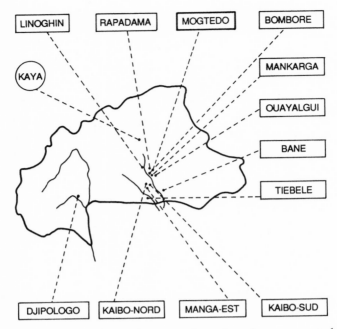

Map 9. Location of the twelve AVV planned settlements created
between 1973 and 1984, the case study settlers' home area
(Kaya), and Kompienga. (AVV 1985c and McMillan 1993:270;
reprinted courtesy of the World Bank Cartography Section. The
boundaries, denominations, and any other information shown
on this map do not imply, on the part of the World Bank Group,
any judgment on the legal status of any territory, or any endorsement or acceptance of such boundaries.)

S. Sawadogo 1986; Skinner 1964b, 1989). What was new in 1974 when the
AVV and OCP were launched was the national state's attempt to provide order
to this historic process in keeping with its own vision of sustainable farming.

The settlers who provide the focus of this study reside in V3 (Village 3),
one of six AVV planned settlements created outside the town of Mogtedo.
Between 1973 and 1985 the AVV created twelve of these village groups—
mostly in the underpopulated river basins of the Nakambe and Nazinon
(map 9). The highest concentration of AVV planned settlements along the
Nakambe, near the main highway that links Ouagadougou with eastern
Burkina, Niger, Togo, and Benin. The decision to focus the case study on
V3 was dictated by the fact that, purely by accident, 45 percent (twenty
households) of the settlers living at V3 in 1979 were from the same home
village—Damesma. This high concentration of settlers from the same home

village simplified comparisons between the project village and the village of origin.

Damesma is located 10 kilometers outside the regional capital of Kaya, in the heart of Burkina's densely settled Mossi plateau; the project village, Village 3 (hereafter referred to as Mogtedo V3 or simply V3), is one of the AVV planned settlements lying 19 kilometers outside the town of Mogtedo. The two sites are separated by 120 kilometers, or 200 kilometers by the main roads (maps 2 and 9). The trip from Damesma to the outskirts of Kaya can be made in less than two hours by foot, bicycle, or cart via a rocky 8-kilometer footpath. There is a longer 14-kilometer route that a sturdy truck can ply during the dry season.

Kinship and Community in Damesma

From the air Damesma looks like a collection of tiny walled towns. These clusters form seven neighborhoods, or *saghse* (sing. *saka*).[1] Each saka contains several compounds or *zaghse* (sing. *zaka*) (see Skinner 1989:27). A compound residence, or zaka, comprises all or some of the dwellings of a single extended family or *yiri* (pl. *yiya*)—usually a man, his brothers, their wives, their unmarried children, married children, and their children's families. The majority of the houses in the compounds are round, made of sun-dried bricks and topped with a thatched roof. Interspersed among them is an occasional rectangular house with a tin or mud roof, representing in most cases money from family members working in Côte d'Ivoire.

At Damesma the seven saghse—which in January 1979 ranged in size from sixty to three hundred inhabitants (fig. 2.1)—group together the local residents of a *boodoo*. In contrast to saka (neighborhood) or zaka (compound residence), boodoo refers to a unit of people related by descent, not by residence. Such a descent-based group and the component lineages comprising it is probably the most meaningful unit of rural social and political organization in Mossi society. Skinner (1989:20) defines the word *boodoo* (what Hammond [1966:109] refers to as the *booyalengo* in the Yatenga region) as the "patrilineal groups that anthropologists would normally call clans, maximal lineages, major lineages, or minor lineages." Hammond (1966:109) uses the concept of "exogamous totemic patrisib" to refer to the same unit.

The members of a boodoo (maximal lineage) claim descent from a common founding ancestor. Although the members of a boodoo generally cannot trace their precise kinship, the relationship is symbolized by a shared totemic object (what Hammond [1966:113] refers to as the sib totem) like an animal or a tree that represents their group (McMillan 1983). Members

Mogho Naba
(Special Title, "Ruler of the World," of the
Paramount Chief of the Ouagadougou Kingdom)
↕
Boussouma Naba
(Provincial Chief at Boussouma)
↕
Kombere Naba
(District Chief/s*)
↕
Tenga Naba
(Village Chief at Damesma)
↕

Saka Naba (Neighborhood or Quarter Chief)	*Boodkasma* (Oldest living member of the Boodoo who has ritual, social, and political obligations for the group)
↕	↕
Saka (Neighborhood or Saka)	*Boodoo* (The clan or maximal lineage claiming descent from the same founding ancestor and sharing a totem)
	↕
	Zakkasama (Oldest living member of the zaka with ritual, social, and political obligations for the group)
	↕
	Zaka/Yiri (The household or compound residence. The extended family or sublineage, usually a cluster of patrilocal families, who claim approximate kinship, usually a shared grandfather, and who live in the same enclosed geographical unit or compound. Often composed of one or more nuclear families that work and eat together)

* Intra-village rivalries that could be traced to political conflicts after independence account for the fact that four of the seven sakse at Damesma were allied with the same district chief as the village chief (the Sanmetenga Naba at Kaya and three with the Piiktenga Naba at Delga.

(In the Mossi kinship system, kin groups are flexible. There is tremendous variation in the composition and strength of identity within and between groups. This figure is intended to provide only a brief outline.)

Figure 2.1. Social and political groups in the "traditional" Mossi system at Damesma.

of the boodoo are not allowed to eat their totemic animal or to cut down a totemic tree. The oldest living male member of each boodoo, referred to as the *boodkasma* and/or *ni kiema* (see also Finnegan 1976; Hammond 1966:113; Skinner 1989:21–22), performs important ritual and social duties like arranging marriages and arbitrating disputes. If a new boodkasma is living away from a village when he assumes his new position (as many are), he must return.

Skinner notes that the Mossi do not make any terminological distinction between the different levels of their segmentary lineage system (1989:20). Nevertheless, the literature shows that all Mossi groups recognize and use the status differences between these units to limit the access of each unit to the corporate assets of the boodoo. These corporate assets include a household's original claim to inherited land-use rights to the village as well as traditional ritual positions. In the early 1960s, Hammond observed a similar phenomenon among the Mossi in the Yatenga region:

> The economic ties that unite all members of the sib [boodoo] are activated most vigorously and continuously within its component lineages. First there is the fact of collective ownership of land by all agnates, the spirits of their ancestors, and the future generations of their descendants. Only through membership in the sib can the Mossi acquire the right to land use, and only through proper land use can they retain this right. This requires adherence to traditionally sanctioned patterns of land tenure—those established by the ancestors, assured by training, and reinforced by the elders. (1966:110–111)

Skinner refers to the component lineages (or minimal lineage units) of the boodoo as a *babissi* (literally, "father's brother"), which is a large extended family composed of relatives who have a common ancestor from three, four, or at most five generations back. Hammond observes that within these component lineages of the sib (boodoo), the living members rarely belong to more than three generations (1966:111). At Damesma the component lineages are referred to as the *boodoo bila* (literally, "small boodoo"). These are families who can detail their precise genealogical relationship to one another, usually those related by the same great-grandfather. They are presided over by the *zakkasama*.

The shallow genealogies of most Mossi lineages reflect the fact that while kinship can be described as the "basic organizing principle in Mossi society" (Hammond 1966:109), genealogy is not that important. Hammond notes that "most Mossi are ignorant of all but the chronologically most recent and relevant details of their genealogies" (1966:110). This point is confirmed by Finnegan (1976:130–139), Schildkraut (1978:30), and Skinner (1989: 22), who observe that few nonroyal Mossi (that is, those without inherited claims to a chieftaincy) can remember the names of an elder accurately beyond the generation of a father's father.

If this description of kinship categories and the Mossi system for reckoning kinship relationships seems confused and confusing, it is. Finnegan notes that "the main difficulty in describing Mossi social structure, besides the shallow genealogies, is a lack in Moré [the Mossi language] of specific terms for different levels of social organization" (1976:140). Hammond argues that the attitude of the Mossi toward this genealogical ignorance and imprecise kinship terms, despite the great attention they give to kinship, is reflective of the functional unimportance, perhaps even the *functional advantage*, of such ignorance. Especially important, "The record is sufficiently accurate to validate and sanction relations between the living, but not so rigid that occasionally necessary genealogical adjustments are ever likely to threaten lineage continuity" (Hammond 1966:111). Finnegan (1976) and Hammond (1966) both stress the important role played by flexible kinship terminologies in facilitating the incorporation of outside immigrants and groups with radically different social status, since it allows such "outsiders" to claim relationship to one of the established patrilineal lineages after only a few generations. As a result, one typically finds that "the segments of non-noble lineages tended to be scattered throughout a district [and] . . . interacted only when they were physically close" (Skinner 1989:22).

In 1978 the seven saghse at Damesma contained only the locally resident members of the seven boodoo. Other members of the boodoo were dispersed throughout Burkina and Côte d'Ivoire. At that time the immigrants' principal contact with the maximal lineage and minimal lineage (symbolized by the boodkasma who headed each of the seven maximal and component minimal lineages) was for performing the rituals associated with marriages or deaths, in negotiating marriage alliances, or when recent immigrants were forced to regulate a dispute with a family from another clan or lineage at Damesma (McMillan 1983).

Early History of the Region

The subdivision of Damesma into the seven neighborhoods (saghse) and maximal lineages (boodoo) has its roots in the historic settlement of the Kaya region. Before the imposition of colonial rule, Damesma and the surrounding Kaya region were administered as part of the Mossi states. Historians agree that the first ancestors immigrated north from the Mamprussi and Dagomba regions in present-day northern Ghana between the twelfth and fifteenth centuries (Fage 1964; Skinner 1964b; Zahan 1967). The various founding myths relate how a group of conquerors (known collectively as the *nakombse*) came north and colonized an area that was populated by an indigenous people known collectively as the *nyonose*.

Although frequently described as the Mossi Conquest, this movement north was probably more similar to present-day agricultural migration than to a pitched battle between the Mossi conquerors (nakombse) and the indigenous inhabitants (nyonose). Fortes (1971:6) describes how the population of the entire Voltaic region of West Africa was "constantly being redistributed by migration of small groups. . . . The fact that such migrations have gone on in the central area suggests that these migrations were the result rather of ecological pressures and social forces than of large-scale conquest." These generalized movements account for many of the shared social, linguistic, and political characteristics in what is called the Voltaic Culture Area—a classification applied to various ethnic groups in the regions of northern Ghana, Togo, and Burkina that are drained by the Volta rivers and their tributaries.

From the fifteenth to the late nineteenth century, the invading nakombse consolidated a loose confederation of tribal states known as the Mossi kingdoms. Tenkodogo to the east was reportedly the first to be established. It was followed by Ouagadougou in the center and Yatenga to the north. At the head of each kingdom was a *moro naba*, or paramount chief, who had under him a hierarchy of lesser provincial and district *nanamse* (sing. *naba*) who "drank the nam," or received the authority of their chieftaincy from the moro naba. Each of these lesser chiefs had the power to appoint village chiefs, who would inherit or acquire subregional power bases for themselves.

The interrelationships between different levels of the political hierarchy were loose. In their most visible form, they were symbolized by a range of ritual, labor, and in-kind tribute relationships. Each village chief and his following, for example, owed a certain number of labor days on the fields of a more powerful district chief, or *kombere naba*. Both village and district chiefs were often given the right to arrange the marriages of girls from the chiefly and nonchiefly families under them. A chief was expected to lend military support and to follow his overlord on outside alliances and judicial decisions. In return, the lesser chief and his people received protection and arbitration in intervillage disputes such as negotiating the return of a runaway or stolen wife or gaining compensation for livestock damage to crops. Some of the more powerful chiefs exacted taxes from caravans using the trade routes crossing their jurisdiction.

When the Mossi moved into a new area to cultivate, as did the farmers who left Damesma for the northern plateau in the 1930s and 1940s, they would ask one of their home chiefs or a powerful chief in the new area to appoint them a chief. In some cases the chief would appoint one of the migrants as his political representative. More often, the superior chief would send one of his "own children." Although the chief's "child" might have only a distant relationship to the actual chief, his physical presence in the village would link the village to the higher levels of the political hierarchy.

An example of this is reported in the origin myths of Damesma. According to legend, groups of Mossi from Ouagadougou (that is, from the south) began moving into the area in the eighteenth century. These Mossi settlers acquired the right to cultivate land from the indigenous inhabitants, or nyonose. According to legend (stories differ slightly among clans, who always wish to emphasize their historic claim to the chieftaincy), these settlements united in asking the moro naba in Ouagadougou to send them a chief. The moro naba granted their request, promising the settlers one of his own sons, a child, whom they could return to get when he was older. They would be able to identify their chief by his limp. Years later, when the settlers' delegation went to Ouagadougou, the moro naba presented them with a group of young men. When asked if they could identify their chief, they could, since there was only one candidate who limped. To this date, the subdistrict chieftaincy in the area near Damesma is known as Puetenga, land of the club-footed or lame one.

Before settling at Damesma, Naba Piko (the lame-footed chief) lived for short periods in several neighboring villages. He eventually arrived at Damesma with an entourage of allied "servitor" clans. Each servitor clan acquired a separate land grant and became a distinct neighborhood (saka). The residents of the saka Ouidi were the chief's traditional warriors and looked after his horses. The eunuchs for the chief's court were reportedly selected from the saka Gando. The inhabitants of the saka Poedogo (the Poece), served as Naba Piko's fetish priests and soothsayers. The chief's saka, Natenga, regrouped several lineages—one that was eligible for the chieftaincy, one in charge of guarding the chiefs' tombs, and a third composed of hereditary court griots. The saka Tangan (which means "hill") included the original nakombse immigrant households who requested Naba Piko. The inhabitants of the remaining two saghse, Nabodogo and Pousguin, moved into the area at a later time.

Except for a few immigrant households, most of the families at Damesma claim descent from the pioneer (or, depending upon your perspective, invading) Mossi nakombse. In the colonial period when official papers made surnames important, these individuals all took the *sonda* (what Finnegan [1976:143] refers to as *sonderé*), or clan name, Ouédraogo. Previously only the chief's lineage had been referred to by this name at Damesma. Although the descendants of the original inhabitants of the land (the nyonose) adopted the clan name Savadogo, live in a separate subvillage, and do not constitute a saka of Damesma, they are considered to be Mossi. A Ouédraogo man can marry a Savadogo woman and vice versa. The main restriction is that a Savadogo cannot hold political office. The Savadogo, however, do have exclusive right to the position of *tengasoba*, or earth priest, who holds special power over the rain, land, and supernatural phenomena. Although the position of earth priest is outside the Mossi political hierarchy, it is considered essential to the well-being of the land and sustains an alliance between the Savadogo and other groups.

Political Structures

When the French conquered the Mossi at the end of the nineteenth century, they built their administration on what they perceived to be a fixed hierarchy of chiefs within a single unified kingdom (Skinner 1957, 1960b, 1964b, 1970a, 1970b, 1989). The moro naba at Ouagadougou was made paramount chief, or king; the two other moro nabas at Tenkodogo and Yatenga were placed under him. Some of the powerful district chiefs were made chiefs of administrative cantons and given duties under the new administration, including tax collection and labor recruitment for construction projects and the colonial army. Villages were assigned to specific canton chiefs, thus "fixing" what had previously been a system of shifting alliances. Overlapping this hierarchy of chiefs was the civil administration, which consisted of a regional *prefecture* and a subregional *sousprefecture*.

Until 1983 the village chief, or *tenga naba*, was the people's most direct link with the new national government (fig. 2.1). The chief was charged with collecting the annual head tax and witnessing all requests for official papers, such as birth certificates and identification cards, required for travel outside the immediate area. The bureaucratic wheels moved slowly on requests from illiterate farmers, and the chief was often asked to use his influence to speed up the process. The chief was also charged with communicating government edicts to the village and orchestrating village health and agricultural development programs, food aid, and national elections. These administrative duties were channeled to the chief through the Kaya *sousprefecture*.

Each saka was represented by a political chief, or *saka naba*. Unlike the boodkasma, the saka naba was a political post that was appointed by the naba. The Damesma naba was head of his own saka (Natenga); each of the other six saghse was headed by its own saka naba. In the past, the saka nabas were appointed by the district chief at Delga (the Piktenga naba) but were under the political authority of the Damesma naba. This was a dual commitment that was the source of much conflict in the early 1970s, when village chiefs like the Damesma naba started to assume a more independent stance following national independence. While the office of village chief (naba) was made elective after independence, in most cases it continued to pass from father to son.

Patterns of Religious Conversion

Ancestor veneration is at the core of traditional Mossi religious behavior:

> The recent ancestors are notified, through sacrifices, of the important events in the lives of their descendants, and they are expected to aid in solving everyday problems. The ancestors also invoke their sanctions against antisocial behavior among their descendants. Once a year, the Mossi people, in concert with the Moro Nabas, appeal to their individual and collective ancestors for good crops, large families, and for the preservation of the dynasty. (Skinner 1958:1103)

Damesma was one of the first villages in the Kaya region to have a chief (the grandfather of the present chief) who converted to Islam. By 1979, Islam had become an important mechanism for reinforcing the unity of, and social distinctions between, the traditional structure of clans and saghse. The spread of Islam has not been even but instead has been closely identified with the three saghse (Natenga, Pousguin, and Tangan) that have the strongest present and past claims to the village chieftaincy. The inhabitants in these saghse place considerable social pressure on their relatives to adopt Islamic practices, including daily prayers, style of clothing, and abstinence from alcoholic beverages.

Professed Catholics and animists are found in the four saghse that group the four "servitor" clans, which are less closely identified with the chieftaincy (Gando, Nabodogo, Poedogo, and Ouidi). In 1979 most of the Catholics were young household heads and single men and women. Many had first been exposed to the religion while working abroad. Every Sunday the courtyard of the village Catholic church would be packed with the shiny bicycles and motorbikes of returned migrants. The Catholic diocese provided a lay preacher, who resided in the village but drew no salary.

Land-Tenure Rights

Saul (1988:259) emphasizes that in Burkina, as in most parts of Africa, permanent farming rights are usually held by descent groups similar to those outlined above. Although the colonial government recognized the right of certain individuals to register land and transform it into private property, these principles were never widely applied (Boutillier 1964; Hammond

1966; Saul 1988:259). Too much emphasis on the concept of kin-based land tenure, however, can obscure the fact that at their origin, these types of kin-based land-tenure rights are personal. Saul notes that

> most cultural groups in Burkina maintain the idea that land use rights originate by an individual farmer clearing virgin or unoccupied bush. He [the farmer] thus establishes a special relationship that has spiritual and economic facets with the site in question. This special relationship is not extended to his collateral lineage fellows but is later transmitted to all his descendants in the male line. The ritual office and use rights devolve in fact to the senior elder of this group, but no descendant can be rightfully excluded from this land. The corporate group around which a piece of land emerges later, with the succession of the generations and as a result of a growth in the number of descendants of the first clearer who is the initiator of the rights. (Skinner 1958:1103)

The fact that descent-based cultivation rights are "personal at their origin" (Saul 1988:260) is reflected in the traditional patterns of land tenure and new lands settlement in the settlers' home village.

Original Settlement Patterns: The Settlers' Home Village

A household's original claim to land ownership in Damesma is through membership in the boodoo, or clan. The seven clans and individual sublineages within each clan differ in both the area and quality of land to which they have access—in particular to the choice lakeside and low-lying areas.[2] This distribution of land has its roots in the way in which the village was first settled.

Village legends recount that the residents of the saka Tangan were the first nyonose (conqueror) group to inhabit the present village area. This explains why their lands are the most extensive of the seven saghse. The ancestors of Natenga (the saka of the present chief) and the servitor saghse— Ouidi, Gando, and Poedogo—arrived in a second wave of in-migration. Legends describe how the later settlers received smaller initial land grants. Political power, however, was not necessarily associated with bigger and better land holdings. When the Damesma land was divided, the chief's clan chose the sandy bissiga soils closest to the settlement. In these early times land was plentiful, and the light, sandy soils were appreciated because of their ease of cultivation and their proximity to the village. Moreover, although the chief's family always worked, their income was supplemented by the gifts and tribute, including grain, animals, and kola nuts, they received from their subjects.

A similar situation was found among the other clans that in the past had strong ties to either the Damesma village or the Puetenga district chieftaincy. In the precolonial and early colonial periods, the clan of the Poece or Korrogo (inhabitants of the present-day saka of Poedogo) were the soothsayers, clairvoyants, and special fetish priests to the district chief and received gifts for their services. When colonial rule was imposed, many of the traditional judicial and protective roles of the chiefs were replaced by the government. As a result, the village chiefs and people were less willing to contribute to the maintenance of the district chiefs and servitor groups like the Poece. The reduction in gifts made it difficult for the Damesma Poece to support themselves on their small land holdings, which in 1979 were among the smallest in the village. This was the primary reason given to explain why this clan, which represented less than 20 percent of the home village itself, comprised more than half the settler households that had immigrated to the AVV project by 1979.

Land-Tenure Categories: The Settlers' Home Village

Although a household's original claim to land was through membership in the boodoo, in 1979 the boodkasma or ni kiema retained little direct control over land disposition and use. The fields belonging to a specific household were clan fields that had become identified with its sublineage through inheritance. At Damesma these lands were referred to as mampasago or mamsolem ("my right"). Proprietorship over specific fields was determined by patrilineal descent within the elementary family—from father to elder son (fig. 2.2). Other tracts of land that could not be inherited were associated with certain kinship and political offices. These were described as lands of "customary right," to distinguish them from holdings that passed through inheritance. At Damesma the boodziiga was an area of clan lands that came under the control of the boodkasma when he assumed leadership of the boodoo. As the oldest living member of the boodoo, he had special social and religious duties for the group. At the death of the elder, the right to cultivate these fields passed to the man who replaced him—presumably the second-oldest living male.

A third land-tenure category embraced the clan lands whose distribution was the special prerogative of the chiefs (both village and neighborhood). Such fields were known as nabaziise (sing. nabaziiga) and supplemented the holdings that a village or saka would inherit (mamsolem) from his predecessor. Since the village chieftaincy usually passed from father to son, the distinction between chiefly and inherited land was often unclear. The naba-

Damesma

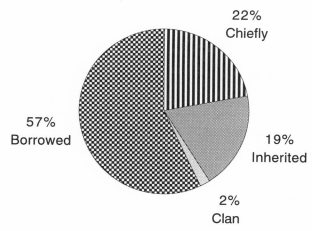

Figure 2.2. Land tenure categories in the settlers'
home village (Damesma), 1979. Methodology:
Percent of total land area planted. (McMillan
1986:264)

ziise for the village and neighborhood chiefs had special rituals associated
with their cultivation that could only be performed by the man duly vested
with the office. If a boodoo lost its claim to stand as a semiautonomous
saka with a politically appointed saka naba (as happened with one boodoo
at Damesma), the nabaziiga of the old neighborhood chief was taken over
by the chief who absorbed the group.

A system of institutionalized borrowing provided the means by which
land identified with specific groups of people could be exchanged. If the man
who headed a family unit had proprietorship over more fields than he could
cultivate, any member of his extended family might ask and expect to receive permission to use a portion of the extra land. To refuse a request for
land from someone in the same clan was to risk serious punishment from the
ancestors (see also Boutillier 1964 and Saul 1988:264–266). At Damesma,
as throughout Burkina, this reallocation took the form of a loan, with the
proprietor retaining his permanent rights to the land and the borrower obtaining usufructuary rights only. While first priority was usually given to
members of the same clan, a loan could be made to someone outside the
patrilineal kinship group. When this occurred at Damesma, however, it was
often between groups that had already formed an established relationship
through intermarriage. Nonfamily loans could also follow what Hammond

(1966) calls a "bond relationship" of mutual aid and friendship. In 1979 an estimated 57 percent of the land cultivated by the farm families in the settlers' home village was classified as borrowed.

Because of historical circumstances that influenced their original land rights, certain clans cultivated a higher percentage of borrowed land than others. This accounts for the fact that in 1979 over 60 percent of the land borrowed at Damesma belonged to people outside the clan of the borrower. Over time these exchanges assumed patterns. For example, farmers from the land-poor saka of Natenga borrowed heavily from farmers at the land-rich Tangan saka. In 1979 over 75 percent of the farmers in the farming systems survey at Damesma had borrowed more than one-third of the total area that they farmed, and over 50 percent had borrowed more than two-thirds. Since the fields that a farm family lent tended to be their worst fields or the fields that they were about to leave fallow, cultivating a high percentage of borrowed fields was associated with lower income.

This correlation between a high percentage of borrowed land and living standards was very different in the other two Kaya villages that were included in the baseline research. Although the study showed that 39 percent of the measured fields were planted on borrowed land, this figure was inflated by the fact that six of the seven households with more than two-thirds of their total land area classified as "borrowed" were first- and second-generation immigrants to a "new" area located next to a large seasonal lake. Because of their length of residence and the fact that many of the loans had already been inherited, they considered their land rights to be secure, although technically they were still classified as loans. Ironically, with increasing population pressure in the more established central neighborhoods and growing demand for dry-season irrigated crops, these once marginal lakeside lands had become some of the most valuable village lands by 1979.

The disproportionately high rate of land borrowing in Damesma despite high population pressure can be attributed to the village's high rate of outmigration. When immigrants left, their inherited land was reabsorbed back into the holdings of their respective kin groups. The redistribution of this land to kinsmen and nonkinsmen outside the immediate family occurred through borrowing. In theory, no matter how long a member of one of the established Damesma lineages stayed away, he or any of his descendants could return and reclaim at least some of "his father's fields." Therefore by 1979, although the high rate of out-migration from Damesma to agricultural areas like the Vallée du Kou and AVV made more land available through borrowing, it did not result in a more permanent reallocation to households with less land. Certain families were still required to farm a much higher percentage of borrowed holdings. Thus when the AVV settlers stated that they immigrated for land—they were often referring to their frustration with cultivating a high percentage of borrowed land, rather than to lack of access to land in and of itself.

If a borrower continued to satisfy the loan conditions (that is, did not give the impression that the land belonged to him) and the lender did not have a pressing need to reclaim the land, a borrower's son could inherit one of his father's loans. Before cultivating it, however, the son usually had to come to the proprietor and request a loan as if for the first time. This act of renewing the loan was another way of recognizing the proprietor's permanent rights to the field. Social pressure made it difficult to reclaim long-term loans or loans that had been inherited. There were, nevertheless, recorded cases in which children had recalled loans that their father had made as much as twenty to thirty years earlier. Normally, however, after the death of an original borrower, a field became an inherited loan that the borrowing family could continue to regard as its own.

Land Tenure and the Household Life Cycle

While the male household head had primary control over the allocation and use of the land he acquired through inheritance, customary right, or borrowing, the cultivation of this land was subdivided among different household units. Certain fields referred to as *pugo* were worked collectively. The harvest was stored apart and provided for the household's main subsistence needs. Any income from the sale of these crops was under the control of the household head. Other fields known as *belogo* were cultivated as private fields by individuals such as married women, sons, and brothers, as well as unmarried sons and brothers who still owed the bulk of their labor to the family's cooperative fields. The person in charge of the field had the right to the harvest. Although women did not inherit the right to use land, a woman could request a land loan from either her own or her husband's extended family. When she died, the fields she had acquired in this way would sometimes pass to her son.

Two examples of this type of inherited loan occurred in the fifteen households included in the farming systems survey at Damesma. This system of overlapping land rights had major implications for the organization of the family farm. In 1979 the typical farm at Damesma consisted of twenty-one fields in four or five distinct locations, for a total of 5.8 planted hectares. A field, as the term is used here, refers to an area sown in one dominant crop and controlled by one person. The geographical area of contiguous fields with a distinct tenure arrangement (for example, inherited by the household or borrowed from a certain group) is referred to as a terrain. One terrain might include as many as eight separate fields—with different crops and different persons or groups of persons responsible for their cultivation.[3]

Equitable distribution of household land through inheritance and subdivided cultivation rights was always difficult in a densely settled village like Damesma. When a man died, the control over his inherited fields passed to his eldest son. If the son was too young, responsibility for the fields would be taken up by a younger brother of the deceased and returned to the son when his status changed. The ideal was for a man's sons, their wives and children, as well as the father's wives and underage children, to continue as one household after the father's death. In fact, however, it always became difficult to resolve the recurrent conflicts between corporate and private interests as the size of each brother's family grew. Thus, as a rule, most brothers divided their father's corporate fields and granaries after his death. One household in the sample at Damesma—a man and his married nephew— underwent such a fission in 1979. In 1978 the uncle and the nephew cultivated the main cotton and sorghum fields together. The nephew also maintained a large area of private fields for himself. During the 1979 season the nephew's young family (wife, newborn baby, and elderly mother) subsisted entirely off the grain harvested from the private fields they planted during 1978 and ceased to work with the uncle, although they still shared a common courtyard.

Such intrahousehold conflicts over land often appeared even before a father's death. As a man's sons married and started families of their own, they typically increased the size of their belogo and the amount of time devoted to these holdings. Although the father gradually increased his access to clan and lineage lands, usually this did not keep pace with the growing size of his family. Over time there was inevitably less inherited land per person and one of the sons was shortchanged. These situations could be dealt with through alternative patterns of residency and work, including borrowing land from households affiliated with the mother's patrilineage in a neighboring village, resettling some part of the family in a less populated area, or wage labor abroad.

If a farmer could not get the loan he wanted locally, he could request land in a neighboring village through association with his mother's or grandmother's patrilineage. If he could claim no local kinship ties, he could request land from the chief or from another family that served as his sponsor. If the village was close by, the farmer and his family often went there only to cultivate. However, as they acquired more permanent rights they might be joined by other relatives and come to form a new lineage segment. In 1979 most villages in the vicinity had at least one lineage segment that had immigrated from Damesma and had acquired land through such alliances. Sometimes a farmer who had left a village would return once he had access to larger holdings at home. This could occur because of a death in the family or because family members left to cultivate or work abroad. There might also be a change in the status of the individual; for example, becoming an elder or a chief would give him access to lands other than those acquired through individual inheritance.

Two of the twelve households in the farming systems study in Damesma in 1979 were headed by men who had returned to the village as recently as 1977. One of them came back to assume the role of boodkasma (clan elder) after fifteen years of cultivating in a less populated Mossi area farther north. Almost 100 percent of the land that the elder cultivated in 1979 was boodziiga (clan fields), which could not be inherited by his middle-aged son. For this reason, the son's desire to leave his elderly father and to start a new farm in the southwest, outside Bobo-Dioulasso, was well known. The second returned migrant came back to Damesma when his father died and his brother retired as a pensioned veteran from the Burkinabè army.

Just as land needs could increase in the normal development cycle of a family, they could also decrease. As a man aged and had fewer dependent children, he needed fewer fields. The eldest son would then typically expand the size of the private fields cultivated by his own nuclear family until they became the main cooperatively worked fields. Migration could also sharply reduce the size of a household and cause semiautonomous production units to merge. In 1978, one study farmer shared his compound at Damesma with his nephew, the son of a deceased brother, though the two families worked and ate apart. At the end of the 1978 agricultural season, one of the farmer's other brothers returned from Côte d'Ivoire, married, and set up a joint household with the study farmer. The returned brother did not, however, accompany the study farmer to the AVV in February 1979. Instead, he merged his fields and his immigrant brother's inherited fields with those of the nephew (the dead brother's son), forming a new, fused household. This is a good example of how household structures could change to meet changing family needs.

Traditional Patterns of New Lands Settlement

With the imposition of colonial rule, many of the social barriers to more distant immigration were reduced. In the 1920s and 1930s there was a major movement north from Damesma to the less populated Mossi lands near Barsalogo, which had vast stretches of low-lying land. During the 1960s a growing number of Mossi settlers from the Kaya region began moving to Burkina's higher-rainfall southwest and southeast, which were the traditional homelands of the Bissa, Dagari, Bobo, Gourmantche, and others. This movement was given impetus by the 1968–74 drought. At least fifty households left Damesma for the Vallée du Kou irrigation scheme located outside Bobo-Dioulasso in the early 1970s.[4] In the one-year period between May 1978 and May 1979 (McMillan 1983), out-migration resulted in a 10 percent decrease in the total population of Damesma. The highest percentage of individuals who left and did not return during the preceding five years could be classified as agricultural migrants in search of "new" or better land.

Borrowing, and the mechanisms whereby borrowed holdings could over time be converted to the status of inherited lands, was the chief means by which the Mossi acquired land in less populated regions. The typical pattern was for immigrants to first request land from the indigenous inhabitants in a less populated region. In areas with abundant land, this land loan was usually a straight grant, with little expectation that it would ever be reclaimed. By giving a new settler land and perhaps extra food, an indigenous farmer made an investment in future social ties with the new immigrants. By granting land and some initial subsistence and social support, an indigenous farmer gained a potential friend and political ally. Special rituals and sacrifices provided additional opportunities to formalize the incorporation of the immigrant family into the indigenous host community. By passing through the customary channels to acquire land, a borrower acknowledged the indigenous lineage and village leader's right to control the final disposition and use of village lands.

Early Damesma immigrants typically sponsored the immigration of later ones. When this occurred, however, the male head of the family usually took the newcomer to the same indigenous farmer who had first sponsored him. The more established settler thus increased his family's allies while, at the same time, increasing the allies of his indigenous sponsor. By granting land, the indigenous sponsors gradually increased their power in the new hybrid community. In some cases these social bonds were further reinforced by intermarriage between the lineages of the indigenous host grantor and Damesma migrant grantee. Over time these linkages were expected to create the same sort of dispersed lineage segments from Damesma that were characteristic of earlier in-migration zones.

This traditional pattern for colonizing and acquiring new land worked as long as land was plentiful. When land became scarcer, the system broke down. A critical factor was the unwillingness and, indeed, demonstrated inability of local inhabitants to resist sudden, dramatic increases in immigration. Thus, immigration might continue into an area long after it had surpassed the local carrying capacity of the land with the existing base of crop production technology (Agrotechnik 1988, 1989; Remy 1973, 1975, 1981). As population densities increased, land loans were made for shorter periods of time (Boutillier 1964; McMillan 1980, 1983; Saul 1988), and the immigrants who arrived later in an area were generally awarded less choice pieces of land (Nana 1989c; PNGTV 1989a; Saul 1988:263).

This increased pressure on an older settlement's land resources inevitably resulted in rising levels of social conflict among settlers, hosts, and pastoralists. Recurrent sources of conflict included livestock damage to settler crops as the new settlers' herd sizes increased, shortages of potable water because of higher demand, pastoralist resentment at being denied access to former grazing areas and water points, and a diminished supply of easily accessible fuel wood (Hartog 1979; McMillan 1983; McMillan, Painter, and Scudder 1992; Nana and Kattenberg 1979; D. Ouédraogo 1979). By the time these crises occurred, the levels of social conflict were often very high. At this point in the settlement cycle, "the most ambitious farmers controlling a larger or growing work force and movable wealth adjust to the situation by migrating out of the 'saturated' zones to places where it is easier to obtain large tracts" (Saul 1988:263).

Conclusion

When the AVV started in 1974, agricultural new lands settlement was already an established tradition in the settlers' home village of Damesma. Under the traditional land-tenure system, final inherited land rights remain vested in the descendants of the first individuals to clear and farm a given area. While the users gained usufructuary rights, the grantors (and their descendants) retained final allocation rights. Borrowers were reminded of their land-tenure status through a series of interdictions regarding what types of crops, trees, or buildings could be placed on a land. The traditional system worked to guarantee the members of all established lineages—regardless of their historic land endowment—with at least minimal access to land. This same system, and the flexible system for lineage reconstitution, provided the means for outside immigrant groups without established lineage ties to a village to acquire more permanent land-tenure status in less populated areas over time.

Ethnographers argue that this traditional pattern of colonizing new land was made possible by the flexible kinship system, political structures, and land-tenure rights of the Mossi and the smaller, less hierarchical ethnic groups along their periphery (Finnegan 1976; Hammond 1966; Saul 1988; Skinner 1964b, 1989). The same flexible social and political system provided the means for the Mossi to replicate past patterns of social and political behavior. Lesselingue notes:

> The cases of cultural assimilation [of Mossi immigrants] are rare. They do not exist in the traditional zones of in-migration because there the immigrants are on the road to becoming the future. . . . They are self-sufficient among themselves. Nor does it exist in the more recent areas of in-migration . . . because the immigrants are few in number in comparison to the indigenous population and must bind together in terms of "ethnic survival." (1975:464, translation mine)

Lesselingue's findings are similar to those of Schildkraut, who worked with first- and second-generation Mossi immigrants to Ghana. In her book, *People of the Zongo* (1978), she describes the immigrants' changing concepts of ethnic identity over several generations, the persistence of certain ritual, political, and social ties to their parents' home villages, and the reestablishment of Mossi chieftaincies in areas located hundreds of miles outside Mossi territory.

> As Mossi migrate towards the borders of Mossiland they often settle in villages which are inhabited by members of different ethnic groups. It is in these areas that the gradual process of cultural integration takes place and the basis for an undifferentiated Mossi identity is created. Non-Mossi become politically incorporated as they accept the authority of Mossi chiefs and, in some cases, assume political offices. Intermarriage occurs, and ties of economic interdependence are created, all of which are factors contributing to the integration of diverse ethnic communities in Mossi society (Schildkraut 1978:30–31).

For the Damesma settlers at the AVV, immigration to the project was a variation on this centuries-old theme of agricultural immigration. The key difference after 1974 was the AVV's attempt to "rationalize" (the term used in project documents) the underlying foundation of this traditional immigration process by creating a new system of state-mandated individualized land-tenure and "democratic" institutions.

3

The AVV Project Vision

The massive spontaneous immigration away from the Mossi plateau to Burkina's less populated southwest was well underway when the OCP began in 1974. The AVV planned-settlement program was a deliberate attempt to off-set the rapid, uncontrolled forest clearance and spontaneous new lands settlement in the river basins affected by control. The problem was attacked at three levels. The first level involved a presidential edict declaring that the river basins were the property of the state. A second level involved zoning to reserve specific areas for protected wildlife and forests and to designate other areas for intensive crop and livestock production. At a third level the project restricted the amount of land that individual households could clear and required settlers to adopt a prescribed package for intensive agriculture and new "democratic" institutions designed to encourage sustainable cropping. The underlying assumption behind the project's land-tenure, settlement, and local government policies was that once removed from their "traditional" norms and values, the settlers would be freer to experiment. Planners also hoped to avoid accusations of Mossi colonization of the numerically less dominant peoples of the south.

Land-Tenure and Zoning Policies

Especially important to the AVV project plan was the fact that settlers' access to land was accorded by the state, which guaranteed the settlers' rights to a

10- or 20-hectare project farm as long as they respected the project's proposed program for intensive cultivation. This system of state-accorded land-tenure rights differed markedly from the social and political mechanisms by which Mossi settlers had traditionally acquired new settlement and cultivation rights. The legal basis for the AVV land-tenure policies dates from a series of government edicts created between 1906 and 1956 that introduced the legal concept of private and state ownership (*régime réglementaire*) parallel to the system of traditional land tenure. On the basis of these edicts, Burkinabè could claim private ownership of land on which they had constructed any sort of permanent structure or other major improvement (AVV 1985d; McMillan, Nana, and Savadogo 1993).

A legal distinction was made between public domain and private domain lands. Public domain lands encompassed natural resources as well as certain man-made resources (such as buildings and infrastructure) that by their nature or social importance should not belong to any private individual. This category included rivers, roads, lakes, river and lake banks, bridges, military bases, and public transport. The Burkinabè state inherited this dual system of legal and customary land-tenure rights and modified it by other edicts. A law enacted in 1960 (No. 77/600/AN, 20 juillet 1960) made the state the final proprietor of all land not already registered by that date. This was followed by a later act (No. 29/63/AN) in 1963 that authorized the government to reserve for the state any land that benefited from state investment in infrastructure development, and to declare as property of the state all less populated lands or lands distant from major population centers (AVV 1974, 1985d; McMillan, Nana, and Savadogo 1993; F. Ouédraogo 1976).

On the basis of these laws, the state was able to use a presidential ordinance (September 5, 1974) to declare that the river basins were state property. The appropriated area was legally defined to include almost 30,000 square kilometers—over 10 percent of the total land area of the country. On the basis of this ordinance, the AVV outlawed all cultivation rights outside the official AVV areas. In theory, this included all immigrants who had moved in on their own, as well as the few preexisting settlements. In most cases the indigenous inhabitants of the areas in which the AVV decided to build village clusters were given the option of moving or reconstructing their homes and fields within one of the planned AVV villages.

Before emigrating to the AVV, the recognized male head of a settler household was required to sign a *contrat de mise en valeur*, which stipulated the project's obligations to him (acting on behalf of the entire family) and his obligations to the scheme. This included the settler's assurance that

1. his decision was voluntary;
2. he had a minimum of three suitable workers in the household labor force;
3. he would abandon his old fields in his home village;
4. he would follow the agricultural techniques promoted by the extension agents;
5. he would clear and destump his own fields.

It was understood that the settler's family had the right to cultivate their AVV farm as long as they respected the obligations outlined in the contract.[1]

Once an area was selected for planned settlement, the AVV conducted additional surveys to determine the "carrying capacity" of its soil and water resources (calculated as the number of households that can be supplied with at least 200 liters of water per day and 8 hectares of "good" land per family [AVV 1973a:5]). Based on these calculations, each settlement was designed to contain between twenty-five and seventy-five 10-hectare farms. This preliminary village and regional layout included the delineation of areas to be set aside for forests and livestock grazing. Each farm consisted of a 1.0-hectare homesite in the main village and six 1.5-hectare bush fields. Each of the six bush fields was located in a spatially distinct cultivation band that the AVV soil surveys determined as having good agricultural potential. These cultivation strips were better adapted to animal traction and tractors than the settlers' traditional pattern of grouped fields (fig. 3.1). The strips also made it easier for the extension agent to ensure that the settlers followed the prescribed crop rotation and cultivation techniques.

DAMESMA HOME VILLAGE   **DAMESMA SETTLERS AT AVV**

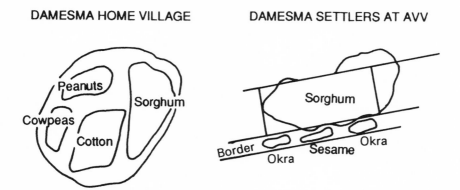

Figure 3.1. Comparison of the AVV field structure and traditional field structure in the settlers' home village. (McMillan 1983:125)

Resettlement, Extension, and Local Government Policies

The AVV invested heavily in basic infrastructure, including access roads, a school, a warehouse, and a dispensary for each cluster of six to seven project villages. For individual villages, wells and extension-worker housing were provided. Most of these construction projects were carried out with the AVV's own tractors, bulldozers, and well-digging equipment. In addition to trained recruitment agents, the AVV made extensive use of radio broadcasts in local languages to advertise its program. When a male settler expressed an interest in emigrating to the project, the recruitment agent conducted a personal interview to determine his eligibility. The basic requirement was the size and stability of the man's family labor force. A settler household had to include at least two adult workers, preferably more, and at least one married couple. Once selected, candidates were notified in the late fall.

At the start of the dry season in January or February, an AVV project vehicle would transfer the family, their food stores, possessions, farm equipment, and animals from their home village to the project. Upon arrival, each family was assigned a household plot by the male extension agent. While a family head could request that his family be sent to the planned settlements nearest to his home village or to a settlement where they might already have kinsmen, this was not always possible nor even condoned. Early documents advocated that the project install settlers as far as possible from their home village. This policy was based on the argument that if the new project farm was nearby, the settlers would consider it as an extension of their traditional farm area (AVV 1973b). The project also had a deliberate policy of intermixing settlers from different ethnic groups and scattering those from the same home village to diminish the influence of the settlers' extended family structures and traditional chiefs.

The settlers' first task was to clear the 1.0-hectare homesite and build a temporary shelter. Until this temporary housing was completed, the settlers were provided with housing under a communal straw shelter. In addition to the 1.0-hectare homesite, each settler family received two of their allocated six bush fields during the first year. They were responsible for clearing one of these fields by hand; the AVV cleared the other with a bulldozer. Both fields were then plowed with an AVV tractor before planting. Each household received an additional field each year for the next four years until they had received a total of six 1.5-hectare fields or six 3.0-hectare fields in the case of a very large labor force. In each case, the settlers were responsible for field clearance, after which the fields were plowed by an AVV tractor. Until the first harvest, each household received a bimonthly ration of grain, fish, and oil based on the number and age of family members. These rations were provided by the United Nations World Food Program (Programme Alimentaire Mondial, or PAM), with the AVV paying only the costs of transportation and storage. Each household also received an initial stock of heavy-duty tools to assist with field clearance.

In return for the right to cultivate a farm in one of the improved project villages, the AVV required the settlers to adopt the project package of intensive cultivation techniques. Basic elements of the package included

1. a new system of land allocation to centralize field layout and to restrict the total area cleared and farmed per worker;
2. a new crop rotation system that required settlers to grow a six-year cycle of sorghum, cotton, cotton-peanuts-cowpeas, sorghum-millet, followed by two years of fallow on each of the six bush fields;
3. new production techniques such as monocropping (cultivating only one crop per field at a time), sowing in lines, thinning, and after the second year in the project, cultivating with an ox-drawn plow;
4. the use of high levels of mineral fertilizer and insecticides as well as new high-yielding varieties of seed (see Murphy and Sprey 1980 and McMillan 1983).

Most of the recommended inputs and technology could be purchased on credit from a centrally placed project warehouse in each village cluster. Short-term credits for fertilizer and insecticide were deducted from the amount the farmers received from the project-coordinated sale of their cotton harvest; long-term credit to purchase ox-drawn plows was deductible over five years.

Planners knew that the proposed crop production package would require much higher levels of cash investment and labor than the settlers were accustomed to. That is why the AVV attempted to restrict the amount of land that the farmers cultivated to between 1.5 and 1.6 hectares per worker, which was assumed to be the maximum area that an adult could farm using the recommended cultivation practices. The project used a system of labor equivalents to determine what portion of the 1.5- or 3.0-hectare fields could be farmed. Larger families were allowed to cultivate a larger area; smaller families, less. The acceptable area to be farmed was marked off by the extension agent at the beginning of each cropping season.

Labor potential was measured by a system that assigned labor values to persons in the family according to age and sex (table 3.1). Since an adult male was considered to have the work capacity most readily transferred to a variety of tasks, this became the standard unit and was assigned a value of

Table 3.1
Index of Labor Equivalents by Sex and Age

Age	Male	Female
0–12	—	—
12–14	0.5	0.25
15–55	1.0	0.75
55–65	0.5	0.25

SOURCE: AVV.

1.0. Women and children were assigned lesser values (0.75 for adult women, 0.50 for teenage boys, 0.25 for teenage girls). Based on their total labor index (the addition of all the different labor values for family members), a household was classified by farm type. For example, Farm Type IA, which was the smallest labor force, included families with a labor index of 1.75 to 2.25. To fall within this category, a family could consist of a man and wife (1.0 + 0.75 = 1.75) or a man, wife, and teenage boy (1.0 + 0.75 + 0.50 = 2.25). Smaller families (Farm Types IA–III) received a 1.0-hectare home-site and six 1.5-hectare bush fields over a five-year period. Larger households (Farm Types IV–VI) received a 2.0-hectare homesite and six 3.0-hectare bush fields. Each dry season the extension agent would recalculate the labor force of the settler households under his supervision to account for the addition or loss of family members. Based on the settlers' farm type, the extension agent marked off the amount of each 1.5-hectare field that the family was supposed to farm.

To promote the intensive agricultural program, the AVV employed one male extension agent for every twenty-five families and one female extension agent for every fifty. It was assumed that once the settlers grew accustomed to the new technical package, this ratio could be reduced. Project planners anticipated that the higher costs of the proposed crop production methods would be offset by higher yields and higher incomes. Moreover, they expected that the settlers' crop yields, per-capita food production, and cash income would increase every year. During the first three years this increase would derive from the annual addition of one new bush field in the project cultivation bands. After the third agricultural season, any subsequent increase would result from more intensive use of mineral fertilizer and labor on a fixed 10- or 20-hectare project farm.

Each project village was required to adopt the AVV model for elected government. This system represented a dramatic break with the prevailing historical system of inherited village and provincial chieftaincies described in chapter 2. The basic administrative unit of each village was the village *groupement,* or extension group. There was one groupement for men and one for women. Each groupement had an elected committee of officers presided over by a chief or president. The village committees were then united into bloc committees. These democratically elected committees were the principal organs through which the AVV issued its directives about farming and natural resource management. Planners assumed that the elected village groupements would continue to operate after the project ended.

AVV Mogtedo and the Case Study Village

The Mogtedo region is characterized by the same sudano-sahelian climate as the central plateau region near Damesma. There is a short rainy season from May to September, followed by a longer dry season from October to April. In the mid-1970s the average recorded rainfall was slightly higher (800 versus 700 to 750 millimeters) and more evenly spaced over a longer period of time than the rainfall at Kaya in the settlers' home area (F. Ouédraogo 1976; SAED 1976). Mogtedo's soils have a higher clay content than the central plateau soils near Kaya and are prone to heavy surface runoff during the short four-month rainy season. The vegetation is described as "degraded arborous savanna" (F. Ouédraogo 1976:28). In 1974 this vegetation included a thick covering of small trees, an occasional baobab, and underbrush. Wildlife was abundant, including birds, rats, antelopes, monkeys, and snakes. This thick vegetation and wildlife stood in sharp contrast to the stark horizons of the settlers' home village.

Location and Basic Infrastructure

From 1974 to the reorganization of the AVV in 1982, the planned settlements at Mogtedo and in the neighboring blocs of Linoghin, Rapadama, Mankaraga, Oualgui, Tanema, and Mogtedo-Bombore were part of an AVV administrative sector that stretched the length of the Nakambe (formerly White Volta) River. Project plans called for the successive installation of additional blocs of similar size and infrastructure over a twenty-year period from 1974 to 1994. These settlement areas would then form a relatively solid band of settlement, interspersed with areas reserved for forestry and wildlife along the Nakambe and linked with similar types of development along the Nazinon (formerly Red Volta) (map 8).

The Mogtedo bloc was created in a 10,000-hectare area of which an es-

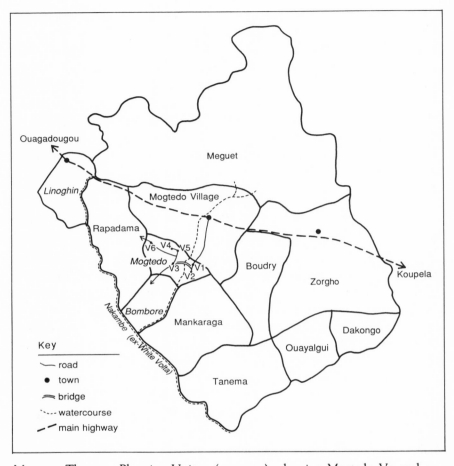

Map 10. The AVV Planning Unit 1 (AVV-UPI), showing Mogtedo V3 and the blocs of Linoghin, Mogtedo, and Mogtedo-Bombore. (McMillan 1993:271)

timated 3,200 hectares were considered suitable for agriculture (map 10). The area was bisected by the river Bombore, a branch of the Nakambe. Although the Bombore was little more than a chain of water holes during the dry season, it became a fast-flowing river once the rains began. As such, the Bombore made it difficult for the indigenous inhabitants to locate permanently on the far side of the river. To guarantee year-round access to the heretofore isolated area, the AVV constructed an all-weather access road and bridge across the Nakambe.

Six planned settlements were created over a six-year period between 1974 and 1980 (map 10). Although the AVV encouraged the settlers to give the villages traditional names, the extension staff and settlers still refer to the planned settlements by their French plat identification numbers of V1, V2, V3, V4, V5, and V6 (Village 1, Village 2, etc.). The first settlement, Mogtedo V1, was created in 1974 on the Mogtedo side of the Nakambe River (map 10). V1 is linked to the other five settlements by a concrete span bridge. The case study village, Mogtedo V3, was created on the other side of the river in 1975 (map 10). The other four villages were installed in 1976 and 1977. In 1978 the main road linking Mogtedo town with V1 and the five villages on the southwestern side of the Bombore was expanded to link with Mogtedo-Bombore, a new 10,000-hectare AVV bloc with seven planned settlements.

The water table for V3 is deep; about 40 meters, as opposed to 15 to 20 meters in the settlers' home village. Under these circumstances it would have been impossible for the settlers to meet their water needs with a traditional or concrete-reinforced tunnel well. The AVV's hydraulic service supplied each planned settlement with at least two bore wells. Each well was equipped with a metal hand pump. At least one settler per village was trained to perform minor pump repairs. In addition to improved wells and roads, the AVV built a number of concrete structures in each of the planned settlements. These included a warehouse for storing farm equipment, a village grain bank, and three two-room houses for extension workers at V3. V3 also included a number of buildings and services that served the entire village cluster, including a four-room office-home for the head extension agent for the six village cluster, a two-room elementary school, two four-room houses for schoolteachers, and a grain mill. Other AVV structures that served the entire bloc were located in V1. These were the main warehouse, a cement and mud-block infirmary and nurse's house (later replaced by a permanent infirmary and nurse's housing at Mogtedo-Bombore), and housing for the veterinary assistant.

When the AVV topographers first arrived to lay out the 10,000-hectare bloc of six settlements, they found only a few areas that were already being farmed by seasonal migrants from the adjacent villages and Mogtedo town. The land was still claimed, however, by several neighboring villages (Weogtega, Tissyone, Toyoko, Budama, Missri, and Naboulegre). The only permanent village located entirely within the 10,000-hectare area designated for the bloc was Taptoin. In 1976, Taptoin was estimated to contain about ten households with a total population of fifty (F. Ouédraogo 1976:33). Taptoin was created by immigrants from the adjacent village of Naboulegre in the late sixties and early seventies. As such, the Taptoin farmers were classified as indigenous inhabitants and were entitled to reimbursement for any loss of land due to AVV development. In 1977, however, the Taptoin farmers were rallying behind a Protestant religious leader who rejected the AVV's demands that they relocate to a project settlement. The Taptoin farmers were ultimately successful and did maintain their independence.

Prior to development of the planned settlements in Mogtedo and Mogtedo-Bombore, the river basin had been an important grazing site for the seminomadic FulBe, particularly during the rainy season when the FulBe moved their herds away from settled agricultural zones. One accurate sign of the change of seasons in Mogtedo was the FulBe leaving the river basins for their more densely settled home village sites in the plateau. When I first visited AVV Mogtedo in 1977, the woods adjacent to the Bombore River were brimming with FulBe campsites. By 1979 these campsites had been displaced by the new AVV bloc of Mogtedo-Bombore.

In 1974 only two areas were actually being farmed in the area now occupied by V3. One of these areas was sharecropped for a civil servant in the provincial capital of Zorgho. When the civil servant's fields were displaced by an AVV cultivation band, the administration gave him another large farm in an adjacent AVV village. The second area belonged to an elderly man who farmed with his wife and daughter. Since he was considered too old to "start a new life" in the AVV, the old man was allowed to continue farming as he liked. The only stipulation was that he move the location of his house from an area designated as a cultivation band. Although the old man never joined the project, the AVV assisted him by mechanically clearing the land for his new house and occasionally plowing his fields. Both the civil servant and the old man were valuable allies for the V3 settlers during the early years.

Planned Settlement

It was originally planned that all the households scheduled for V3 would be installed in 1975. This plan was frustrated, however, by recurrent delays in almost all aspects of bloc development, including road and well construction. As a result, the village was settled over three one-year periods, from 1975 to 1977. Although the first year of living in an AVV-sponsored settlement was always the most difficult, it was especially difficult for the settlers who arrived in 1975. Almost none of the basic infrastructure had been completed and the project was plagued by a host of mechanical and supply problems. The tractors were late in getting to the village, so only the cotton fields were mechanically plowed a second time. Few of the settlers bothered to plant in rows or to follow the AVV's recommendations on monocropping during this arduous first year. When the village wells went dry, neither the settlers nor the extension service had any motor transportation, and for a couple of months all water had to be carried five kilometers by hand, head, and donkey cart from V1. Nevertheless, at the end of the first season, the cotton harvest was good. The sorghum harvest was poor, however, due to the irregular tractor plowing. To ease the situation, the AVV agreed to provide the V3 settlers with half rations for a second year.

In spite of these initial setbacks, most settlers felt that they were making progress by the end of the first year. The accounts of their newfound prosperity circulated back to Damesma, and as a result, another ten Damesma households enlisted in 1976. Eight of the ten new immigrant households from Damesma were assigned to V3. Twenty more households were installed in 1977—three from Damesma and fifteen from Koupela and Kaya. The first immigrants from Damesma tended to be from extended families or clans with limited claims to inherited land or political power. There is little doubt that some of the first settlers were attracted by the project's promise of supplementary food. Although the settlers who came in 1976 and 1977 were more prosperous, they were still from groups who cultivated a high percentage of borrowed land. Few of these early settlers could have afforded the transportation and food costs of immigrating on their own to the more traditional immigration sites in the southwest.

By 1979 the settlers' immigration decisions were being influenced by their desire to join other family members in the project. This accounts for the fact that by 1979 some of the wealthiest households from Damesma and the Damesma-founded frontier villages to the north were moving to the adjacent bloc of AVV Mogtedo-Bombore. Unlike those who immigrated in the first year, almost all the farmers who immigrated after 1975 visited the project before making the decision to move. At least two of the Damesma settlers at V3 in 1979 were men whose wives had left them during the year before they immigrated. Another farmer who attached himself to a Damesma settler was faced with a runaway wife who made his life miserable with constant, public taunts about his reputed impotence. Three of the V3 households had wives that were "disputed"—that is, women whom the farmers had married in spite of the fact that they were promised to other men or had abandoned their former husbands. Each of these three men risked having their wives reclaimed if they returned to Damesma. Other settlers reported bitter disputes with brothers or clan elders in the year before leaving. By 1979 approximately fifty families in AVV-Mogtedo and the neighboring AVV bloc of Mogtedo-Bombore claimed Damesma as their traditional home village.

Not all of the male heads of household who claimed Damesma as their official "home village" had actually lived there. At least half had left the village as children or teenagers. Despite such long absences, these immigrant farmers continued to claim Damesma as their home village and the homesite of their family artifacts and boodoo (clan). Immigration to the AVV was only one of several possible immigration destinations open to them. The key difference was the government's attempt to subsidize, control, and "rationalize" this new immigration trend.

4

Initial Settler Adjustment and Settling In,
1974–1979

In the original project plan, the settlers' homesites were supposed to be randomly allocated. This policy was intended to prevent the reinstatement of the settlers' traditional social ties and political institutions. Because of the unintended delays in developing the basic infrastructure, this policy was not followed at V3 (see chapter 3). As a result, by the third and final year of organized population transfer at V3, the project village was divided into three neighborhoods based on broad areas of origin. One neighborhood grouped Mossi settlers from Damesma; the second, Mossi settlers from the Ouagadougou and Kaya villages other than Damesma; and the third, Mossi settlers from Koupela. The lone FulBe family was installed in between the Damesma and Ouagadougou/Kaya groups on a plot adjacent to the head extension agent's house. It should be emphasized that this high concentration of settlers from one village (Damesma) was an aberration that was only made possible by the early construction delays.

Despite these geographical differences, the initial period at the scheme was characterized by a sense of intense bonding of all the settlers, regardless of their region of origin or previous social status. In interviews the first group of settlers, who came in 1975, and first extension agents described how the two groups banded together to share the difficult task of lugging water by hand or donkey cart from the one functioning well five kilometers away. Until the first extension agents' houses were built, both the agents and the settlers lived under the same woven straw shelter. The same spirit of camaraderie was reflected in the settlers' nostalgic tales of pooling their knowledge of local flora, fauna, and medicines. The settlers and agents were especially concerned about their increased vulnerability to wildlife, especially snake and scorpion bites. They were more vulnerable because they were unfamiliar with the traditional medicinal plants and healers in the new area. One of their first cooperative activities in 1975 was to pool the medical cures and knowledge they had brought with them.

The same sort of collaboration seems to have characterized intervillage relations during the first three years, with a new batch of settlers arriving each year. Established settlers made a concerted effort to help those who arrived after them. Although the most intensive support was reserved for members of the same extended family, community aid was not related to strict lines of either area of origin or kinship. I personally witnessed the spirit of pan-village bonding among the new settlers who immigrated from Damesma to the planned settlements at Mogtedo-Bombore in 1979. In contrast to V3, these villages typically had only two or three other families from Damesma or the Kaya region living in them. Although the new settlers always emphasized their ties to home village families, they also went to great lengths to introduce me to their new neighbors, who were often from outside the Kaya region.

This same initial period was characterized as well by high levels of dependence on and a high frequency of interaction with the village extension agent. It was the agent who allocated the fields and who distributed new tools and food aid. When the settlers first arrived, they received daily instruction from the village extension agent on where, what, how much, and when to plant. The extension themes embraced field clearance, plowing, planting, first weeding and thinning, second weeding, mounding, harvesting, grain storage, and cotton marketing, as well as forestry and cooperative management. During the first three years the sound of an extension agent beating an empty metal drum to summon the male heads of household to village meetings was an almost daily part of life. Since the majority of settlers did not know one another, the extension agent's home was the main place that men congregated in the evening after work. In most cases, the agents also appointed the first village president and officers.[1] At V3 the wife of the male president was appointed to lead the women's group.

The gradual shift to a more independent transition period was signaled by the decentralization of evening talk sessions from the extension agent's house to the homes of the emerging village leaders. At V3 these included the homes of the AVV-appointed president, the *marabout* (Muslim holy man considered to have supernatural powers), the senior elder of the Poedogo lineage, a Ouagadougou merchant who was also a Koranic scholar, and a second Koranic scholar. Except for the two Koranic scholars, all the settler leaders were from Damesma. It is in this second "transition" period that the villagers subdivided into groups based on shared area of origin and extended family ties. This period was also characterized by the creation of new economic and political distinctions based on differential achievement in the project. New project-accorded political status was also important. The same transition period was associated with the selective reintroduction of certain traditional social and political relationships.

Creating New Social and Economic Categories

The first distinction settlers made among themselves was based on area of origin. This pitted the settlers from the north-central plateau near Kaya against Mossi settlers from the eastern plateau region of Koupela (see map 2). After an initial period of pan-village cooperation that lasted about three years, the two groups ignored each other. By 1978 they were actively hostile.

An incident that symbolizes the change occurred when a Koupela settler began to give generous gifts to the male head of one of the wealthier Damesma families, whose daughter's marriage alliance had just collapsed—the Burkinabè equivalent of being "left at the altar," with all the associated social stigma. By 1979 the settler's gifts had become increasingly grand, culminating in the presentation of two carts of gravel to pave the path to the family compound. In response the Damesma settler demanded that the gift-giver attend a group meeting of the Damesma settlers, at which the Koupela farmer was informed that if he was making the gifts in the spirit of friendship, that was acceptable. If, however, he was hoping to win a Kaya daughter in reward for the exchange, he was mistaken: "Kaya farmers do not sell their daughters to the highest bidder like a sack of peanuts."

As relations worsened between the two largest home village groups, the Damesma settlers were prone to band together at the slightest whiff of insult. An example was the eruption that resulted from the rumor that a Gourmantche (that is, non-Mossi from the southeast) neighbor of a Damesma settler in another AVV village had courted the fiancée of a settler from a village located near Damesma. Although there was no "proof," one of the wealthier Damesma settlers, who was not particularly well liked by his comrades, ordered a meeting of the Damesma settlers. The reunion quickly degenerated into derogatory slurs about the Gourmantche neighbor and other settlers from his area. In the end it was decided that no one who was "with them"—that is, no one who was a friend of the settlers from Damesma— would be allowed to speak to the accused man. The Damesma settlers then threatened to ostracize one of their fellow villagers from Koupela who was the accused man's friend unless he denounced his friend. The Koupela settler refused to denounce his friend. From the Koupela settlers' perspective, both they and the Gourmantche settler were being "set up" as convenient whip-ping posts to deflect attention away from the growing divisions among the Damesma settlers themselves.

One of the most glaring new divisions was created by the differential immigration from Damesma's seven clan-based neighborhoods. Over half the Damesma settlers were from just one of the seven clans—Poedogo— which, although large, still represented only 20 percent of the population living at Damesma in 1979. A high percentage of the Poedogo settlers were from a single subclan (maximal lineage) known as Poebila, or little Poedogo. During the same year one of the traditional leaders of Poebila immigrated from the home village and brought some of the subclan's fetishes with him. This meant that, in contrast to the other subclans from Poedogo and six other clan/neighborhood groups from Damesma, the Poebila settlers could negotiate marriage alliances and perform all but one of the important tradi-tional sacrifices without returning "home."

This second transition period was also associated with new changes in economic as well as social status. Almost immediately, three large families emerged as the top cotton producers and vied with one another to be ranked as number one. By 1979 this mostly friendly competition was being ex-panded to include competition for the purchase of consumer products and improved housing. In that year the male heads of two of the three top-ranked households purchased motorcycles and the third purchased a second moped. A second tier of successful project households began to emulate and to ally with them.

Another new source of conflict was centered on the elected post of village president. Although the extension agents emphasized that the V3 president was not a "chief" in the traditional Mossi sense, he still was accorded special privileges and respect. The village president, for example, was usually the first settler to be consulted about a new AVV rule or extension theme. Just like the "traditional" chief's wife at Damesma, the V3 president's wife was appointed and later elected to head the women's group. Just as they did for the Damesma chief, the village children and women danced in front of the V3 president's door at major feasts, and prestigious outside visitors were ei-ther housed or dined in his compound. What concerned the V3 settlers was not the current relationship of the village president to the AVV administration, but rather the future, when the AVV would cease to operate and V3 would be integrated into the surrounding province as an independent administrative unit. Then the elected village presidency was likely to be transformed into a traditional village chieftaincy. Although traditionally the members of the Poedogo clan were not in line for the Damesma village chieftaincy, certain members were rumored to aspire to the office of AVV village president. It was at this point that the numerical dominance of the settlers from Poedogo began to threaten the power and prestige of the other clans that had outranked them at Damesma.

Creating New and Reintroducing Old Crosscutting Social and Political Ties

The same transition period was associated with the creation of new and selective reinstatement of old social mechanisms to bridge the settlers' diverse ties to one another, to the surrounding indigenous inhabitants, and to the families and political leaders who remained behind in their home area.

Mutual Aid

One reflection of the importance that settlers attached to the development of strong social ties was the large quantities of grain and other aid they gave to new settlers. This aid was given most frequently to settlers from the same extended families. In fact, many of the family ties were quite distant. The average and more successful sponsored households generally tried to sponsor at least one new settler family each year. In addition, each one of the sample households hosted short visits from the new settler wives during the 1979 corn harvest. The corn harvest coincides with a brief lull between the more labor-intensive weeding and the main harvest. Although it was customary for female guests to work a few hours in the host family's fields, the women spent most of their time gathering leaves (*voaga*). After three or four days, the women returned to the new settlements carrying large sacks of gift corn, dried voaga, and a better understanding of the new area's wild foods. In one poignant case of open-handed generosity, a fifth-year settler lent his moped to a first-year settler he was assisting so that the new settler could transport his sick child to the Ouagadougou hospital. The moped was stolen by vandals, but the owner refused to accept any compensation or even to act perturbed over the loss. Indeed, he continued to lend material and food aid to the afflicted family.

Although I saw a few cases in which a first-year settler helped harvest the fields of an established settler who was his sponsor, such an act was seldom more than a gesture. More typically, the first-year settlers showed their gratitude with small, largely symbolic gifts of oil and sardines received as food aid from the project. This pattern of nonreciprocated aid differs markedly from patterns observed in other parts of Africa and in Latin America, in which new settlers usually worked the fields of their sponsor. The main explanation seems to be that the AVV settlers considered that the long-term value of the social relationship reinforced by their sponsorship far outweighed any short-term gain from a cash payment or labor aid.

Fictive Kinship, Joking Relationships, and Bond Friendship

Other crosscutting ties were created through the reciprocal exchanges associated with fictive kinship and joking relationships. A Damesma settler from Poedogo might refer to a Damesma settler from one of the other clans—or in one case, an indigenous farmer—as the "people of my mother." The actual relationship could be as distant as one of his father's, grandfather's, or even great-grandfather's wives coming from the other settler's neighborhood, lineage, or village. These distant kinship categories were used less often to identify someone than to reinforce a preexisting alliance between two friends. There was a much more open observance of joking relationships (see Hammond 1964) at V3 than in the home village. In the most widely observed joking relationship, a woman would tease, joke, and give gifts to a male relative to whom she was related by marriage. The two partners in the exchange would refer to each other as *rakeni*. Another joking relationship that I observed only in the early years was that of a joking husband or joking wife (*dem rawa* or *dem paga*). A child would select a joking spouse of the opposite sex to whom he or she would give small gifts on holidays. These joking marriages were generally between children who were so separated by age or background that there was no possibility of their relationship being taken seriously. Parents encouraged their children to choose their joking spouses from nonrelated families with whom they were trying to build alliances.

In addition to these ties of real or fictive kinship, a number of settlers established special friendships, or "bond" (see Hammond 1966:133–136), relationships with nonkinsmen. These relationships normally occurred between two men of about the same age. Bond friends would come together to render mutual aid, labor exchange, and political support for each other and each other's kin. Over time these friendships were usually reinforced by marriages between their children.

Religious Affiliation

Still other crosscutting ties were created by religion. At Damesma, the ties of religious conversion followed traditional clan lines. The three clans with the closest relationship to the chieftaincy (Natenga, Tangan, and Pousguin) were exclusively Muslim (table 4.1). The less closely allied clans (Nabodogo, Poedogo, Ouidi, and Gando) included a mixture of Catholics and "animists" who adhered to traditional Mossi beliefs. Politics and religion were intertwined in a slightly different way at V3. The Damesma settlers from Poedogo remained Catholic-animist. The settlers from Ouidi, who were allied with the Poedogo settlers by marriage and bond friendship, remained Catholic-animist. In contrast, there was strong pressure on the Damesma settlers from the other five clans to convert to Islam in order to show their solidarity against the numerically dominant settlers from Poedogo.

The Muslim settlers were aggressive proselytizers. They argued that the religion required only a minimal amount of study and ritual observance (see Skinner 1958). Conversion in turn gave the settlers an entree into a wide range of relationships with Muslims in other AVV villages, in the indigenous villages near the bloc, and even in Mogtedo town. This phenomenon was not restricted to Mogtedo. One Christian extension agent recounted how his father, an AVV settler at Kaibo, converted to Islam in order to feel more "at home" in his new village. Catholicism did not give rise to the same passionate pan-village, group identification. One reason was the Catholics' organization into village congregations with a single lay preacher (catechist). In contrast, the Muslims frequented religious observances in different

Table 4.1

Religious Affiliation of Clans at Damesma and in the Project Village

Clan	Damesma	Mogtedo V3
Natenga	Muslim	Muslim
Pousguin	Muslim	Muslim
Tangan	Muslim	Muslim
Ouidi	Catholic-Animist	Catholic-Animist
Poedogo	Catholic-Animist	Catholic-Animist
Nabodogo	Catholic-Animist	Muslim
Gando	Catholic-Animist	Muslim

AVV and non-AVV villages and had a fluid set of religious leaders from different villages. These ties of religious affiliation were expressed in the settlers' attendance at one another's receptions and rituals. Up to one hundred men, women, and children attended a typical Muslim naming ceremony. In addition to the V3 Muslims from Damesma, Ouagadougou, and Koupela, these included at least one representative of the Muslim groups in each of the other project villages, and one or two of a farmer's Muslim friends from indigenous villages and the pastoralist FulBe communities. Few Christians and animists would attend a Muslim naming ceremony. The same small number of Christians and animists might attend the work party of a Muslim neighbor. In the same way, Muslim participation at Christian labor invitations and baptisms was low.

Marriage

Throughout Mossi history, the bonds created by marriage were the most permanent means of forging alliances between nonblood kin. Marriage also united groups with different levels of political power and natural resource endowments (Dim Delobsom 1932; Hammond 1966; Skinner, 1960a, 1964a, 1964b). Marriages did not occur between households from the same saka, or clan/neighborhood, at Damesma. In the other two Kaya villages, where all but a small minority of first-generation immigrants claimed descent from the same founding ancestor and therefore claimed to belong to the same clan, it was rare to find a wife who married a man from the same village. The typical pattern was for a girl's marriage into a particular household to be only one of many alliances of exchange and mutual assistance between the two families. One pattern was for a household or extended family to exchange brides with three to five large, extended families over several generations.

A second pattern was for a young man to pay suit to a family with numerous daughters. In such a case, the young man would visit the head of the girl's family on holidays, assist the male head and perhaps the girl's mother with cultivation tasks, and make gifts to the girl's father and the head of the extended family. If everything went well, the suitor might be allowed to marry one of the family's daughters. It was virtually impossible, however, for a young man to carry off this sort of suit alone. The difficulty and expense of negotiating a good marriage alliance was one reason that labor migrants tried to maintain their home ties (see Skinner 1965). If a young man was well thought of, his kinsmen cultivated cordial relations with various families through which he might ultimately receive a bride.

A third way for men to obtain new wives was through alliances with the family of their present wife, their brothers' wives, or their fathers' wives.

Thus, the AVV settlers encouraged their wives to return home after harvests and make generous gifts to their extended families. If a wife was happy, and if her husband's family showed proper respect to her family, she might be given a young girl to award as a bride. The girl would often be brought to live with her female kinsman (aunt) while she was young—both to help with household tasks and to minimize the chance of her eloping. Such a girl is known as a *ma yiri paga* ("wife of my house"). When the ma yiri paga reached maturity, by custom she would be married to one of the unmarried sons in the household or to one of the families allied with that household.

Most brides who married settlers during 1979 were awarded through alliances that predated the settlers' immigration to the project. A second wife was awarded to one middle-aged household head in the study sample by the family of his first wife. That family lived in a village 60 miles north of Damesma. In the year before the bride arrived, the prospective groom visited her family twice. One of the groom's oldest friends from Damesma was responsible for making the final gifts to the girl's family and escorting her to the project. A second male family head received a wife from his mother's home village to award to his thirty-year-old unmarried brother.

As the settlers strengthened their economic and social ties to the new community, they preferred to marry their daughters to other families in the AVV, usually a family from the same home area with whom the bride's family already had some preexisting tie. The ideal was for the girl's father to consult the home village clan elder before making the match and for the elder to give his consent. Although the clan elder was consulted, he did not necessarily take an active role in negotiating the match. The settlers' gesture in consulting the elder, however, reinforced the elder's role as the official family head. The elder's benediction also gave the entire clan a vested interest in supporting the marriage. This vested interest was especially crucial in the event of a divorce or the death of either partner. The lengthy negotiations involved in marrying the daughter of one of the older Damesma settlers into one of the larger, wealthier settler households illustrate the dual economic and social role of these alliances. The alliance was considered propitious because the groom's family would give the bride's family a firm ally in the village, access to supplementary farm labor, and long-term insurance against hunger should the male family head become ill or die. Before arranging the match, however, the girl's father wrote to the Damesma chief, who was also the head of his clan (Natenga). The Damesma chief agreed with the logic of the match. After receiving the chief's authorization, the prospective groom's father held a lavish Muslim *doaga* (offering) at Damesma—not in the project village. At this doaga the chief of Damesma, in his role as titular head of the girl's father's clan, announced that he, not the girl's father, was awarding the girl. As of early 1980, the prospective groom's family was acknowledging its part in the alliance by continuing to show respect for and assisting the girl's father. Negotiations concerning the precise date of the marriage and the choice of groom (one of the household head's younger brothers) were also under way.

Young men who attempted to bypass the long process of exchange and mutual alliance between families were rebuffed. One instance involved a Damesma settler from a neighboring AVV village who was constantly visiting and assisting one of the older V3 settlers. The older settler had an unmarried fourteen-year-old daughter. After several months he reminded the young man that if he was hoping to win the hand of his daughter, she was already promised. He did encourage the young man, however, by noting that he had other young daughters who were not far behind the fourteen-year-old. Accepting the challenge, the young man continued an active alliance with the older settler and eventually did get a bride.

Without these sorts of long-term economic and social relationships between families, it was virtually impossible for a young settler to get a wife whose past was not complicated by a series of nasty disputes over broken engagements. The settlers recognized the extremely high economic and social costs of the conflicts that could be caused by broken engagements. Therefore, before committing themselves to a special relationship of support and mutual aid with a new family at the project, a household would generally conduct a rational assessment of the potential marriage possibilities that the alliance held.

Not all of the prearranged and arranged marriages went smoothly. One daughter of an AVV farmer had been promised to another farmer in the home village since her youth. When the daughter came of age and the fiancé inquired about the marriage date, the girl's father informed the groom that he would first have to convert to Islam. The fiancé protested that the girl's father had not objected previously to his religious status and refused to convert. Since the father was unwilling to break the agreement with the potential groom's household, negotiated through the clan elders at Damesma, and since he refused to back down on the issue of religion, he was rumored to hope that the girl would quietly elope. She eventually did.

Serious disputes could erupt when a clan elder exerted his right to award a specific girl without the consent of the girl's father. I observed only two cases of contested arranged marriages at Damesma during the year I followed the village marriages most closely. In both, the father was forced to back down. Almost immediately after doing so, both fathers left the village. The only socially acceptable alternative to an arranged marriage was for the promised girl to run off with another man and to stay away from Damesma until she had several children (the usual number was three, because there were cases of a fiancé's family reclaiming a woman with only one or two children). The girl's mother and father could then maintain that the girl was acting against their wishes without publicly breaking with either the elder or the fiancé's family. Two V3 couples eloped during 1979. Although both girls' families made elaborate expressions of public outrage, the villagers agreed that both elopements were a sensible solution to an impossible pre-arranged engagement.

For a father to renege on a marriage alliance was to tear at the very fabric of the Mossi lineage and alliance system. The repercussions that followed from a case in which a settler did renege from a marriage alliance in 1980 discouraged others. This particular situation involved a settler who had two fifteen-year-old daughters. The clan elder at Damesma had promised one girl to an older AVV settler who was from a village adjacent to Damesma. Although the man was well respected, his family was small, he was old, and he adored his first wife. The second girl had been promised to a household head in his mid-thirties who had a wife he had inherited when his elder brother died but no wife he had sought on his own. While the father maintained the second alliance, he chose to award the first girl to a younger household head at V3 who was obviously on the way to becoming one of the wealthiest AVV settlers. His decision unleashed a vicious feud between the rejected fiancé's friends and family and the girl's father, including threats of death and evil-doing. Not one of the other settler households was willing to publicly support the father's break with the elder. When the two marriages finally did occur, they were held quietly, with no public celebration or gift exchange.

Relations with the Indigenous Inhabitants

The V3 settlers passed through several stages in their relationships with the indigenous inhabitants in adjacent villages. When the settlers first arrived, they were disturbed by the animosity of the local people. Over time, however, most settlers established a relationship with at least one indigenous host family. Their first exchange with a local farmer was often to acquire native seeds and medicinal plants. Further, it was not uncommon for one or more indigenous farmers to seek advice from the V3 marabout or to visit the homes or the ceremonies of wealthier settlers. The first major change in intergroup relations came when the new settlers consulted one of the indigenous earth priests in order to locate a suitable burial ground. A second spate of interaction was catalyzed by a long drought during planting. Again the settlers asked the indigenous earth priest to prepare a sacrifice on their behalf.

The year 1979 (four years after the first AVV settlers arrived at V3) brought several new types of interaction between settlers and hosts. The first involved increased intergroup livestock purchases and sales. The settlers and hosts also collaborated in the establishment of a new village market. This was also the first year that the indigenous villagers voluntarily sent a delegation to the V6 celebration that ended the Muslim Ramadan fast. This event was especially significant because the AVV cultivation bands at V6 were located in areas that had been actively farmed by the neighboring indigenous villages. This was also the first year that the head Muslims of V3 made regular visits to the courts of the local chiefs and to ceremonies of other indigenous Muslim groups.

Relations with the Home Village

The settlers' persistent ties to the home village were evident in five major areas: landholding, ritual, marriage alliances, return visits, and political linkages. In theory, any Damesma immigrant or his descendants could return to the home village and reclaim all or part of his father's inherited fields. In practice, most settlers had few inherited fields, which was often why they had left in the first place and why return migration was not anticipated, except to assume a special ritual office. It was clear that if the Damesma settlers left the project, it was to colonize yet another frontier rather than to return home (McMillan 1983). Nonetheless, their ties to the home village remained strong.

This persistent linkage with the home village was reflected in the dual-level structure of the two most important harvest sacrifices—*Kiougou* and *Kitwaga*. Both sacrifices celebrate the current generation's unity with the ancestors. At Damesma, each sublineage organized its own Kiougou, which it celebrated through its recognized leader, usually the oldest member of the clan. Thus, it was possible for Kiougou to be celebrated in a migrant settlement. With the arrival of the two recognized leaders of the Poebila clan segment in 1979, the members of this subclan were able to celebrate Kiougou in their new settlement. One leader was a wealthy farmer from Damesma, a cattle trader; the other was a wealthy farmer who had spent most of his life in one of the frontier settlements created by Damesma immigrants in the 1920s and 1930s. This event symbolized an important turning point in the permanency of the move. In contrast, the Kitwaga sacrifice was cele-brated on behalf of the entire clan and had to be performed by the bood-kasma, or clan elder. While the head of a sublineage could acquire some of the clan's fetishes and live in another section of the country, the clan elder in charge of Kitwaga *had* to be resident at Damesma, where the clan fetishes were stored.

The settlers' need to guarantee the networks through which they obtained wives reinforced their persistent identification with the Kiougou and Kit-waga rituals, which symbolized their unity with the village chief, lineage elders, and clan leaders remaining at Damesma. Although the settlers' chil-dren increasingly married other settlers' children, the majority of marriages were still orchestrated through the traditional elders and/or village and saka chiefs. Not surprisingly, the older settlers' visits home were almost always linked to creating new and maintaining old marriage alliances.

Two periods were especially popular for home visits. The first was in Oc-tober for Kitwaga. An individual's age was calculated from Kitwaga to Kit-waga, and so it was the traditional time when a girl's father decided whether or not she was ready for marriage. For this reason, it was particularly impor-tant for the male head of a household who hoped to receive a bride to be present during the festivities. Many of the AVV teenagers went home simply to enjoy the celebrations. The second wave of home visits took place im-mediately after harvests. Wives returned more frequently and for longer pe-riods than their husbands. If the household head returned after harvests, it was usually only for a short visit to attend to a specific problem, such as transporting an elderly parent or new bride to the project or selling cattle.

Until 1979 the most direct linkages between the AVV settlers and the Damesma chief were for taxes and official papers.[2] In that year the provincial administrator insisted that the AVV settlers' taxes be paid through him, not the home village chiefs. Even without this official link, most of the Da-mesma settlers stayed in at least yearly contact with their chief; a few even paid their taxes in both places the first year. The Damesma settlers knew that in the event of a misunderstanding with another Damesma descendant, a marriage alliance dispute, or other problems such as recovering children from a runaway wife or getting a child out of jail, a settler was helpless without the support and allegiance of a powerful chief. While the AVV ex-tension agents could sometimes play the same role locally, they were totally ineffective in resolving matters in other parts of the country or across na-tional frontiers. Given the high percentage of Mossi living in Côte d'Ivoire, the latter was an important consideration. Three Kaya chiefs visited V3 in 1979—the Damesma chief, the chief of a small village near Damesma, and the chief of one of the seven Damesma clan/neighborhoods. It was impossible, however, to compare the power of the other chiefs with that of the Damesma naba.

In 1979 the chief was an active man in his mid-forties who had extensive dealings throughout the central plateau as well as in Ouagadougou, Bobo-Dioulasso, Côte d'Ivoire, and now the AVV. His strong relations with the national administration developed from his early support of both the political party in power and the district chief at Kaya. His extensive relations with Côte d'Ivoire, southwestern Burkina, and the AVV were routed through the thousands of Damesma immigrants and their descendants who lived in these areas. Each year the chief spent one to two months visiting different groups of Damesma migrants and Damesma descendants in Côte d'Ivoire and Burkina's southwest. His visits to the AVV in 1979 and 1980 were celebrated with feasting, gifts, and dancing. Although the AVV settlers recognized that the Damesma chief was not officially involved in the selection of their new chief, his endorsement would affect the new chief's authority.

There was a strong precedent for the way the Damesma chief extended his authority, either consciously or unconsciously, into the AVV. The customary pattern was for a new immigrant community to request that a powerful chief send his representative (Izard 1965, 1970, 1971; Skinner 1957, 1960b, 1962b, 1964b, 1970b). By sending a relative to be his representative or acknowledging the de facto immigrant leader (often by referring to this individual as having a distant kinship tie to himself), the chief created a mechanism for integrating the new frontier settlement into the Mossi hierarchy of village, regional, and provincial chiefs. This hierarchy, in turn, expanded the chief's power to get things done over a much wider geographical area.

Evolving Patterns of Conflict Resolution

The strong emphasis the settlers placed on alliance formation resulted from their sudden, unnatural removal from the traditional mechanisms for acquiring land in new, less populated zones. The settlers realized that the ties of neighborhood and the village extension group, or *groupement*, that were introduced by the project were dependent on high levels of support from the project. Once project support was withdrawn, they could not be relied upon. The lack of any strong base of preexisting social ties to the indigenous hosts forced the AVV settlers to invest a great deal of energy and resources into the reconstitution of extended family ties.

Despite this substantial investment in the new "communities by design," these ties remained weak, as evidenced most clearly in the adjudication of disputes. In the home village most livestock and marriage disputes between individuals were resolved locally through informal visiting and mediation. The nightly ritual of visiting one's kinsmen and allies was essential to community life. While sharing gossip, villagers defined and redefined values, shared news, and reached a group consensus on issues and disputes. If the dispute involved two members of different lineages in the same clan, it would usually be worked out in consultation with the neighborhood/clan chief and/or an informal council of lineage and sublineage elders. Only rarely, when a case involved litigants from different villages or clans, would a case be appealed all the way to the village chief.

These informal channels of adjudication were disrupted at the project. The problem was especially serious for settlers who immigrated without other members of their extended family. During the early years most conflicts were negotiated through the AVV extension agent. These included claims brought against the FulBe herders for livestock damage to crops[3] and disputes over livestock ownership, as well as settlers' personal problems. By the fifth year (1979), however, settlers were using other methods to resolve disputes, including social ostracism and mediation through the V3 marabout. As a respected holy man and member of the Damesma chief's clan, the marabout was careful to avoid the disputes of any single settler faction. He also counseled a steady stream of indigenous farmers and extension agents. Since both parties to a dispute would usually talk to him, the marabout was well informed. He was also discreet. Having heard both sides, he was often able to make an objective negotiation of a problem. In return for his efforts, the marabout received cash gifts. This income allowed him to hire a man from the home village to work his fields while he met with his clients.

In the absence of established, recognized channels for diffusing conflict, the stress of reconciling new social and economic conflicts could be volatile. Two events that occurred in late 1979 and early 1980, slightly less than five years after V3 was founded, are illustrative. The first situation erupted when a wealthy Damesma farmer beat his neighbor's wife.[4] The neighbor was from a village near Damesma in the Kaya region. In spite of the fact that the Damesma settler's sons begged her forgiveness, she insisted on seeking her own justice and went to the home of one of the other Kaya settlers to ask him to call upon the non-Damesma Kaya households to assist her. If they had been at home, she said, she would have asked her blood brothers, but since they were at the AVV, she had no other recourse. She refused to discuss the case or compensation due her with any of the AVV extension agents and appealed to the national police based in the provincial capital at Zorgho. The offending settler was imprisoned for a short time before being released in preparation for a trial.[5]

The second event erupted when a settler from Damesma died in a nearby planned settlement. The settlement had a mixed population of Mossi from different regions; only three of the households had immigrated from Damesma. When the young man died, his non-Damesma neighbors refused to bury him. To add insult to injury, the dead man's neighbors ignored the death and continued on to market. The settlers cited the dead man's religion as their principle reason for refusing to participate or to assist. As loyal Christians and Muslims, they could not be expected to participate in the rituals of an unclean, beer-drinking animist. Shocked by this stark reminder of their fragile ties to nonrelated settlers in the new "communities by design," the Damesma settlers from the surrounding villages came to bury him the next day.

Conclusion

The AVV land-tenure and settlement policies were a deliberate attempt to break with the traditional social mechanisms by which the Mossi had long colonized new land. Over time, however, the settlers showed a pattern of selective adaptation to the project policies and selective reinstatement of their traditional social roles and relations. These patterns of adjustment were quite similar to those observed in successful settlements throughout the world (Chambers 1969; Colson 1971; Goering 1978; Nelson 1973; Scudder 1981, 1984, 1985, 1991).

During the first three years of settlement, when the planned transfer of population to the new village continued, the settlers made a deliberate attempt to minimize their preexisting social and economic differences. This period was also characterized by high levels of dependence upon and interaction with the AVV extension agents and low levels of interaction with the indigenous inhabitants. The transition to a second, more dynamic stage of community development was signaled by the settlers' subdivision into different groups based first and foremost on area of origin. During this period there was a growing number of new conflict situations whose origins could be traced to increased economic competition and the greater importance of religion.

This second stage was also characterized by the creation of new and the reintroduction of old social mechanisms to bridge the settlers' diverse backgrounds. These crosscutting mechanisms included the formation of new interest groups based on religion and economic status as well as area of origin and kinship. Also during this period, the settlers attempted to increase their social, political and economic ties with the sometimes hostile spontaneous settlers and indigenous inhabitants. In addition, they reinstated certain traditional rituals and ceremonies. In one group of Damesma settlers—those from the clan Poedogo and the subclan (lineage) Poebila—economic success meant sponsoring the immigration of additional members from their unilineal descent group. This ultimately led to the reconstitution of one of the traditional subclans in a group of neighboring project villages. In contrast, a second group of farmers used the same social grid to create a new base of social networks with other successful settlers from outside their traditional kinship group. These settlers typically broke some of their traditional obligations to their Damesma-based patrilineal clan. They also made little attempt to foster the immigration of additional family members. This new pattern of kinship ties created by marriage and reinforced by reciprocal non-market exchanges of labor and food helped the Damesma settlers to create a united social presence in the project and in the region. Although this presence was not "traditional," in that the primary social ties between households were not based on patrilineal descent, the newly created social ties were still vitally important. Moreover, these ties were an important factor undergirding the group's new economic success in the project.

By 1980 the V3 settlers were well aware of the deep social rifts that divided them. They were also aware that a large part of the distinctive flavor of V3 was derived from the high concentration of settlers from Damesma. Although this high concentration gave the Damesma settlers an early advantage over other immigrant groups, over time it caused them to have more difficulty reconciling their new and former economic and political statuses. This sort of realignment of status relationships was the norm in immigrant Mossi communities (Ancey 1974; Benoit 1973a, 1973b; Benoit and Lahuec 1975; Schildkraut 1978; Schildkraut and Finnegan 1974). At the AVV, however, the process was made more difficult by the artificial selection and rapid development of the sponsored settlements. In contrast, a typical spontaneous community contains a diverse mixture of outside settlers and local hosts. This self-selection generally occurs gradually, with family members sponsoring the arrival of later family members over one or two decades. In this way the new community has an opportunity to reincorporate gradually rather than in one or, at most, three years.

Although many problems had appeared at V3 by 1979, they seemed to be ones that could eventually be resolved. Ample evidence from older planned settlements worldwide indicated that settlers could often rework a project model for community development into an operational social framework over time (Apthorpe 1968; Apthorpe and MacArthur 1968; Barnett 1981; Brokensha and Scudder 1968; Butcher 1971; Chambers 1969; Colson 1971; Gaitskill 1959; Hammond 1959a, 1959b, 1962, 1963; Hansen and Oliver-Smith 1982; Scudder 1962, 1968, 1969, 1971, 1981, 1985). Scudder considers such reworking of the project model and/or reweaving of the social fabric to be a prerequisite for settlers to begin to feel "at home" in their new habitat (Scudder 1981:114). He argues that this "feeling at home" could be assessed through a wide range of indices, such as a growing willingness to travel to off-farm locations; the use of local, new, and transferred names for physical land forms, plants, and animals; the reestablishment of community organizations; and the formation of new organizations to represent the settlers vis-à-vis the government and the world at large (Scudder 1981:19). In 1979 there were many such indicators. Especially important was the growing power of the Catholic and Muslim communities, the partial reinstatement of traditional harvest and circumcision ceremonies, increased participation in the ceremonies and rituals of the indigenous inhabitants, and an increased ease in dealing with outside civil authorities. Studies worldwide showed that this type of creative reworking was generally most successful when there was a strong economic incentive for cooperation, like a profitable irrigation scheme or commercial rain-fed crop. In 1980 the economic prospects looked good.

5

Early Economic Changes and Assessment, 1979–1980

Both the AVV farm-monitoring survey, with a sample of 313 households in 1979, and the intensive case study of the Mogtedo V3 settlers show that the Damesma settlers experienced high levels of crop-income growth during their first five years at the project. Yet they were not reinvesting this higher income in intensive farming. Indeed, both studies show that with longer periods of residence in the scheme, the average household gave less attention to the proposed crop extension package. Based on these results, researchers concluded that the AVV was unlikely to attain its long-term goals for sustainable income growth from farming.

The results of the case study agreed with the farm-monitoring survey's conclusions about the settlers' production practices. The case study demonstrated, however, that an exclusive focus on the success or failure of the recommended package overlooked other areas of significant and positive change. These included an increasingly diversified investment of time and money in areas outside the recommended program. The settlers' more diversified strategies included clearing new fields outside the project area as well as investing more in livestock and working at nonfarm jobs. When the income earned from these other activities was included, the Damesma settlers showed a substantial increase in total income. Based on this analysis, I concluded that the settlers living in the case study village were on the brink of a new stage of more dynamic economic growth and diversification. The settlers were not, however, adopting the proposed program for intensive farming, nor were they engaged in sustainable forest management.

Results of the AVV Farm-Monitoring Survey

A central part of the original AVV project's design was a monitoring unit referred to as the Statistical Service. The service's goal was to provide information on the success or failure of specific technical innovations, as well as on the more general effects of the agricultural program on settler income and welfare. The primary mechanism for data collection was an economic survey of a random sample of households in all the major AVV village clusters. The unit of research was the household, defined as the residential unit that cultivated one of the 10- or 20-hectare AVV farms. This same household unit was the focus of project extension policies. The male who was recognized as the official household head represented the family unit in all contractual dealings with the AVV (such as for insurance, equipment purchases, credit, and crop sales). Moreover, it was assumed that crops planted on the project farm would be cultivated cooperatively under the supervision of the male household head. The farm-monitoring survey included 132 households in 1978 and 313 in 1979, representing about 11 percent and 18 percent respectively of the settlers living in the AVV-sponsored settlements in those years (Murphy and Sprey 1980). (See appendix A for a more detailed discussion of the methodology.)

This research provides clear evidence that the AVV was indeed successful in its attempts to increase crop yields and raise settler incomes (Murphy and Sprey 1980). Although the average yields for sorghum were below those projected, they were still two to three times higher than those the case study recorded for the home village farmers (700 to 900 kilograms per hectare versus 200 to 350). Even with the much higher production costs associated with the project (fig. 5.1), the settlers' net value of crop production was two to four times higher than the recorded average in their home village (table 5.1). The average figures recorded for the smallest farm sizes (Types IA and IB, 1.75 to 2.25 and 2.50 to 3.25 labor units respectively) were 200 percent greater than the net first-year income that was projected by the AVV in 1973 in all of the blocs except Kaibo South (Murphy and Sprey 1980:64; AVV 1973b, 1974). The AVV farm-monitoring survey shows, however, that these higher yields and income were primarily the result of the expansion of the total area cultivated and the natural fertility of the new soils rather than the successful introduction of the recommended package of technical innovations. Specifically, Murphy and Sprey (1980) found that

Early Economic Changes

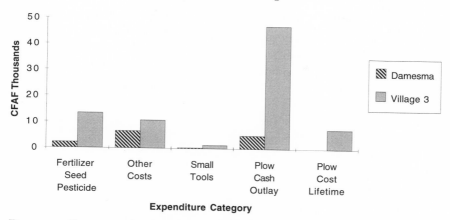

Figure 5.1. Crop expenditures, 1979. (McMillan 1983:149; Murphy and Sprey 1980:20, 59)

(1) settlers who had been at the project for shorter periods of time tended to follow the extension package more closely than those who had been there longer and (2) cotton was the only crop on which the recommended package of cultivation techniques, including fertilizing (fig. 5.2),[1] monocropping, using pesticides, planting in rows, thinning, and timely weeding with animal traction, was consistently applied. This difference in adoption of agricultural innovations on particular crops according to length of residence in the scheme was attributed to a higher level of supervision by the extension ser-vice in the early years and the extension service's emphasis on cotton, which was used to reimburse settler credits.

Results of the Case Study Farm-Monitoring Survey

The case study research with the V3 settlers (n = 12 households in the AVV and 35 households in the settlers' home area in 1979–80) agreed with the general conclusions of the AVV farm-monitoring program. Where the case study distinguished itself was in its ability to gather information on areas outside the proposed agricultural innovations that were being moni-tored by the farm-monitoring survey. Specifically, the case study revealed important differences in the organization of family labor, the settlers' living standards, crop production, and sources and levels of household income, as well as changes in intrahousehold roles and relations that were not and probably could not be observed in the more broadly based farm-monitoring survey.

Table 5.1

Net Crop Income per Adult Labor Equivalent (ALE) for 1979
and Net Profit from the Sale of Traction Animals After Repurchasing
New Animals (in CFAF)

Village Groups	N	Net Income[a]	Net Income[b]	Net Profit from Sale of Traction Animals
AVV				
Mogtedo and Mogtedo-Bombore[c]	(97)	—	—	—
1-year settlers[d]	—	48,000	—	—
2-year settlers[d]	—	75,400	—	—
2-year settlers	—	66,400	—	—
3–5-year settlers	—	56,600	—	—
6-year settlers	—	65,800	—	—
Mogtedo V3 (3–5-year)				
All households	(9)	86,701	75,566	+13,611
Selling animals	(5)	78,566	67,431	+20,777
KAYA HOME VILLAGES				
All	(35)	—	30,100	—
Without animal traction	(22)	—	26,916	—
With donkey plow	(7)	—	29,976	−670
With ox plow	(6)	—	37,271	−9,397

SOURCES: McMillan 1983; Murphy and Sprey 1980.

[a]Cash value of production minus cash costs of inputs and "real" costs of animal traction equipment and animals based on potential resale value of the animal, depreciation of the plow, and upkeep of the animals and plow (Murphy and Sprey 1980:59,70).

[b]Cash value of production minus cash costs of inputs and recorded cash costs of payment and upkeep of equipment and animals (McMillan 1983:411).

[c]The Statistical Service Survey data are subdivided into five groups of farmers according to the stage of farm development and equipment. First-year settlers are new settlers who farm their 1-hectare homesite plus two official bush fields, both plowed by the AVV tractors. Second-year settlers are in their second year and have three bush fields to cultivate, one of which is plowed by the AVV. A distinction is made

Table 5.1 *continued*

between settlers who have purchased animal traction and the few who have not. Third- to fifth-year settlers are authorized to farm four bush fields, one of which is plowed by the AVV. It is assumed that by the third year, all households have animal traction. From the sixth year on, settlers are authorized to farm four of their six bush fields (two of the six are supposed to lie fallow at any point in time). Having received all six of their official bush fields, these households no longer receive any mechanical plowing.

dWithout animal traction.

Changing Patterns of Household Labor

Both the farm-monitoring survey, with a sample size of 313 households in different AVV blocs, and the case study of the Damesma settlers at V3 revealed important changes in the organization of the settlers' farms. These changes included a 40 percent increase in the average land area farmed per worker using the AVV system of calculating Adult Labor Equivalents (ALE) by sex and age (Table 3.1) (from 1.4 to 1.95 hectares per ALE) and a 260 percent increase in the percent of cropped areas devoted to cotton (from 8 to 29 percent) (fig. 5.3). Especially important from the settlers' perspective was a 100 percent increase in total labor hours (from 622 to 1,256 total weighted labor hours per ALE), in large part because of the expanded area planted in cotton (fig. 5.3).[2] Cotton required four times the labor expenditure per hectare of sorghum (1,520 weighted hours per hectare for cotton

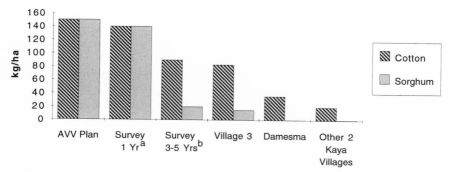

Figure 5.2. Fertilizer use, 1979. (AVV 1973:18–19; McMillan 1983:390, 392, 393; Murphy and Sprey 1980:15)

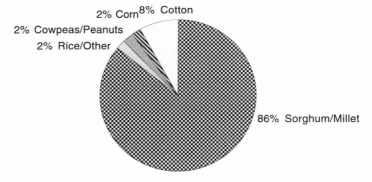

A. Damesma (1.4 ha/unit labor)

2% Corn 8% Cotton
2% Cowpeas/Peanuts
2% Rice/Other

86% Sorghum/Millet

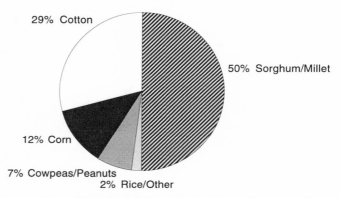

B. Village 3 (1.95 ha/unit labor)

29% Cotton

50% Sorghum/Millet

12% Corn

7% Cowpeas/Peanuts
2% Rice/Other

Figure 5.3. Area planted in different crops, 1979 (percent of
total area). Includes both cooperatively worked family
fields and privately worked fields. Percentage represents the
percent of total area cultivated by the sample farmers in
each group. (McMillan 1983:119)

versus 394 hours for white sorghum [McMillan 1983:397]). Harvests were
especially time-consuming. In a good year the average cotton field could be
picked three times. This agricultural calendar varied from Damesma, where
the main crop activities ended after the sorghum harvest in November. The
dry-season months from December through April were the traditional times
for farm families to engage in handicrafts, trade, and house repair. In the
project this period of low agricultural activity was reduced to less than two
months. If settlers were still in the process of field clearance and destumping,
there was little respite.

Although the AVV extension package did increase total labor, it did not affect the principal sources of farm labor. As in the home villages, family members performed the majority of crop activities. Few settlers had family members from the home village to call on to assist them during peak labor periods. Those who did come complained that the work was too hard and the pay scale (one sack of cotton for five to six days of picking) ridiculously low. In 1978 one of the favorite evening entertainments at Damesma was a deaf-mute's mime of how hard he had to work during his short visit to relatives in the AVV.

Traditionally, the principal source of nonfamily labor is the work party, or *sosoga* (see Saul's [1983] discussion of work parties in south-central Burkina Faso). Farmers issue invitations for work parties on a particular date. Anywhere from 20 to more than 100 persons might attend. In gratitude for his or her friends' agricultural labor, the host provides food, drink, and occasionally musical entertainment. Although an invitation can provide supplementary workers during peak labor periods, it also plays an important social and political role. One of the special prerogatives of a chief is to issue labor invitations to assist his family in the cultivation of his fields, which are much larger than the fields of the average farm family. In turn, attendance, duration of work, and the number of workers each family provides are an illustration of political loyalty.

The most frequent use of labor parties in the settlers' home village was for weeding (McMillan 1983). Weeding was also the task whose timing and quality had the most critical effect on yields. In one of the neighboring two villages where chiefs were less prominent, work parties were used primarily for the arduous but noncritical task of threshing. Work parties figured less prominently among the Damesma settlers at V3, especially in the early years, when everyone was involved in the heavy work of establishing new fields (McMillan 1983). When they were organized, it was most often to help small families who were at a disadvantage because of illness or age.

Another source of supplementary workers that was quite visible at the AVV was classified as "aid" labor. In contrast to the labor parties, the aid laborers volunteered their services. Aid workers were most often the wives of close friends or new settlers who would volunteer to assist an individual with his cotton or corn harvests. In return, the volunteer workers would receive several baskets of cotton or corn as gifts. The gifts usually far exceeded the actual cash value of the volunteers' labor. Since the timing of neither the cotton nor the corn harvest was especially critical, the function of the portion of the harvest that was given in remuneration was primarily to reinforce a social link between the farmer and the volunteers' families.

The most striking difference in the use of nonfamily labor at the two sites was the increased use of hired labor. This increase could be measured in absolute hours (392 weighted hours versus 12) and as a percent of average total labor hours worked (9 percent versus 0.4). Despite high labor demands for weeding, only 2 percent of the weighted hours for the first weeding and 7 percent for the second weeding were hired during the 1979 crop year. The difficulty of acquiring hired labor for weeding placed a premium on settlers being able to retain and motivate male and female family workers. To cope, several small families recruited nonrelated young men from the home village or local villages to work and board with them for the entire agricultural season.[3] The terms of the boarder relationships were seldom explicit. Cash and kind payments were construed as "gifts" and the boarder's visit was portrayed as one of "checking out" the AVV. Had we coded this in-residence, boarding labor as "hired," then the total figure for hired labor would have been much higher than 9 percent. Prenegotiated hired labor was more easily acquired during the nonpeak labor periods before planting and at cotton harvests. In 1979 hired labor accounted for 60 percent of the weighted hours for clearing cotton stalks before planting sorghum and 17 percent of the weighted labor hours for the cotton harvests (McMillan 1983).[4] The use of hired labor to harvest cotton enabled the settlers to pick the same field two or three times. Family members seldom wanted to harvest a field more than once.

Although the settlers continued to rely primarily on family labor, there were important shifts in the organization of farm labor. A typical farm in the settlers' home village contained twenty to twenty-five parcels in four to five distinct locations, or terrains, each with a distinct land-tenure arrangement. One terrain might include as many as eight separate parcels with different crops and different persons or groups of persons responsible for their cultivation (fig. 3.1). Certain fields were farmed cooperatively, with the entire family benefiting from their production. The head of the household dictated what crops were to be cultivated on these fields, the timing of the operations, and use of any products produced. Grain produced on cooperatively worked fields was used to feed the household members. Any monetary gain from the sale of food or cash crops from the cooperatively worked family fields was controlled by the male or female household head.

In addition, all individuals in the household had the right to cultivate a certain amount of land for their personal needs. Most women farmed at least one plot of a food grain, one or two plots of peanuts (groundnuts) or ground peas, and at least one vegetable patch. Unmarried children usually farmed one parcel of grain or a cash crop such as peas or cotton. Subhousehold groups composed of married sons or brothers and their families also farmed an area of food and cash crops that was separate from the household's cooperatively worked fields. Any crops or cash income from the sale of crops produced on a private field was under the control of the person responsible for the field. These privately produced crops were stored apart. Wives and unmarried and married children also had small herds of animals and engaged in a variety of off-farm income-earning activities like petty trade and handicrafts. Grain produced on the women's fields was seldom sold. Instead, it was typically used to provide a woman and her children with an extra meal during the period just before harvest, when food stores ran low. Wives were also responsible for the sauces eaten with the sorghum and millet porridge. Vegetables for the sauces were grown in small vegetable gardens. During the dry season the sauces were complemented with dried baobab leaves and wild plants. The women's revenues from trade and handicrafts were spent for oil and spices for the family sauces as well as for clothing, medicines, and other supplies for themselves and their children. Products produced on married children's private fields provided food and income for the special needs of married sons and brothers, their wives, and children. These patterns of production meant that a sizable proportion of total family income from and labor for crop, livestock, and off-farm employment was under the direct control of women and nondominant male family members. In addition, this privately produced food and cash income played an important role in determining the nutritional well-being and living standards of the entire family unit. As such, the "traditional" Mossi household functioned as a series of overlapping units of production and consumption.

In contrast, the AVV project assumed that the settler household would function as a unified production and consumption unit with a single decision-making locus. The male household head was the official representative of the family in all dealings with the project. The farm family's rights to land and any debts were incurred in his name. Thus no consideration was given to private production activities in the original design of the AVV fields or extension services.

Increased Economic Diversification

During the early years at the project, the settlers were involved in the heavy work of clearing fields. Families were small, and there was little time or money for noncrop activities like livestock and trade. By the fifth year the settlers had accumulated stores of reserve grain and had paid off all or most of their initial debts to the project. Moreover, most households had substantially increased in size because of the immigration of additional family members. This increase in household size on a fixed 10- or 20-hectare land base was an incentive for the successful settlers with large households to move away from the recommended program by investing in noncrop activities like livestock and trade and by expanding cultivation into areas outside the official boundaries for the project fields as a strategy to increase family income (fig. 5.4). The successful settlers were also motivated by the need to accommodate a second generation. Children who had immigrated to the project in their teens were now approaching the age when they would start families of their own. In the original project model, it was predicted that this population increase could be absorbed by farming more intensively. Therefore only a few farms were reserved for the next generation's fields. Larger families were encouraged to split, sending part of the family to one of the new blocs being developed within a 50-kilometer radius of Mogtedo.

The concept of splitting the household, especially when the father was still alive, ran counter to Mossi extended-family values. Traditionally, a household's wealth was most strongly correlated with the size of the family labor force, and the best security for the family had been to retain as many of the older sons as possible. One function of the system of borrowing land between families was to allow younger family members to increase their private land holdings temporarily. Then, as the father aged, the elder son would generally take over the father's inherited fields. Toward the end of their lives, the elders at Damesma usually cultivated only a small amount of land as private fields. The settlers were familiar with this traditional pattern of household expansion and increased subdivision within the household, followed by reconsolidation into a new household with an elder son as the male household head. Their big fear was that their married children and older adult children would become frustrated by the family's fixed 10- or 20-hectare farm and leave. An additional incentive for diversification was the desire of the less wealthy households to move away from a singular dependence on agriculture in the face of a high level of uncertainty about the total amount and spacing of annual rainfall, as well as the project's future. There were also, by the fifth year in the village, more opportunities for commercial endeavors and specialized trades such as masonry and mechanics.

Livestock / In the absence of fundamental changes in national banking institutions, livestock continues to be the principal source of investment for rural farmers, which augments their income as well. For pastoralist populations, livestock provides the principal source of income and—to the extent that livestock or livestock services are exchanged for grain or used for meat and milk—food (see Delgado 1979 and Finnegan and Delgado 1980). The manure livestock provides figures in any long-term strategy to develop sus-

A. BUSH FIELD OF SORGHUM

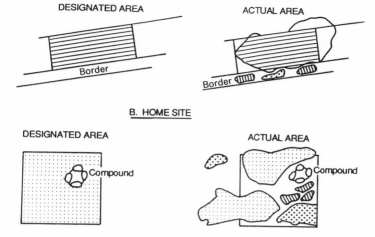

B. HOME SITE

C. BUSH FIELD FOR COTTON, PEANUTS, AND COWPEAS

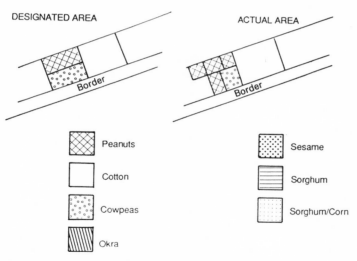

Figure 5.4. Designated vs. actual field structure at V3, 1979.
(McMillan 1983:120)

tainable cropping systems. Livestock is also one of the most important sources of income and investment for women.

It is not surprising, therefore, that the first investment to which the larger, wealthier settler households turned was livestock. By 1979 two of the three top cotton producers had accumulated large herds, each with more than forty cattle and oxen. The third top producer household had a sizable herd that numbered twenty head. The project model for on-farm animal husbandry was very different from the traditional model of boarding large livestock with pastoralist herders. Indeed, there was a rule against letting herders guard their animals on project fields. Traditionally, the chief constraint to keeping cattle on-farm was labor, especially during the rainy season, when the animals were at risk of trampling a neighbor's planted field. Theft was also a problem. Cattle rustlers knew that most households owned at least one pair of fat, well-tended oxen. Aided by the large area of surrounding uncut bush, along with good AVV access roads, vandals could steal, slaughter, and export the carcasses without being seen. The nearby Ouagadougou market provided an insatiable demand for meat. By 1979 four of the forty-seven households still living in V3 had their animals stolen. The result was that households with limited labor were increasingly reluctant to keep large livestock on-farm.

The settlers were equally reluctant to board their cattle with the FulBe living along the edge of the AVV-sponsored settlements. Here again, due to the isolated location of the planned settlements and their lack of historical relations with the FulBe, the animals were highly vulnerable to theft. Initially, some of the AVV settlers continued to board their animals with familiar pastoralists near their home villages. Others dealt with the problem by boarding their animals with the one FulBe settler household living in V3. By 1979, however, this single household was no longer able to adequately supervise the growing herds. Prompted by increasing problems with stolen and lost cattle, two of the largest cattle herders negotiated herding contracts with immigrant pastoralists living just outside the project village in early 1979. Assuming greater safety in numbers, several of the smaller, less wealthy households then boarded one to four animals with these herders. In return for boarding the animals, the herdsman had the right to sell the animal's milk, to receive an annual gift of cash or grain (estimated to be the equivalent of 1,000 to 1,500 CFAF per head of cattle per year in 1979), and to keep a portion of the calves born while the animals were under his care.

Nonfarm Employment / Most farmers' nonfarm income-earning activities consisted of small-scale commercial enterprises such as trade, manufacturing, and services. Only a few families had someone who engaged in the more lucrative year-round enterprises. For this reason the case study distinguished the second category of settlers as having "secondary occupations" and analyzed their income apart (table 5.2). In 1979 there were five outstanding examples of settlers with secondary occupations at V3: a storekeeper, a merchant who resold bread and beer, a butcher, a mechanic, and the village marabout. All five individuals had lived at the project for at least four years and began these activities two to three years after coming to the project. Two of them were in the study sample (table 5.2); our information on the other three is based on interviews and observations.

The storekeeper stocked a small general store with basic items such as soap, needles, kerosene, candy, bicycle parts, razor blades, kola nuts, and the gas-oil mixture used for mopeds. A settler purchased these items with savings from his cotton sales and money earned as a wage laborer on AVV construction projects. If the storekeeper did not have a particular item in stock, the customer could leave a request that would be filled in one or two days. The special-ordered trade goods were then transported from Mogtedo on the settler's bicycle or moped or on AVV trucks moving to or from construction sites. Although the storekeeper's selection was limited and his prices about 10 percent higher than prices at Mogtedo, he had a steady clientele of both settlers and extension agents. We estimated that his net revenue from the store was between 10,000 and 15,000 CFAF ($50 and $75) a month. In 1979 the storekeeper was expecting to enlarge his stock, to build a separate store building, and to expand his trade into the regional market at Mogtedo town and the famous black market center at Puetenga.[5] A second, less active storekeeper was a Damesma settler who periodically bought and resold sticks of bread, beer, and sodas to settlers and extension agents. By 1979 these three items had replaced chickens and kola nuts as the customary gifts given to visitors and extension agents. The bread man gave large amounts of credit that were never reimbursed. Thus, although he enjoyed a large volume, his net revenue was almost nil.

A third Damesma settler had a lucrative business as a butcher. Most of the goats and sheep he slaughtered were purchased from the nearby village markets or at the homes of indigenous villagers or FulBe. The settler butchered his animals and sold the meat in the village twice a week. Although his cash profits were only 500 to 1,000 CFAF per animal, the butcher reaped other benefits from the trade. These benefits included meat for a household of more than twenty inhabitants, the capacity to give meat as gifts to extension agents and other settlers, and, once or twice a year, the sale of accumulated hides.

Table 5.2
Income from Nonfarm Production and Commercial Activities, 1979
(in CFAF)

Source of Income	AVV Damesma Settlers	Kaya Villages		
		Damesma	Other Two Villages	
			2a	2b
Handicrafts[a]	4,864	13,350	2,616	5,847
	(8)	(12)	(8)	(10)
TRADE				
Animals	9,150	5,994	0	0
	(1)	(5)		
Agricultural products	1,525	5,937	150	1,730
	(7)	(11)	(2)	(3)
General merchandise	6,699	5,429	55	7,049
	(6)	(7)	(2)	(4)
LOCAL LABOR				
Manual labor	11,968	4,344	5,000	0
	(3)	(5)	(1)	
Equipment rental	0	5,400	0	5,150
		(1)		(1)
Fishing	0	512	20,401	722
		(5)	(3)	(3)
SECONDARY OCCUPATIONS				
Commercial	202,500	0	0	0
	(1)			
Butcher	0	69,875[b]	0	0
Other (marabout)	154,500	0	0	0
	(1)			
Military pension	0	0	0	510,648
				(1)

Methodology: Figures represent an average over all the sample households that reported income from a particular source.

( ) Indicates number of households that reported income in this category.

[a] Includes income from a variety of production activities, including beer-making, baking, weaving, and metalworking.

[b] Does not include meat guarded for consumption by the family.

The long distances that the settlers had to travel to markets and for return visits home made it increasingly necessary to own a moped or at least a bicycle. With the increased use of bicycles, mopeds, and, after 1979, motor-cycles, there was a growing demand for repairs and spare parts. A fourth settler at V3 operated a small repair and parts business in his home. In 1978 he shifted the focus of his activities from V3 to Mogtedo town. By 1979 the mechanic had rented a stall in the Mogtedo market, where he owned one of the two displays for mechanical parts and repair. We estimated the mechan-ic's net revenues from the repair and the sale of parts to be about 200,000 CFAF in 1979.

The fifth settler at V3 who could be categorized as having a secondary occupation was the village marabout (Muslim religious leader), who also functioned as a combination physician-soothsayer-clairvoyant. Each day in 1979 the marabout received a stream of settlers, indigenous inhabitants, construction workers, woodcutters, and extension agents who sought advice and medicine. The marabout often served as an intermediary between war-ring factions. For his counseling, medicines and amulets, he received cash and kind gifts valued at 100 to 2,500 CFAF a day. The marabout was candid about the benefits he accrued from his profession. These included a new moped, a tin roof, and a middle-aged male boarder to work in his fields. We estimated that his net revenues after deducting entertainment expenses were at least 150,000 CFAF ($750) in 1979.

Another source of noncrop employment was wage labor on AVV public works projects. The average pay for the lucky few who were accepted for road construction was 15,000 to 17,000 CFAF per month. The less desir-able work on the V3 school buildings in 1979 was unofficially reported to be 350 CFAF a day. Settlers could also rent their donkey-drawn carts and, more occasionally, their plows to other settlers. Teenage sons and daughters would sometimes rent their family's plow and/or their own labor to other AVV farmers. These various secondary occupations could substantially increase a household's annual income. Both the marabout and mechanic engaged in similar activities before coming to the project. The income that they earned at the project, however, was much higher. With the exception of the bread and beer sellers, almost all the farmers with secondary occupations had at least one adult male relative or, in the case of the marabout, a boarding worker who supervised the project farm.

High-earning secondary occupations were less frequent in the settlers' home region. There the more typical pattern was for the members of a household to engage in small-scale trade and handicrafts like brewing beer, spinning, and weaving during the dry season. One of the most important changes at the AVV was a drop in the total *number* of different kinds of handicraft and trade activities that the settlers engaged in. The project was also associated with a slight decrease in the recorded net revenue earned from these activities (5,991 CFAF in the home village versus 4,436 CFAF per unit labor (ALE) at the project). There were several reasons for the decline in the actual number of activities. Primarily, the expanded agricultural season left only one month of low activity during the dry season. The greater distance to a major regional market (25 kilometers at V3 versus 14 kilometers at Damesma) was also a factor.[6] The settlers' increased desire for manufactured products also decreased the economic importance of local handicrafts.

The shift from handmade to machine-made goods was especially noticeable for kitchen utensils and cloth. At Damesma the majority of water containers, sauce, and food dishes were handcrafted from clay or calabashes. By 1979 these products were being replaced by tin buckets and porcelain-coated metal plates in the project. In much the same way, the traditional homespun cloth that was still the most common everyday clothing in the home village was being replaced by a less sturdy manufactured cloth in the AVV-sponsored settlements. Women complained that with the expanded agricultural season they had little time for spinning. Moreover, even if they did, it was almost impossible to find a young man who would accept a commission to weave the thread.

Assessment

Although the farm-monitoring survey included questions on the settlers' unofficial crop and noncrop production activities, the enumerators were unable to gather very accurate information on these topics. One of the main reasons for this was the settlers' reticence in discussing their activities outside the recommended program with project personnel. Further, the enumerators for the farm-monitoring survey talked only with the male household heads, thus ignoring a large number of adult men and all of the women who were engaged in these activities. Even if an enumerator was highly motivated and did collect information outside the designated questionnaires—and some of them did—he was constrained by his inability to note the information on a standard form.

The case study avoided many of these problems by concentrating on a small number of households (twelve in the project; thirty-five in the home village), using a flexible questionnaire design, and employing a research assistant who was not part of the extension program and who had previously worked in the settlers' home village. As a result, the case study shed new light on the sources and levels of household income, the sufficiency of food produced and creation of a regional grain surplus, and the project's effect on women.

Project's Impact on Total Income

The original plan for the AVV foresaw a steady increase in the settlers' per-capita revenues from intensive farming. During the first three years this increase would derive from the annual addition of a new project field. By the fourth agricultural season, when the households would have received all of their official project farms, any increase would come from more intensive use of the existing land area. To evaluate this aspect of the project's impact, the Statistical Service used two calculated figures of "net" and "gross" farm results (Murphy and Sprey 1980). Since the farm-monitoring survey did not show the settlers having a substantial income from trade and handicrafts or private production, none of the recorded income from these sources was included in the calculations. The "gross results" for each sample household were considered to be the cash value of the recorded kilogram production of each crop at local market prices (appendix B, table B-9), minus the cash costs of seed, fertilizer, and insecticide, plus the cash value of the recorded kilogram production of the house garden. In the next stage of analysis, the cost of tool purchases, depreciation on the animal traction equipment, and credit were subtracted to obtain the "net result." The analysis of these calculated income figures was broken down by village cluster and length of residence in the scheme. On the basis of this data, it was possible to conclude that the project's expectations for a steady increase in total farm income were unrealistic (Murphy and Sprey 1980). The reason was that as the settlers increased the number of project fields they were authorized to farm from two to four during the first years, they also increased the size of their families.

The analysis did not include any information on income from livestock, trade, or fields that were outside the allocated areas. When the case study included the total cash value of production on the compound fields and "illegal" bush fields that were outside the designated project area, the average household showed a 40 percent increase in the "net farm results" per worker (using the AVV system for consumption and labor equivalents) (table 5.1). In addition, the average household earned 20,000 CFAF in the 1979–80 agricultural season from the sale of their first pair of animal traction animals, even after purchasing a new pair (table 5.1).

The average recorded household income from nonfarm enterprises for households without secondary occupations increased the total income per

A. Damesma

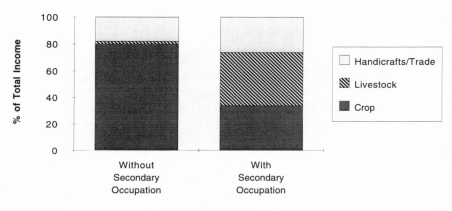

B. Damesma Settlers

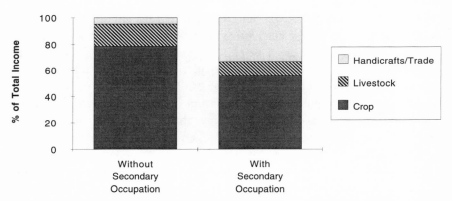

Figure 5.5. Income sources, 1979. Figures represent a weighted average per adult labor equivalent (ALE) for all the households in each category. Most farmers' off-farm income-earning activities consisted of small-scale commercial enterprises such as trade, manufacturing, and services. Only a small number of the study farmers engaged in the more lucrative year-round activities; these farm families were identified as having "secondary" occupations. For this reason, the study differentiated between households with secondary occupations and those without. (McMillan 1983 : 178–79)

worker (ALE) another 5 percent. Nonfarm income comprised 40 percent of the total income per worker for the two study households with high-earning secondary occupations (fig. 5.5). Although the case study sample size in 1979 was too small to draw any statistically significant conclusions about the nature and incidence of this type of economic diversification for the project

Early Economic Changes

Table 5.3

The Recorded Nonagricultural Expenditures per Household in 1979

(in CFAF)

Expenditures	Damesma Settlers		Damesma	
	CFAF	%	CFAF	%
Food	4,399	4	25,280	27
Clothes	7,032	6	3,019	3
Household goods	3,940	4	3,857	4
Services	388	—	62	—
Electrical appliances	2,511	2	534	0.5
Bikes and mopeds	27,773	23	12,335	13
Travel	1,761	1	1,591	2
Medicine	467	—	349	0.5
Education	204	—	187	—
Taxes	1,670	1	2,250	2
Consumption (general)	8,665	7	2,277	3
Jewelry	2,847	2	0	—
Ceremonies within household[a]	4,520	4	23,230	24
Ceremonies outside household	4,842	4	4,805	5
Gifts (general)	26,732	22	15,640	16
Gifts to home	25,549	20	0	—
TOTAL	123,300	100	95,912	100

[a]Includes large expenses for marriages by returned migrants.

as a whole, the results did indicate that an assessment of the settlers' income based only on the recommended crop package overlooked other areas of positive change. These included new sources of income from manufacturing, trade, and livestock.

The settlers' rising disposable income was reflected in their expenditures for food and consumer goods. Food, mostly grain, was the single largest category of expense (27 percent) in the Kaya villages (table 5.3). Even so, it was not uncommon for households to experience a period of hunger during which they ate only one meal per day. Meat was seldom eaten except on holidays.[7] Although 4 percent of the recorded expenditures at the AVV were used for food, this money now went to luxury items such as milk, meat, and spices. By 1979, V3 had one butcher who slaughtered one goat or sheep every three days. Two other butchers slaughtered on holidays. The settlers were also in the habit of commissioning small amounts of meat and fish from the Mogtedo market every third day. During the dry season the settlers purchased fresh milk and yogurt from the pastoralists. In contrast to the settlers' home village, most meat and condiments were purchased by the male household head rather than by his wives. Similarly, the wives' grain production tended to be sold rather than used for family food.

Nonfood expenditures focused on the purchase, maintenance and upkeep of bicycles, mopeds, and motorcycles (23 percent) and gifts to fellow villagers and family members who remained at home (42 percent) (table 5.3). The settlers' expenditures on clothing were not all that different from those of home village farm families.[8] Six of the forty-seven male household heads at Damesma bought new mopeds and motorcycles at the end of the 1979 cotton harvest. When I asked one of the motorcycle owners what he wanted next, he replied, "A truck." With few exceptions, most of the AVV bicycles and mopeds were purchased with income earned from the sale of cash crops. This was not the case at Damesma, where almost all vehicles were purchased with money earned from wage labor in Côte d'Ivoire or Bobo-Dioulasso. A similar situation existed for radios and the more expensive radio-audiocassette consoles.

The higher incomes of the settlers were also reflected in the reduced importance of foreign wage-labor migration as a source of consumer goods and marriage payments.[9] The average young man from Damesma began a cycle of foreign wage labor at age eighteen. Since few migrants had any formal education, they were largely confined to plantation jobs that paid 10,000 to 15,000 CFAF per month. Teenagers immigrated in order to have money for new clothes, bicycles, and radios as well as to pay marriage costs. In a traditional Mossi wedding, the bride was taken to her new home with a minimum of pomp after several years of negotiation and exchange between the bride's and groom's families. The high rates of labor migration, however, contributed to the inflation of these marriage costs. Although the basic alliances between the two families were the same, it became fashionable to have an expensive wedding celebration. A wedding feast plus gifts could easily cost the groom 100,000 to 150,000 CFAF. In 1979 this sum was the equivalent of an entire year's savings from working as a migrant laborer in Côte d'Ivoire or the price of a large, healthy pair of oxen.

Only three of the forty-seven households at V3 had a teenage child who immigrated in 1979. In two of the three cases, the decision to immigrate was primarily motivated by social rather than economic factors.[10] The AVV settler household heads, in contrast to household heads at the home village, made substantial cash gifts to their teenage sons, which could be used to purchase bicycles and clothing. In addition, they paid for virtually all marriage costs. Thus, although foreign labor tours persisted at the project, there were some important changes in both the incidence and the economic role. There was also a much greater expectation that the labor migrants who did leave would return to settle permanently after only one or two years abroad.

Impact on Cereal Production

A second area for reinterpretation relates to the relative sufficiency of grain production and the achievement of the project's goal to create a regional grain surplus. The results of the farm-monitoring survey, which included production only on the official bush fields, led to the conclusion that there was little surplus grain production in the three years covered by the survey (1977–78, 1978–79, and 1979–80) and that, based on these trends, the situation would be unlikely to improve (Murphy and Sprey 1980:77). In contrast, the case study showed that during the 1979–80 crop year, the average production per worker (ALE) of the Kaya settlers was twice the figure recorded by the AVV Statistical Service and three times the average quantity produced in the settlers' home area; this represents an average of 515 kilograms per family above the minimum food standards established by the FAO (fig. 5.6). The substantial differences in results can be attributed to the fact that in 1979 the Kaya settlers of the case study were in their third to fifth year at the project, whereas the AVV farm-monitoring survey during that year included settlers who had been there only one year as well as those who had been there for five. Moreover, the case study measured production on all fields, while the survey focused only on the official fields in the extension program.

Although the case study showed that the settlers were selling only 14 percent of their agricultural products other than cotton (McMillan 1983: 157), this figure did not reflect the overall increase in area planted or the fact that the settlers now had large cumulative stores. The primary factor affecting this appeared to be a substantial increase in the quantity of grain that was given as gifts or in exchange for livestock and hired labor. The largest category of gift exchange in terms of actual quantities involved was the food given to new settlers. In 1979 this typically involved an established settler giving gifts of 100-kilogram sacks of grain to supplement the food rations the new settlers received from the project. In most cases the new settlers could claim some sort of preexisting lineage or affinal tie with their sponsor. By far the major motivation for this type of sponsorship was the desire to affirm, strengthen, and in many cases create new ties between old

A. Total Production (per unit labor)

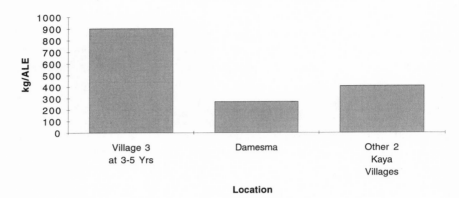

B. Total Production in Relation to Estimated Minimum Food Needs [a]
(per household)

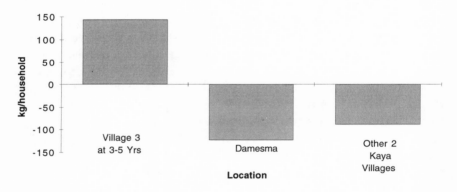

[a] Based on 1975 Project Identification Report of the Dutch Government for the AVV,
which estimated a minimum food requirement of 2,230 calories per person per day. This
is the equivalent of 240 kg cereals and 30 kg legumes per person per year,
including loses during storage (Murphy and Sprey 1980: 22). Figures represent the
difference between the recorded grain per resident and the recommended 240 kg
minimum of cereal.

Figure 5.6. Cereal production, 1979. ALE = Adult Labor Equivalent. Figures represent an unweighted mean for individual households in the
sample. (McMillan 1983:156)

and new settlers. Given the geographical isolation of the AVV villages and the resentment shown toward the project by the existing inhabitants of the valleys, the AVV settlers considered these ties important for ensuring their long-term survival in the region.

Grain was also exchanged for livestock. The case study showed that the majority of settlers used the money they earned from the sale of the first pair of oxen they purchased from the AVV to pay off their remaining debts to the project. In most cases the replacement oxen were purchased from the local FulBe in exchange for grain. The cost of the animals did not appear in any of the data on marketing but was discovered during the research on purchase and resale of livestock.

The farm-monitoring survey was unable to gather very detailed information on either gift or bartered grain. Although the data from the case study were imperfect, in that the case study—like the farm-monitoring survey—was primarily concerned with production and market sales, it suggested that lack of information on nonmarket exchange and the settlers' production in areas outside the official fields might have camouflaged some of the increase in sorghum production that was associated with the project.

Impact on Female Settlers

A third area where the case study suggested a variance in interpretation was the effect of the AVV on women and the internal organization of the households. At Damesma, the settlers' home village, women traditionally farmed 20 to 25 percent of the total planted area as private fields, from which they alone controlled the harvest (fig. 5.7). These fields were usually positioned along the edge of the cooperatively worked fields to reduce traveling time between sites. Women also had an active role in animal husbandry and trade.

No consideration was given to these personal activities in the original design of the AVV fields or the extension services. Moreover, the AVV villages were generally farther from major markets than the settlers' home villages, which prevented the women from reinstating many of their former trade activities. This disregard of women's traditional economic roles in the "official" project plan and the associated decline in income earned from private crop, livestock, and trade activities led Murphy and Sprey (1980) to conclude that the planned-settlement program was having a very negative effect on women. Guissou (1977) reached a similar conclusion based on her research with one hundred farm women in the settlers' areas of origin and eighty-six female settlers in six AVV groups (8 percent of the AVV adult female population in that year).

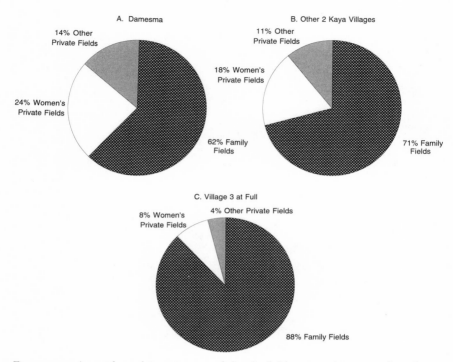

Figure 5.7. Area planted in private and family fields, 1979 (percent of total area). Figures represent unweighted means that are calculated over the entire group. (McMillan 1983:158, 388)

The case study concurred that there was little time for private production during the first three to five years of living at the project. The much higher labor demands associated with the proposed crop-production package were exacerbated by the layout of the project farms. In contrast to the settlers' home village, each of the settlers' six official bush fields were located in a different part of the village. Thus, it was more difficult for women to squeeze in one or two hours of work on a private field in the early morning and at the end of the day. Despite these constraints, most of the Damesma settlers' wives did manage to reinstate a small area of private fields by the third to fifth year of living at the scheme, which was 1979 (fig. 5.7).

To reduce travel time, the first women's fields were created in the borders between the cultivation bands and the homesite (fig. 5.4.A). As the settlers became more daring in defying the prescribed boundaries, they created new private fields in the low-lying marshy basins outside the official cultivation zones (fig. 5.4.B). In addition, it quickly became customary to subdivide the project field that was designated for legumes into private cow-pea and pea-nut fields for women (fig. 5.4.c). By 1979 these "illegal" private fields represented 12 percent of the total area farmed (versus 38 percent at Da-mesma); 8 percent of the total area farmed by the Damesma settlers at V3 was women's private fields, versus 36 percent at Damesma (fig. 5.7) (McMil-lan 1983:388, 413).

To compensate for the decline in women's private crop production, the male household heads began to make cash gifts to their wives after the sale of the cooperatively produced cotton. The settlers also reinstated a system of harvest gifts whereby the male household head gave gifts of twenty to thirty dried ears of corn to the wives of close friends and allies in the village. Over the course of the harvest, a woman could receive 100 to 200 kilograms of "gift" corn in this manner.

In contrast to practice in the settlers' home area, almost all the women's grain that was either grown or acquired through gift exchange was sold rather than used for family consumption, and the male household head was responsible for the purchase of sauce condiments (to accompany the staple cereal dish), school materials, and clothing. The income that the female family heads earned from cash payments and the sale of food goods was usually used for personal needs and investments such as jewelry, travel, clothes, gifts, trade goods, and livestock. These and other changes in pro-duction and consumption patterns show that the actual impact of the AVV on women was less negative and more complex than could be deduced from an analysis based on a point-in-time survey limited to the agricultural project itself.

Conclusion

Both the farm-monitoring survey and the intensive case study show that the AVV settlers experienced high levels of crop income growth during their first five years at the project. Yet this higher income was not being reinvested in intensive farming. Indeed, both studies showed that with longer periods of residence in the scheme, the average household gave less attention to the proposed crop extension package. Based on these results, researchers con-cluded that the AVV was unlikely to attain its long-term goals for sustainable income growth from farming.

The results of the case study agreed with the farm-monitoring program's conclusions about the settlers' production practices. The case study demon-strated, however, that an exclusive focus on the success or failure of the recommended package overlooked other areas of significant and positive

Table 5.4
A Four-Stage Settlement Model

Stage One	Planning/Recruitment, Initial Infrastructure/Development, and Population Transfer
Stage Two	Settling In and Transition
Stage Three	Economic and Social Development
Stage Four	Handing Over and Incorporation

SOURCES: Scudder 1981, 1984, 1985, 1991.

change. These included major changes in total labor demands and the organization of farm labor, and an increasingly diversified investment of time and money in areas outside the recommended program. The settlers' more diversified strategies included clearing new fields outside the project area as well as additional investment in livestock and nonfarm employment.

These successive patterns of adjustment share many characteristics with successful settlements worldwide (Chambers 1969; Colson 1971; McMillan, Painter, and Scudder 1992; Nelson 1973; Scudder 1981, 1985, 1991; Scudder and Colson 1982). Scudder describes four stages (table 5.4). The first stage refers to the period that precedes and accompanies the initial population transfer. Policy decisions made at this stage can have a lasting effect. Especially important are decisions made about village placement, farm size, road development, recruitment, and crop extension themes. Scudder's second phase, "Settling In and Transition," refers to the initial three to five years during which settlers adapt to their new economic and social setting. He argues that while "learning the ropes," most settlers

> adopt a conservative stance, their first priority being to meet their subsistence needs. They favor continuity over change; and where change is necessary, they favor incremental change over transformational change. Where possible, they cling to the familiar by moving into new settlements with relatives, former neighbors, and co-ethnics. They also try to transfer area-of-origin house types, farming practices, and other skills even though they may not be suited to the new habitat. (1984:16)

This transition stage ends when enough settlers "shift from a conservative stance to a dynamic, open-ended one, hence initiating a third stage of 'Economic and Social Development.'" The shift occurs only after settler security has increased as a result of the production of sufficient food and the settlers' feeling more "at home."

Once settlers have made the shift from the risk-adverse second stage to the risk-taking third stage, they tend to follow the same sequence of investments (Scudder 1984:18). Scudder observed that initially settlers invest in education for their children. Subsequently, additional farm land is share-cropped, leased, and/or purchased, and the farming system is expanded into cash crops (including labor-intensive, higher-risk crops), livestock, and non-farm activities. Scudder's fourth stage, "Handing Over and Incorporation," emphasizes that no settlement is truly successful until the local leadership has been taken over by a second generation. This fourth stage also refers to the process by which a new lands settlement becomes an integrated part (rather than a special enclave) of the region within which it is situated. The stage also implies the devolution of many project administrative tasks onto local, regional, and national authorities.

In line with Scudder's model, it was during the first three years, when the settlers were just beginning to adjust to their new social and production environment and during which they showed the highest level of dependence on the extension agent (Scudder's second stage of "Settling In and Transition"), that they were most willing to follow the prescribed agricultural program. Between years three and five, when they were feeling more at home in their new community and were able to adequately feed their families, they became more willing to experiment. This experimentation included a willingness to deviate from the prescribed package as well as a greater willingness and desire to invest in nonproject areas such as livestock and trade. The settlers also showed a greater interest in education, reflected in the fact that each study household had at least one child enrolled in elementary school. At this point the chief cost of education was the opportunity cost of the child's labor (for herding and other light agricultural tasks), not the direct cash costs (table 5.3).

Based on this evidence and Scudder's model, I predicted that the V3 settlers in 1980 were just beginning a new period very much like Scudder's third stage of "Economic and Social Development," during which we could expect more rapid increases in production, net income, and nonfarm employment (McMillan 1983). During this time I expected to see a continuation of the trend toward greater diversification into livestock and nonfarm employment such as trade and a gradual reinstatement of private crop and livestock activities by women and non-household-head males. I also expected several of the wealthier families to move part of their families into Mogtedo town to engage in trade. Based on Scudder's stage model, I predicted there would be a gradual warming of social relations between the Mossi settlers and Mossi indigenous inhabitants and that the evolving pattern of economic differentiation would increase social conflict within the settlement itself.

Two events seemed to symbolize the shift from a more conservative, dependent transition phase to what I thought was a more dynamic, independent stage of development at V3. The first involved the creation of a village market. Between 1974 and 1980 the AVV designated three sites for a centrally located market in the Mogtedo village cluster. Only one of the three proposed markets was still functioning in 1979. The extension agents attributed these early failures to the lack of cooperation among the settlers and the settlers' strained relations with the indigenous inhabitants. In 1979 the V3 settlers created their own market in collaboration with the neighboring indigenous villages. The extension agents were informed only a few days before the official opening. The new market was backed by all of the important village leaders. One of the three wealthiest farmers, a man who dominated economic life at V3, promised to purchase at least one tin of grain from each settler. The purpose of his underwriting the grain market was to encourage settler participation and, in so doing, to make the local market more attractive to wholesale merchants from Mogtedo. To further encourage participation, the Muslim leaders rescheduled the village's Ramadan feast to coincide with opening day.

The second event, which followed not long after, was the settlers' insistence that the project renegotiate the date set for cotton sales. The event was catalyzed by the head extension agent's announcement that because of complications in the ginning schedule, the settlers would have to sell their cotton at two, rather than one, large project-sponsored markets. The male household heads were unhappy with the new schedule because it meant that they would be required to give two sets of gifts to family members instead of one. The net effect of selling in two separate markets was to reduce the male household head's ability to accumulate a cash reserve. Despite repeated visits by the supervising extension agent, the settlers refused to budge. The project ultimately conceded and gave them a later market date.

The new market and the cotton strike were part of a general shift toward more independent settler attitudes and investments at V3. In 1980 the prospects for continuation of these trends looked good. At the regional level the AVV had just installed a new group of seven villages at Mogtedo-Bombore, adjacent to Mogtedo. Mogtedo V3 was strategically placed on the main road that linked the Mogtedo and Mogtedo-Bombore planned settlements to Mogtedo town. Plans were also underway to develop two new blocs with six to seven planned settlements each. Monday through Friday the road was frequented by construction workers, heavy bulldozers, and supervisory staff.

Every third day a reverse stream of settlers from Mogtedo-Bombore would sweep past V3 in route to and from Mogtedo town. The V3 settlers were enthusiastic about the opportunities that these traffic patterns held for developing a village market, retail stores, and bars. Some of the wealthier settler families planned to construct homes and businesses in town. In short, the settlers appeared to be on the brink of a new stage of dynamic economic growth and development and expansion into the wider region.

6

New Economic Options and Settler Choices, 1980–1989

If a new lands settlement is successful, it creates a variety of economic options and a group of settlers and hosts with greater economic resources. If the successful settlers' ambition and energy are harnessed by new opportunities, they can become a driving force behind new investments. If these opportunities do not exist, the settlers are likely to move. This pattern of upward mobility and development has been observed in successful colonization schemes all over the world (Nelson 1973; Salem-Murdock 1989; Scudder 1981, 1985).

Short restudies of the Damesma settlers in 1983 and 1986 showed a continuation of earlier trends toward increased cereal and livestock production, decreased use of fertilizers, and a desire for profitable off-farm employment. In 1988 the entire focus of the study changed when eight of the twenty-five farm families that were included in the 1987 restudy left the project. These were, with one exception, the project's success stories—the top commercial farmers in V3. They did not return to Damesma but immigrated to the town that had developed at the construction site of the Kompienga Dam (map 11). The main motivation behind their move was the perception that the Kompienga region offered greater opportunities to develop dry-season irrigation and trade.

A full ten-year restudy carried out in 1989 revealed that the settlers who moved were part of a larger group of farmers who left AVV Mogtedo and AVV

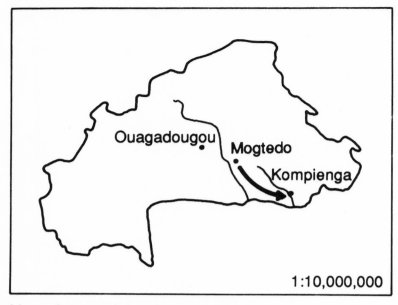

Map 11. Location of Mogtedo and Kompienga.

Mogtedo-Bombore between 1988 and 1989. The same restudy showed that the rate of settler dropout was much lower in the neighboring AVV planned settlements at Linoghin. These different rates of settler dropout could not be attributed to uneven physical endowments. Both Linoghin and Mogtedo were characterized by approximately the same soils and the same prescribed package for intensive farming. A more powerful explanation lay in the various factors that affected the settlers' opportunities to develop nonfarm employment.

The Changing National Context

The early success of the AVV settlers attracted massive numbers of spontaneous or self-directed settlers into the land between the sponsored settlements and the Nakambe River (see fig. 6.1). This settlement was most pronounced at Linoghin and Rapadama, both of which are located along the paved highway linking Ouagadougou with Burkina's eastern border, Togo, and Niger (AVV 1985c, 1988, 1990). Lower rates of self-directed settlement were recorded in the more isolated settlements at Mogtedo and Mogtedo-Bombore before 1987 (AVV 1985c; S. Sawadogo 1988b).[1] The second large

New Ecomomic Options

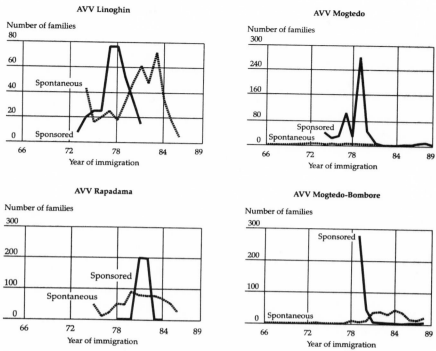

Figure 6.1. Sponsored and spontaneous immigration in connection with the AVV planned settlements at Linoghin, Mogtedo, Mogtedo-Bombore, and Rapadama, 1966–1989. Data are incomplete after 1985. (AVV 1985c; AVV-UPI 1989b; S. Sawadogo 1988b).

group of spontaneous immigrants was the pastoralists (AVV 1984b, 1985c; Rochette 1976a, 1976b). The Upper Nakambe Basin had long been an area to which pastoralists would bring their animals in the rainy season to avoid crop damage in the settled zones. Even before disease control started, a growing number of pastoralists were shifting their permanent camps farther south into the river basin (AVV 1984b; Nana and Kattenberg 1979:9; Rochette 1976b). Later arrivals were attracted by the cash and kind payments that would accrue from boarding the successful AVV settlers' cattle.

Some of the clearest evidence of the wider economic effects of this increase in sponsored and spontaneous settlement comes from the growth in area markets. The impact could be measured in terms of increased market activity and increased grain sales, as well as in the expansion of the area's administrative and market centers. Only three of the twenty markets frequented by the settlers living in the AVV planned settlements at Mogtedo,

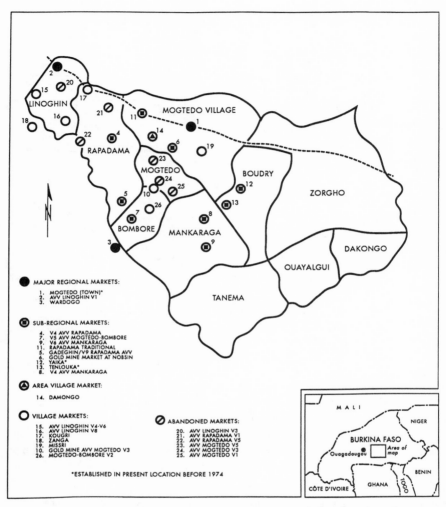

Map 12. Location and relative importance of existing and abandoned markets
frequented by settlers living in the AVV-sponsored settlements at Mogtedo,
Mogtedo-Bombore, and Linoghin, 1988–1989. (McMillan, Nana, and
Savadogo 1993:75; reprinted with permission of the World Bank. The
boundaries, denominations, and any other information shown on this map
do not imply, on the part of the World Bank Group, any judgment on the
legal status of any territory, or any endorsement or acceptance of such
boundaries.)

Table 6.1

Settlement and Development in the Town of Mogtedo, 1960–1989

	1960	1968	1975	1980	1985	1989
			(number)			
Households in town						
Indigenous	60	60				
Immigrant		200				
Inhabitants	200	1,300	3,374	—	4,550	6,050
Stalls in central market	—	—	100	300	600–650	800
Business in separate buildings	—	—	5	14	—	75
Mills	—	—	1	—	—	10
Etalagistes (semidetached stores)	—	—	—	—	—	122
Persons selling in boutiques and market[a]						
—market day						1,914
a. rainy season (August 1989)						4,000
b. market day, dry season[b]						273
—nonmarket day						

SOURCE: F. Kabore and J. Guigma, Enquête Marché, August 1990, in McMillan, Nana, and Savadogo 1993.

[a]Persons selling (not attendance) in boutiques, the market, detached businesses, and étalagistes.

[b]Estimated "normal" attendance. A restudy of the market in March 1990 failed to confirm this figure. Indeed, the number of people selling actually decreased after August 1989. This was attributed to the large number of Mogtedo merchants selling at new markets created at the gold-mining sites.

Mogtedo-Bombore, or Linoghin in 1989 existed prior to 1974 (map 12). During the same fifteen-year period, the town of Mogtedo was itself transformed into a prosperous market and administrative center.

By 1989 Mogtedo included more than 6,000 inhabitants, 75 shops in separate buildings, 122 businesses in semiattached buildings, and 10 grain mills (table 6.1). We counted 1,900 male and female merchants in the shops and central market area on two rainy days during August 1989. Even in the

Table 6.2

Number of Market Stalls and Estimated Dry-Season Attendance at the
Linoghin Market, 1975–1989 (August–September)

Year	Number of Stalls	Average Number of Persons Attending		
		Linoghin AVV Farmers	Linoghin Spontaneous Immigrants	Persons/ Merchants from Ouagadougou and Outside[a]
1975	32	60	18	0
1976–78	40	100	40	20
1979–81	80	120	80	25
1982–84	130	200	100	60
1985–87	200	600	1,300	400
1988–89	300	800	2,500	1,700

SOURCE: F. Guira 1989, in McMillan, Nana, and Savadogo 1993.

[a] In contrast to other area markets, the largest Linoghin markets usually occur during
August and September because large numbers of seasonal migrants from Ouagadougou are resident then. Settlers' relatives are also numerous at this time.

rainy season the market hosted seventy merchants (three full busloads) from
Puetenga—one of the largest, most active markets in the country. Market
activity was reportedly even greater during the more active dry season. By
1983 the Mogtedo market was reported to have eclipsed the market at
Zorgho, the provincial capital, in both size and sales; by 1989 it was rumored
to be on the verge of surpassing the large Koupela market. As a result of this
rapid growth, the entire Mogtedo region was made a separate administrative
department in 1985.

The market created by the AVV sponsored settlers at Linoghin in 1974 is
the second most important market on the paved highway between Ouagadougou and Koupela (map 2; table 6.2). It now numbers some 300 stalls.
Market officials indicated that as many as 5,000 people might attend the
market during the dry season. In 1989 the market included five free-standing
business enterprises (one large boutique, two bars, one coffee shop), as well
as open-air restaurants and service centers (bicycle mechanics, tailors). Market officials estimated that fewer than 20 percent of the persons attending
the Linoghin market were actually from the AVV sponsored settlements
when we conducted our research in August 1989.

A census of wholesale grain and livestock merchants highlights the pivotal position of area markets in redistributing agricultural products. On a single market day we counted more than thirty-five people employed as wholesale grain merchants (eight based in the national capital of Ouagadougou and twenty-seven based in Mogtedo town), nine wholesale peanut merchants, twenty-two wholesale goat and sheep merchants, seven wholesale chicken merchants (with sixty-five assistants), and seven wholesale cattle merchants (five from the region and two based in Ouagadougou).

We counted 375 sacks of grain (45,000 kilograms) leaving the Linoghin market on a single market day during August 1989 (F. Guira 1989). Market officials at Linoghin estimated that transporters from outside the region purchased an average of 400 sacks of grain per market day (the markets are held every third day) during the rainy season; during the dry season the figure could rise to as high as 800 sacks (96,000 kilograms). Eight hundred sacks of grain represent the annual cereal needs of 400 persons, based on the FAO estimate of 240 kilograms as the yearly food grain needs of an adult (Murphy and Sprey 1980:74). During the same August market survey we counted 150 goats and sheep sold.

Other new economic options were more random and included the discovery of gold at several sites near AVV Mogtedo in late 1987. The associated "gold rush" increased in-migration and market activity throughout the surrounding area. Four sites were immediately adjacent to the AVV planned settlements at Mogtedo. Next to each site a market developed where miners could sell their gold as well as spend their earnings on raw and cooked food, alcoholic beverages, water, fuel wood, consumer goods, video shows, and prostitutes. A few of the male household heads and sons struck it rich. One settler at V1 reportedly sold a nugget for 1,000,000 CFAF ($4,000); another young settler at V3 bought a motorcycle with the money he earned. The most active gold miners were younger male household heads, older women with grown children, and unmarried sons and brothers. Many women settlers were actively involved in selling water and raw and cooked food at the mining sites.

We counted a daily average of 705 miners at the four Mogtedo sites over a four-day period from April 4 to 8, 1990 (McMillan, Nana, and Savadogo 1993). During the same study period we counted a daily average of seventy-four merchants at the four sites. Most of the merchants came from either Ouagadougou or Mogtedo town. Only four (two selling small merchandise and two selling kola nuts) of the seventy-four merchants counted on that particular day were from the AVV sponsored settlements.

Another change was the creation of Burkina's first hydroelectric dam at

Kompienga, more than 250 kilometers from Mogtedo (Agrotechnik 1988, 1989; Dr.-ing 1987; A. Guira 1989; SAED 1980). The original plan for the AVV proposed four dams to eventually irrigate an additional 75,000 to 260,000 hectares (AVV 1974:6). The Bagré dam, in the central southern part of the country on the Red Volta, was to be the largest, with a projected irrigation potential of 40,000 to 140,000 hectares (AVV 1974:6). Bagre was to be the first dam constructed. Because of difficulties in obtaining outside donor support, however, the government decided to proceed with Kompienga as a demonstration project for Bagré (16 megawatts) and, ultimately, with an even larger project at Noumbiel (60 megawatts) on the Côte d'Ivoire border. Although the original plan indicated that the Kompienga dam would also supply a small irrigated perimeter as well as seasonal flood irrigation, there was no provision for this in the original project budget. Kompienga's primary purpose was to generate hydroelectric power for Ouagadougou.

The extreme southeastern edge of Burkina, where Kompienga is located (near the Togo and Benin borders), was sparsely populated in comparison with the rest of the country. Living in small, scattered, low-density settlements, the indigenous Gourmantche and Yansé shunned cultivating the fly-ridden, low-lying areas. Until preparations for the Kompienga dam began, the area was quite isolated. Construction of a road linking Fada with the proposed dam site dramatically increased immigration to the Kompienga River basin in the mid-1980s (fig. 6.2). A second, smaller wave of immigration involved the sponsored importation of skilled construction workers from Europe, Canada, and other parts of Africa and the unsolicited spontaneous immigration of large numbers of unskilled workers. The labor migrants were accompanied by merchants and farmers hoping to supply food and services to the dam workers. Most skilled workers left after the official inauguration of the dam in April 1989. Their exodus coincided with a fourth immigration to Kompienga town, the dam construction site. In contrast to earlier immigrants, these settlers, like those who left the AVV, tended to be agriculturalists who were attracted by the area's prospects for irrigated dry-season farming to produce commodities for international trade. In August 1989 the town of Kompienga numbered 3,239, not counting civil servants. Ninety-eight percent of the inhabitants had immigrated since 1985. Only 63 (15 percent) of the heads of household indicated that they had worked for the dam, and 310 (75 percent) of the household heads reported that either agriculture or livestock production was their primary activity.

At the same time the settlers were experiencing these new economic

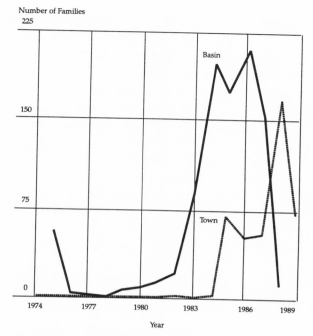

Figure 6.2. Year of immigration for settlers in the
Kompienga Basin and the town of Kompienga,
1989. (Agrotechnik 1988; McMillan 1989)

options, their opportunities for foreign wage labor decreased. About one million Burkinabè were estimated to be living in Côte d'Ivoire in 1985, many of them employed in commercial plantation agriculture. With the dramatic decline in world cocoa prices beginning in the early 1980s, this type of foreign wage labor was no longer the profitable option it once had been. Although precise figures are lacking, the net flow of out-migration from Burkina was reduced. In addition, large numbers of Burkinabè migrants who had settled in Côte d'Ivoire began returning and were attracted to the underpopulated river basins. The lack of opportunities abroad also increased the younger settlers' incentives to develop profitable farming opportunities.

Another important influence on new lands settlement in the OCP river basins was the increasing conflict between the AVV-sponsored settlers and the indigenous hosts, pastoralists, and spontaneous settlers in the surrounding area. These relationships became increasingly hostile as human and animal population densities increased. This hostility was translated into numerous petty acts of aggression, which reduced the settlers' sense of security in the new area. The spontaneous settlers quickly learned that although the AVV could threaten to expel them, it could do little to implement such threats because of the legal ambiguity of the settlers' land tenure (McMillan, Nana, and Savadogo 1993). While the 1974 presidential decree creating the AVV declared that the OCP river basins were the property of the state, the national legal code still recognized the hosts' customary land-tenure rights. The result was to confuse the issue of whether the AVV had any real power to revoke the spontaneous settlers' rights to remain on project lands. With no clear-cut land-tenure rights, the pastoralists moved farther and farther away from the sponsored settlements. Those who remained nearby or who crossed the AVV territory risked having their animals wander into settlers' fields. The high social and economic costs of these conflicts meant that many of the pastoralists with large herds moved their animals farther south to "new," less populated river basins (see Sowers 1986).

After 1981 the AVV underwent a major reorganization toward a more decentralized planning model (appendix B, fig. B-1).[2] The reorganization was largely a response to donor pressure for the project to deal more effectively with the increasingly complex settlement issues in the valleys and to lower costs (appendix B, table B-7) (AVV 1985c; Reyna 1980, 1983, 1985). It was also prompted by the desire of many donors to move away from central funding to funding particular projects for which they alone could take the credit. It is a process that disgruntled administrators referred to as the "Balkanization" of the AVV. The overall goal of "coordinated action and planning for the development of the zones liberated of onchocerciasis" was maintained, but the emphasis was changed to incorporate the hosts as well as the immigrants. The new reorganization also emphasized integrating the project with regional development organizations and reducing the cost of basic infrastructure. The need to develop more environmentally sound crop and livestock technology was emphasized as well (AVV 1981a, 1981b, 1983; Baris et al. 1983; Kabore, Brilleau, and Badolo 1985; Vayssie 1982; Yanogo 1988).

After 1982 the administrative unit for the AVV's regional development programs became the UP, or Planning Unit (map 10; appendix B, fig. B-1). A UP was a geographical unit having a certain homogeneity of planning problems and opportunities. Each UP was composed of several UDs, or Development Units. Each of the older AVV blocs of planned settlements, like Mogtedo, was converted into a UD. UDs were created to cover the neighboring plateau regions as well. Planners hoped that each UP would be funded by one or more donors. Under the more decentralized model, all the planned settlements along the Nakambe River (formerly the White Volta) were re-grouped into Planning Unit 1, or UPI (map 10) (AVV 1984a; see also AVV-UPI 1986, 1987, 1988, 1989a, 1989b). The AVV-UPI included eleven UDS. Seven were former groups of planned settlements, or blocs (Linoghin, AVV-Mogtedo, Mogtedo-Bombore, Rapadama, Ouayalgui, Tanema, and Mankaraga); the other four UDS (Meguet, the area surrounding Mogtedo, Boudry, and Zorgho) coordinated extension and development for groups of indigenous villages in the higher plateau region. A twelfth planned-settlement group at Dakongo was still in the planning stages in 1989. The agro-pastoral zone at Gadeghin was also part of the decentralized AVV-UPI.

The reorganization brought about a sharp decrease in project staff in the older sponsored settlements. There was also a long period of adjustment, during which it was difficult for the project staff to implement its new programs to arrest soil erosion and to incorporate spontaneous settlers. The net result at the local level was to increase the settlers' and extension agents' anxiety over the long-term stability of the government's interventions. The settlers' anxiety was further complicated by the increasingly unstable national politics. Especially important was the creation of a new revolutionary government after 1983.

On August 4, 1983, Captain Thomas Sankara seized power in Burkina and proclaimed the creation of the Révolution Démocratique et Populaire by the Conseil National de la Révolution (CNR). Sankara's new revolutionary government represented a decisive break with the country's earlier regimes (Savadogo and Wetta 1991). On August 4, 1984, the first anniversary of the revolution, the government announced a program for agrarian and land-tenure reform. Central tenets of the act included nationalization of all land rights and the appropriation of usufructuary rights to those who cleared land.[3] One result of the land-tenure and agrarian-reform act was to provide a firmer legal base for the land-tenure rights of the AVV-sponsored settlers. The law thus increased the spontaneous settlers' willingness to participate in the AVV's new experimental programs to incorporate those living near the AVV-sponsored settlers into a single, unified extension and land-management program.

In 1985 the government established a new program for village land management, called Programme National pour la Gestion des Terroirs Villageois, or PNGTV.[4] The goal of the program was to help villages and regional development authorities implement the themes advocated by agrarian reform. The PNGTV concept, theme, and approach were heavily influenced by the AVV's experiences (Guyon 1986:12; PNGTV 1989a, 1989b). One of the first PNGTV pilot projects was initiated in the area surrounding the AVV-sponsored settlements at Rapadama in 1988 (AVV 1988).[5]

The 1989 Restudy

It was within this context of expanding regional development, new national options, reduced international opportunities, local social conflict, and political change that I conducted a ten-year restudy of the Damesma settlers through the Institute for Development Anthropology. The research was funded by UNDP and executed by the World Bank (see appendix A).

Limited Prospects for Agricultural Income Growth

The restudy showed a continuation of the earlier low levels of adoption of the proposed crop production methods. This trend was especially remarkable for total fertilizer use, which showed a steady decline at Linoghin and Mogtedo-Bombore as well as Mogtedo after 1983 (fig. 6.3). In the beginning

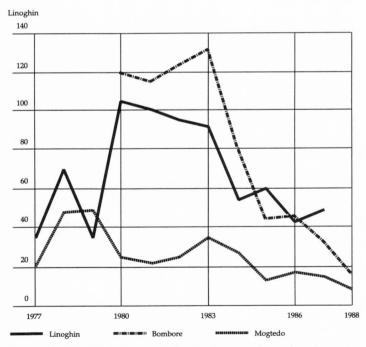

Figure 6.3. Total fertilizer purchases in the AVV planned settlements. (AVV/UD extension records)

the AVV practiced a circular logic, blaming the settlers' declining cotton-yields and soil fertility problems on the fact that they were not practicing the prescribed package of intensive crop production methods. The settlers' lack of attention to these methods was in turn attributed to the "bad" example of the spontaneous settlers and the rising cost of fertilizer and insecticides due to reduced government subsidies.

Later research by ICRISAT (International Crop Research Institute for the Semi-Arid Tropics), INERA (Institut d'Etudes et des Recherches Agricoles), and the AVV has shown, however, that rainfall in the Mogtedo region is marginal for cotton. Under these conditions there was little return to fertilizer use unless it was combined with either new or traditional water-retention technologies like stone *diguettes* (dikes), tied ridges, or cross plowing (Deuson and Sanders 1990; Jayne, Day, and Dregne 1989; Nagy, Sanders, and Ohm 1988; Sanders 1989a, 1989b, 1990; Sanders, Nagy, and Ramaswamy 1990; World Bank 1989). This new research, plus mounting evidence of soil erosion in the older AVV-sponsored settlements, led to a reorientation of extension themes after 1986 (AVV 1983, 1984c, 1985a, 1985b). In contrast to earlier extension activities, the new program gave farmers a much larger role in village administration and extension. The AVV also launched a concerted effort to promote the use of manure pits and stone diguettes.

Despite this major change in extension themes, the 1989 restudy did not show any increase in the settlers' use of fertilizer on crops other than cotton. There was also only limited adoption of the stone diguettes—and this only on the easily accessible compound fields that were served by a project program to promote adoption by providing free transportation of the rocks. In 1989 there was no recorded "spontaneous" adoption of the new technology on other fields. In 1979 settlers used fertilizer on 87 percent of the cotton fields and on 33 percent of the sorghum fields in the AVV case study. Ten years later fertilizer use was confined exclusively to cotton and at much lower levels than those recommended by the project.[6] By 1988 many settlers had virtually abandoned the prescribed five-year rotation of sorghum, cotton, legumes, and two years of fallow. Instead, there was a growing trend toward continuous cultivation of the more accessible fields, with the better cultivation bands planted alternately with cotton and sorghum. Yet, despite the settlers' failure to practice the prescribed cultivation package, the project records did not show a substantial change in yields. Crop yields were reportedly slightly lower on cotton (800 kilograms per hectare versus 1000 in 1979, according to the AVV extension records) and higher on sorghum (1000 kilograms per hectare versus 800 in 1979).

Table 6.3
Official Prices for Cotton and Cotton Inputs at the AVV, 1979–1989
(in CFAF)

Year	Cotton/kg[a]	Fertilizer/kg		Insecticides/liter	
		AVV[a]	Ministère du Commerce[b]	AVV[a]	Ministère du Commerce[b]
1974	40	35	—	115	—
1975	40	35	—	115	—
1976	40	35	—	115	—
1977	55	35	—	115	—
1978	55	35	—	360	—
1979	55	40	—	400	—
1980	55	40	—	400	—
1981	62	40	—	400	—
1982	62	60	—	400	—
1983	70	60	—	450	—
1984	90	97	—	450	—
1985	100	97	90	450	500
1986	100	120	114	825	800
1987	95	120	91	1,710	1,595
1988	95	106	86	1,260	1,260
1989	95	114	105	1,386	1,582

[a] SOURCE: AVV, Credit Agricole.
[b] SOURCE: Ministère du Commerce, Burkina Faso.

Faced with the huge labor demands per hectare for cotton, rising production costs for cotton (table 6.3), and past experience with uneven, unreliable yields in the zone, the AVV farmers gradually increased the area planted to less labor-intensive cereals (fig. 6.4). Households with larger labor forces continued to grow cotton, fearing from experience that after a plentiful harvest, the price for sorghum might drop (McMillan, Nana, and Savadogo 1993).[7] Smaller households with only two or three active workers tended to grow less cotton. With a smaller labor force, these households were less able to absorb the high levels of risk associated with commercial cotton production in the northern climatic zone. For them the loss of a key family member—through illness or migration—at an important point in the production

New Ecomomic Options

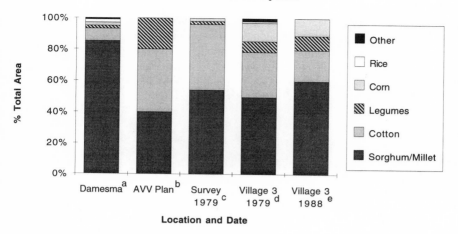

a Source: McMillan 1983: 119.

b Based on project plan for a "Full Farm" in the third to fifth year of settlement in the northern zone (Murphy and Sprey 1980: 66).

c Average based on collectively worked family fields for the sample households at Mogtedo and Mogtedo-Bombore in their third to fifth year at the project. The 1979 Statistical Service Survey did not measure compound fields (Murphy and Sprey 1980: 43).

d Average based on collectively worked and privately worked fields for the nine sample households. Includes compound and bush fields.

e Average based on field measurements of the collectively worked family fields of 20 settler households at Mogtedo Village 3, 2 settler households at Mogtedo, and 2 settler households at Linoghin. Due to small percentage of study farms that we measured (30 percent) and the high concentration of these fields at Mogtedo Village 3, these figures represent a gross estimate of the scale of production of different crops (Savadogo 1989b: 16).

Figure 6.4. Area planted in different crops, 1979–1988.

cycle (such as weeding) could dramatically decrease cotton yields and possibly mean the loss of the entire crop. Even if the crop was lost, farmers were still obliged to reimburse the cost of the inputs, amounting to as much as 30,870 CFAF for one hectare.

Although per-worker (ALE) production of cotton was lower, per-worker production for sorghum was higher in 1988 than in 1979 (table 6.4). This increased production was not associated, however, with a higher cash value. Indeed, when we calculated net crop income,[8] using the median price at which crops were sold based on our survey of crop sales, the average cash value of the settlers' crop production on their collectively worked family fields was 10 percent less than it was in 1979 (fig. 6.5 and appendix B, table B-8; the higher figure for Mogtedo V3 includes both private and col-

Table 6.4

Crop and Livestock Production and Production Expenses per Adult Labor Equivalent
(ALE) in the AVV Planned Settlements, 1988–1989

	Linoghin	Bombore	Mogtedo	Mogtedo V3	Average
Residents per household[a]	10 (20)	11 (20)	11 (20)	9 (20)	10.25 (80)
Labor force (ALE) per household	3.8	4.3	4.3	3.5	3.98
KILOGRAMS/ALE					
Cotton					
1979–80[b]	521	575	575	709	
1988–89	288	100	309	88	
Sorghum, millet, corn					
1979–80[b]	—	391	—	902	
1988–89	1,052	1,086	853	1,397	
CFAF/ALE					
Crop inputs (fertilizer, insecticide)	31,417	11,327	32,876	15,211	
Hired labor (cash and kind)	5,999	2,385	5,625	0	
Rented equipment (cash and kind)	10,564	1,675	277	555	
Net crop income	61,314	54,988	51,071	55,899	
CFAF/MALE HOUSEHOLD HEAD					
Annual livestock income					
A. High-income, low-cost/loss scenario	21,897	6,797	14,764	5,415	8,522[c]
B. Low-income, low-cost/loss scenario	15,570	2,022	7,977	−1,480	6,223

SOURCES: McMillan, Nana, and Savadogo 1993; Murphy and Sprey 1980; Savadogo, Sanders, and McMillan 1989:30.

[a] ( ) Indicates number of households.

[b] Figures for Linoghin, Bombore, and Mogtedo are for "full" households, in third and fifth years of settlement (Murphy and Sprey 1980:78).

[c] Excludes V3 data.

New Ecomomic Options

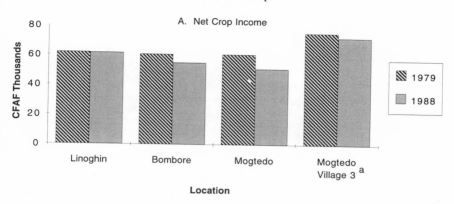

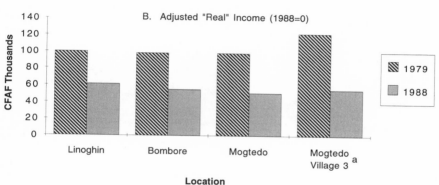

a Includes information on both privately and cooperatively worked fields. Other villages include only
cooperatively worked fields for settlers in their third to fifth year of settlement.

Figure 6.5. Net crop income, 1979–1980 and 1988–1989. (See appendix B, table B.8)

lective fields). When this nominal net-income figure was adjusted for inflation using the IMF price index (appendix B, table B-11),[9] the average income
per unit labor was 40 to 50 percent lower (fig. 6.5; appendix B, table B-8)
(McMillan, Nana, and Savadogo 1993). There were five principal reasons
for this significant decrease:

1. A switch from cotton to cereals, which have a lower median price, but
   lower labor demands
2. The lower adjusted selling price for cotton because higher input prices
   were not entirely offset by the parallel increase in the amount paid to
   farmers
3. The lower median selling price (when adjusted for inflation) for sorghum
4. The fact that settlers' main crop activities were restricted to a 10- to 20-

hectare project farm, with only limited opportunities for using tractors or the cultivation of "illegal" fields (21 percent of the 678 fields in the total AVV sample, which only includes private fields for one woman per family)

5. An increase in average family size

Mixed Income Opportunities from Livestock

Extension records, which usually greatly underestimate the total number of animals, show a steady rise and then leveling off in total number of animals at Mogtedo after 1979 (fig. 6.6). The mean figure for the AVV showed the average farmer owning 4.2 cattle or oxen and 11 goats or sheep (Savadogo 1989c). This average figure, however, masks the growing inequality in large livestock holdings. By 1988, 30 percent (twenty-four) of the eighty farm families in the restudy had no cattle or oxen; 19 percent owned five or more large stock animals. Only about 5 percent of the farm families in all three blocs had large herds of cattle, ranging from twenty to forty head. This trend away from 100 percent ownership of at least two oxen (due to the AVV

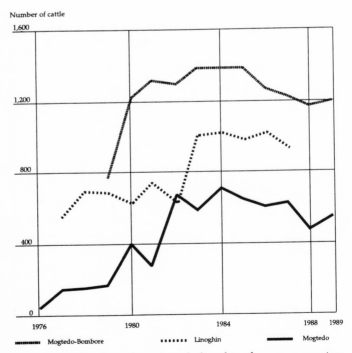

Figure 6.6. Total number of cattle listed in the AVV extension records. (AVV/UD extension records)

requirement that farmers use animal traction after the first year) was observed in AVV Linoghin and Mogtedo-Bombore as well as AVV Mogtedo.

The reduction in livestock ownership can be attributed to the high risk
of both theft and disease. Theft was especially high for smaller families who
either did not have older children to act as herders or whose children were
in school. At higher population densities, the social costs of keeping animals
increased as well. All livestock—but especially large animals—need to be
supervised so that they do not damage a neighboring farm family's fields.
When the risk of loss and theft was factored into the reported annual returns
from animal husbandry (the low income, high cost/loss scenario),[10] the
settlers' returns were much lower than when only current cash and kind costs
for herding services,[11] veterinary care, and feed were considered (the high
income, low cost/loss scenario; Savadogo 1989c). The combination of these
different factors limited the smaller families' willingness to assume the risks
associated with large livestock. The high risks of animal husbandry were
further complicated by the difficulty of negotiating herding contracts. Angry
over the settlers' constant accusations of animal damage to late-harvest crops
like cotton, many pastoralist households were increasingly reluctant to accept the settlers' animals unless forced to by necessity.

Early Rise and Fall of Nonfarm Income Opportunities

The 1979 trend toward the creation of high-earning secondary occupations
did not continue in the planned settlements at Mogtedo and Mogtedo-
Bombore.[12] Only one of the five V3 farmers described in chapter 5 who
had a high-earning secondary occupation in 1979 continued to have one
in 1988–89 (table 6.5). An area-wide drop in net cash income from cotton, the termination of construction activities at the neighboring bloc of
Mogtedo-Bombore in 1981, a fall in income from commercial woodcutting
by 1987, and a gradual cutback in extension personnel all contributed to
the decline in the settlers' disposable incomes. By 1989 the merchant selling bread and sodas, the mechanic, and the butcher had all left the project.
The first separate store—a combination boutique and bar—was opened in
1987 alongside the main road linking Mogtedo-Bombore with Mogtedo and
Mogtedo town. By 1989 it, too, had closed and was soon in ruins. Neither
beer nor soda was available for purchase in the village during the 1989 rainy
season. In early 1990 the most active trade in small manufactured products
like soap, cigarettes, and razors was conducted by the head extension agent's
wife, who was not a settler. While villagers indicated that a wide range of
services were available in the villages, most service activities were available only seasonally. The service trades, moreover, concentrated on provid-

Table 6.5

Average Nonfarm Income from Different Sources for Individuals Reporting Income
from the Source, 1988–1989 (in CFAF)

Source	Linoghin	Bombore	Mogtedo	Mogtedo V3	Kompienga
A. MALE HOUSEHOLD HEAD					
1. Unprocessed agric. products	64,120(1)	—	42,000(1)	—	23,167(3)
2. Processed agric. products	—	—	—	—	8,425(2)
3. Forest and water products	—	—	—	—	87,000(1)
4. Meat and animal by-products	28,500(1)	122,500(1)	38,650(3)	25,000	107,667(3)
5. Commerce	300,000(1)	—	50,250(2)	14,000(3)	81,000(3)
6. Handicrafts	21,300(2)	6,070(6)	1,950(1)	6,950(2)	53,167(3)
7. Gold	—	2,000(1)	36,166(3)	27,721(7)	—
8. Services	4,000(1)	—	5,000(1)	23,700(2)	50,000(1)
9. Agric. labor	—	—	20,000(1)	—	—
10. Nonagric. labor	450,000(1)	—	—	250,000	—
11. Mill	—	—	—	—	550,000(1)

B. ONE WOMAN PER FAMILY

1. Unprocessed agric. products	9,050(2)	—	—	74,200(2)	10,437(10)
2. Processed agric. products	26,043(13)	3,833(5)	3,186(7)	6,642(14)	6,361(11)
3. Forest and water products	30,050(2)	—	—	—	3,000(1)
4. Meat and animal by-products	—	—	37,500(1)	—	—
5. Commerce	2,200(1)	6,000(1)	—	—	—
6. Handicrafts	7,650(1)	8,150(1)	—	—	17,000(1)
7. Gold	—	500(1)	19,691(12)	13,914(16)	—
8. Services	—	—	—	3,500(1)	—

SOURCE: Savadogo 1989a.

( ) Indicates how many men and women provided nonzero numbers.

Methodology: 20 men and 20 women were interviewed in each of the AVV planned settlement groups; 25 men and 25 women were interviewed at Kompienga. Means are taken over these numbers.

ing simple market foods, petty trade (matches, batteries, sugar, soap) and "luxury" food items like cooking oil, rice, and meat.

The failure to develop a strong base of noncrop employment was linked to the difficulty that the settlers experienced in developing local markets. Although each AVV planned settlement had an area designated for a market, few of these markets survived more than a few months. Despite four recorded attempts to create a market at V3 and one at V1 of Mogtedo (sites 20 and 24 on map 12), the only market that survived was in an unplanned village at V5 Mogtedo. Even this market was weak and ultimately failed when trade shifted to the market that sprang up at the gold site at Nobsin in 1988 (map 12). Only two other markets within the planned-settlement blocs survived for any length of time—one at V2 and V5 at Bombore and the other at Rapadama V9 (listed as Gadeghin, site 5, on map 12). The secret of these small markets' success, and of the brief success of the "dead" V5 market, was their favorable location on the edge of the planned-settlement group, which attracted both spontaneous settlers and pastoralists. With the single exception of the AVV village market at Rapadama V4, almost none of the markets located inside a bloc have been successful. Even V4 can be considered a "frontier"/border market since it is located next to several indigenous villages just outside the AVV boundaries.

The settlers' lack of success in developing their own markets contrasts sharply with their substantial impact on regional market activities. In a study of the markets most frequented by settlers living in the blocs of Mogtedo, Linoghin and Mogtedo-Bombore, we found only three—Tenlouka, Mogtedo, and Yaika (sites 1, 13, and 12 on map 12)—that existed before river blindness control and the AVV sponsored settlements began in 1974. Four of the twenty extant markets frequented were located on the main paved highway. Most of the other regional, subregional, and village markets were located either in a frontier zone between the AVV planned-settlement areas populated by indigenous hosts or spontaneous settlers, or at gold sites.

While location was critical to success, attendance was not always determined by ease of access. In 1989 merchants traveling from AVV Mogtedo to Wardogo—one of the largest regional markets, created in 1983—had to cross a tributary of the Nakambe by boat. Wardogo's success was rooted in its location in a frontier zone between the government-sponsored settlements and a large area of self-settled agriculturalists and pastoralists near the Nakambe River. The six markets that survived within Mogtedo, Mogtedo-Bombore, and the neighboring AVV blocs of Rapadama and Linoghin conform to the same criterion of "frontier"/border location.

Although the settlers in the AVV blocs at Mogtedo and Mogtedo-Bombore have been the engine powering the phenomenal growth of Mogtedo, they have not emerged as market leaders. As of April 1990 only one of the AVV settlers from outside the surrounding province of Ganzourgou had constructed a home in the town. This settler, however, has never relocated a portion of his family to the house because of the hostility he encountered from some of the locals. Other settlers requested building sites in town but have never built. In 1989 not one of the prosperous boutiques or businesses in Mogtedo was owned by an AVV settler. Although there were a few AVV settlers who were successful wholesale grain and livestock merchants, they were all from the same Ganzourgou region as the indigenous hosts.

The AVV settlers' lack of incorporation into wider markets can be traced to the original creation of the blocs. When the AVV settlements began in 1974, few of the indigenous host Mossi or FulBe were interested in joining. Nevertheless they were resentful of the AVV's appropriation of the areas that the residents of Mogtedo and the surrounding villages sometimes used for grazing and rainy-season cultivation. In retaliation, they blocked the settlers' later attempts to expand into wider area markets. It did not matter that the majority of AVV settlers and the townspeople were from the same Mossi ethnic group; indeed, this shared ethnicity may have increased the settlers' suspicion about the outsiders' motives. The AVV Mossi settlers from outside Ganzourgou Province were aware of and sympathetic to the indigenous hosts' feelings. Nonetheless, this mutual animosity made it difficult for the AVV settlers to gain "social access" to the higher-earning trade opportunities in Mogtedo town.

Gold Mining

After 1987 gold became an important revenue source in the Mogtedo settlements. In confidential interviews with ten randomly chosen miners,[13] half the male miners reported earning 50,000 CFAF or more after deducting for expenses during the preceding year (McMillan, Nana, and Savadogo 1993). Twenty-eight of the forty women in the Mogtedo sample (Mogtedo and V3) reported an average income of 13,000 to 19,000 CFAF from gold panning (table 6.5). The actual reported incomes (after deducting for expenses) ranged from 1,000 to 50,000 CFAF for the year. The gold mines also created new opportunities to sell food products and water. The sudden infusion of gold income and gold-related trade permitted women to purchase new clothing, which was much in evidence during the annual Muslim and Christian holidays. Other signs of increased prosperity were apparent in the women's purchases of metal dinnerware, locks, windows, cement, and other improvements for their houses.

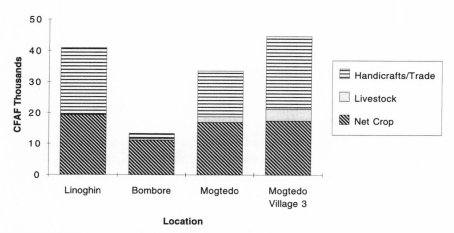

Figure 6.7. Women's net income by source, 1988–1989. (McMillan, Nana, and Savadogo 1993:53)

The women living in the AVV-sponsored settlements at Mogtedo-Bombore were too distant to engage in mining or trade at the gold sites. As a result, the average Bombore woman's income from nonfarm employment was only one-tenth to one-twentieth the average income earned by women in the adjacent planned settlements at Mogtedo (fig. 6.7). The Bombore women argued that without a market, their life was a boring cycle of cultivation and domestic chores, with only occasional trips to other areas to break the monotony. Similar complaints were characteristic of our interviews with women settlers at Mogtedo, in 1983 and 1987 prior to the discovery of gold.

The confidential interviews with male miners confirmed our observations from the expenditure survey that most of the money earned from gold mining was spent on consumer goods. We saw no direct evidence of reinvestment in the development of agriculture or services within the AVV blocs except for funds used to expand the women settlers' food trade. It was symptomatic of the low level of development of services and off-farm employment in the AVV planned settlements that the merchants who operated the larger boutiques, food, drink, and video concessions came from either Mogtedo town or Ouagadougou. Only the small merchants who sold cooked food and water were from the adjacent planned settlements. It seemed unlikely, therefore, that this sudden infusion of off-farm income would be reinvested in ways that would increase nonfarm employment for settlers living in the blocs (McMillan, Nana, and Savadogo 1993). Instead, the most lasting economic effect of the Mogtedo "gold rush" is likely to be to secure Mogtedo's role as an important regional trade and administrative center.

Greater Opportunities to Develop Off-Farm Employment at Linoghin

A very different scenario was recorded in the AVV planned settlements at Linoghin, about 60 kilometers from Mogtedo. There the settlers developed a dynamic market on the paved highway linking Ouagadougou to eastern Burkina, Togo, Niger, Benin, and Ghana (map 12). The economic importance of this market was not reflected in the reported off-farm income for male household heads (table 6.5). Instead, it was more accurately reflected in the higher income levels of the women household heads (table 6.5) and married and unmarried sons and brothers. Even the 300,000 CFAF income recorded for the store owned by one male head of household was actually earned by his married son. The father simply put up the money for the initial investment and shared in the profits. Eighty percent of the women interviewed at Linoghin recorded income from off-farm employment, none of it from gold. Most of this income was from cooked food, homemade beer, and gathered forest products. The average off-farm income for all the women interviewed at Linoghin was at about the same level as income recorded at Mogtedo V3—the village where women gained the most from the direct and indirect benefits of the 1987–88 gold rush (table 6.5; fig. 6.7).

Several factors contributed to the much greater development of nonfarm employment at Linoghin than in the other two blocs. The Linoghin market, in contrast to the Mogtedo market, was created by the Mossi AVV settlers themselves, who therefore could not be accused of stealing trade opportunities from their indigenous Mossi hosts. Linoghin's location was ideal. The market attracted male settlers from all six of the Linoghin planned settlements, as well as female settlers from the nearby settlements at V1 and V2. The settlers' gracious acceptance of indigenous farmers in their market was appreciated, and the fact that a large majority of the AVV settlers at Linoghin were recruited from the same province, Oubritenga, as the hosts and self-settled migrants made it easier for the two groups to collaborate.

One reflection of the greater degree of social integration between the Linoghin settlers and the surrounding host population was the jointly built mosque. Another indicator was a growing trend toward intermarriage. By 1989 we counted five daughters of spontaneous immigrants and four daughters of indigenous inhabitants who were married to settlers living in the AVV sponsored settlements at V1, V2, and V5 Linoghin. We also found six daughters of AVV sponsored settlers who were married to spontaneous migrants. This pattern of intermarriage, cooperation and increasing social integration contrasts sharply with the AVV-sponsored settlements at Mogtedo and Mogtedo-Bombore.

The dynamism of the Linoghin settlers was expressed in other ways as well. In 1988–89 the net CFAF value of crop production per worker (using the AVV system of weighted labor units) was 12 percent higher for the study farmers at Linoghin than at Bombore, and 20 percent higher than for the Mogtedo households. Ten years previously there had been no visible difference between the blocs in terms of net productivity per worker (Murphy and Sprey 1980:69). Linoghin settlers also showed the greatest actual and future potential for diversification into activities other than mining and had average per-household cash and kind expenses for production that were 24 percent higher than at Mogtedo and over 200 percent greater than at Mogtedo-Bombore and Mogtedo V3 (Savadogo, Sanders, and McMillan 1989:43). Seventy-nine percent of the study farmers used some compound fertilizer on their fields at Linoghin, 85 percent at Mogtedo, but only 45 percent at Mogtedo-Bombore (Savadogo, Sanders, and McMillan 1989:34).

The Linoghin settlers also showed the greatest interest in investing in the more labor-intensive soil conservation measures like diguettes and manure pits,[14] presumably because of their greater interest in remaining at the site. To assist farmer groups with the initial development of diguettes, the AVV-UPI provided project trucks. Even after the AVV support for dike building ended, individual farmers continued to expand the number of stone diguettes on their fields. The highest level of interest in diguettes was in the most isolated Linoghin village, V6, which is 20 to 25 kilometers from the Linoghin market. Although too distant from the market for many family members to easily engage in trade, the V6 settlers were close enough to Ouagadougou to develop profitable counter-season crops—in this case fresh corn. In 1989 the V6 farmer with the highest sales sold twenty carts of fresh corn; the lowest amount sold was four carts.

The average household expenditure on education—especially secondary education—was much higher at Linoghin than in the other settlements. Although the Mogtedo settlers invested in education, it was primarily for elementary schooling. For example, only one of the twenty families in the 1989 farming systems survey at V3 had a child in high school. In contrast, most of the twenty households in the Linoghin sample were supporting one and often two children who were away attending high school. Especially remarkable was the development of the first kindergarten in the region. Debt repayment on short-term credits has generally been the highest of all the settlement groups studied. In comparison with the other blocs, the Linoghin group has also had one of the most successful records for the development of group-managed enterprises, the income from which has been used to maintain basic infrastructure like roads and wells.

On the whole, settler turnover has been very low at Linoghin. Although a number of the wealthier settlers have moved into full-time commerce based in Ouagadougou, they have generally left a son or brother in charge of the family farm. Indeed, there has been a great deal of competition to inherit the Linoghin project farms. In one case, when a settler died, the brothers from the home village asserted their rights to inherit the 10-hectare AVV project farm. The AVV finally ruled that the farm could be inherited by the man's eldest son. In contrast, the more isolated, less diversified neighboring blocs of Mogtedo and Mogtedo-Bombore have experienced high turnover. Of the 255 households who acquired AVV farms at Mogtedo between 1974 and 1978, only 58 percent (148) were still living there in 1989. Out-migration was lower but still substantial (81 percent of the 345 AVV households that had claimed AVV farms between 1978 and 1980 were still living at Mogtedo-Bombore in 1989). In contrast, there was virtually no settler dropout from the more diversified Linoghin bloc. Indeed, there was usually fierce intrafamilial competition to replace the few settlers who were forced to return home because of age or illness.

Lessons Learned from the AVV Settlers' Out-Migration to Kompienga

A sizable out-migration of settlers from the older planned settlements at Rapadama, Mogtedo, Mogtedo-Bombore, and Mankaraga to Kompienga focused attention on the important role of developing a more diversified pattern of household production in determining the settlers' long-term investment decisions. In early 1988 more than thirty families left the bloc of Mogtedo, cutting all ties with the AVV. Within about one week the number of children attending the V3 bloc school dropped by one-third. The census of Kompienga town we conducted in August 1989 identified fifty-five households headed by a former AVV settler. Other settlers from Mogtedo joined family members in the southwest, returned home, or immigrated to another AVV site as either sponsored or nonsponsored settlers.

The settlers' main motivation to leave was the greater opportunity to develop irrigated dry-season production and trade. Another factor was the rising tide of conflict between the most successful commercial farmers and those settlers who opted for a more traditional pattern of extensive agriculture with limited cash cropping and on-farm livestock production. By and large, the successful commercial farmers who left had focused on improving the lot of their individual families rather than on investing to improve the living standards of their traditional lineage or extended families. Indeed, in several cases the decisions of these successful commercial settler households to marry their daughters to other AVV settlers were deliberately at odds with the wishes of the traditional clan elders in their home villages. When the successful commercial farmers did choose to consult with their traditional leaders in negotiating marriage alliances or otherwise returning home, they generally dealt with the village chief rather than their clan leaders. Although the chief is important, he has historically been removed from the internal politics of the villages' constituent clans, which are the locus of day-to-day political, social, and economic power in the Mossi kingdoms.

The successful AVV settlers as a group invested less money and time in maintaining strong linkages with their traditional patrilineal extended clans. Instead, they preferred to invest in the development of new economic and social linkages with one another that were more compatible with their new position as commercially successful farmers. The new crosscutting ties were first symbolized by the group's conversion to Islam. After 1979 these ties were further strengthened by intermarriage. For example, only one settler who left for Kompienga was from the clan Poedogo. His decision to break with the Poedogo farmers was signaled when he converted to Islam immediately prior to leaving the AVV for Kompienga. The departure of so many of the leading Muslims contributed to the decay of the once carefully maintained V3 village mosque.

In contrast, the core group of settlers from the Kaya region who did not leave were those from the Poedogo clan who had been unusually successful in encouraging and sponsoring the immigration of additional family members, including subclan leaders. The second-largest group of settlers who remained were those who had allied themselves with this group through marriage and ties of religious affiliation. With a few striking exceptions, the settlers who remained behind practiced extensive cultivation of food crops, with limited livestock and cotton production and little off-farm employment besides gold and small-scale trade at the gold sites.

The decision to move was not made easily or quickly. The first talk of leaving V3 and the first trips to scout out other areas followed the 1983 and 1984 drought years. As early as 1985, leaders of the Muslim community at V3 and their allies expressed concern with what they perceived as a decline in soil fertility. By 1986 the majority of the larger households had reduced the area planted in cotton, but when the rains returned, the grain prices plummeted. The departing settlers argued that prospects for reversing these dramatic market swings looked dim. This period also coincided with large-scale reductions in extension staff. In addition, the AVV was beginning to promote new cash- and labor-intensive soil conservation and water-retention methods.

The V3 settlers who went to Kompienga were attracted by the prospect of developing dry-season irrigated gardening and the potential for trade once the Kompienga dam was completed. Kompienga was also an area to which few Mossi had immigrated prior to construction of the dam. As such, they were less likely to encounter conflicts with other, already established, dominant Mossi groups in developing nonfarm employment. The female family heads liked living near a small urban center with an active market. It is indicative that even in the first years of establishing new farms, many AVV settlers' wives were earning substantially higher incomes from trade than the average woman was earning at Mogtedo-Bombore (Table 6.5) (McMillan, Nana, and Savadogo 1993; Savadogo, Sanders, and McMillan 1989). The settlers were also attracted by the high-quality social services (dispensaries, schools, water points) that the dam construction companies left behind. Thanks to an innovative program in which the dam construction authority provided loans and subsidized materials to encourage workers to construct their own homes, the town was also blessed with a surfeit of cheap, improved housing.

Immigration to Kompienga was not cheap. The cost of renting a truck to transport household goods was 100,000 to 150,000 CFAF, the cash equivalent of the total crop income produced in 1988 by the poorer AVV settler households. On arrival, fifty-two of the fifty-five former AVV settlers purchased their homes from departing construction workers for an average of 100,000 CFAF. Two of the three former AVV settlers who were included in the survey spent 255,000 CFAF ($850) and 418,000 CFAF ($1,395) on housing and housing improvements in the first year and a half alone. The same two former AVV settlers purchased rental properties as well.

One striking indicator of the high level of disposable income of the settlers who immigrated to Kompienga was that the female settlers paid 25 CFAF per bucket to get water from the automatic pumps located in the village, even though free water was available a few hundred meters away on the other side of the main road, in the unimproved area that the dam authority had never zoned. We also recorded high monthly expenditures for milling at privately owned mills and observed almost no hand grinding at Kompienga. By contrast, because the cooperatively run AVV grain mills were inoperable and people had more limited disposable income, a large portion of the grain at Mogtedo and Mogtedo-Bombore was hand ground in 1989. When a woman did not receive money from her husband to pay for grinding or could not afford to pay for grinding on her own, she was forced to spend from two to three hours a day on this time-consuming task. In fact, milling and grinding expenditures at Mogtedo V3 seem to have actually decreased since 1979.

Another group of seventeen settler households left the planned settlements at Rapadama in 1988 (S. Sawadogo 1988a, 1989). The eight settlers who owed the project large credits were presumably unsuccessful settlers. These unsuccessful settlers left for various destinations, some returning home; only one of the debtor settlers from Rapadama went to Kompienga. The other nine households were headed by men who had developed successful commercial activities in the AVV market at V9 Rapadama (indicated as the Gadeghin market on map 12). The V9 market developed into an important area market in the early 1980s. Located on the outskirts of the Rapadama bloc, the market was popular with self-settled spontaneous settlers and pastoralists, as well as with sponsored settlers. In 1987 the AVV was forced to evict several hundred of the self-settled immigrant households when the project created the Gadeghin pastoral zone. Once the spontaneous settlers left, the V9 market collapsed. One year later the successful diversified settler households left the project (S. Sawadogo 1988a).

In the case of the successful settler households, one could argue that the out-migration from Rapadama shared many similarities with the out-migration from Mogtedo and Mogtedo-Bombore. The desire for diversification into trade and more lucrative income-earning activities was the primary factor that influenced the emigration decisions of both groups. As in the out-migration from Mogtedo and Mogtedo-Bombore, all nine of the successful, nondebtor households chose to immigrate to Kompienga and all nine were Muslim. In contrast, we did not find a single Linoghin farmer who was investing or planning to invest at Kompienga.

Conclusion

Although the AVV did not succeed in introducing intensive agriculture, the project did increase the settlers' income. Moreover, various elements of the project—access to new land, supplementary food aid, extension services—did combine to raise settler income and to create new economic options. With new successful economic ventures came a sense of personal empowerment within the wider economy of Burkina and a desire to diversify even further.

At Mogtedo and Mogtedo-Bombore, these commercial ventures were thwarted by the settlers' physical and social isolation from important markets. One group of commercial farmers, including some of the most successful farmers in the region, chose to leave the project for an area where they felt there were better opportunities. Another group adapted to the increasingly isolated social and economic conditions that were resulting from the project's winding down by reintroducing and expanding their traditional patterns of extensive rain-fed agriculture and limited investment in livestock and trade.

In contrast, the greater opportunity to develop trade at Linoghin was a factor that encouraged the most successful settlers to remain living there, despite the constraints that they faced. These constraints included inappropriate extension policies, low cereal prices, limited opportunities for commercial livestock production, and insecure land-tenure rights. None of these were factors that either the project planners or the settlers themselves could completely control. The increased diversification of the Linoghin settlers was not at the expense of additional investment in intensive farming or higher levels of crop productivity. Indeed, after fifteen years of living in the project, the Linoghin farmers had the highest level of investment in variable inputs (such as fertilizer, insecticide, and labor) as well as new soil conservation technologies.

These findings corroborate other research showing that increased economic diversification need not necessarily be at the expense of additional investment in intensive farming or higher levels of crop productivity (Scudder 1981, 1985). Indeed, there is very little evidence from successful settlement areas throughout the tropics of significant numbers of wealthier households withdrawing entirely from agriculture as long as appropriate agricultural markets exist (Scudder 1981, 1985). In terms of environmental sustainability, crop productivity, and positive regional development, one of the most successful settlements in the tropics is Minneriya, which was established in the dry zone of Sri Lanka in the 1930s (Scudder and Wimaladharma 1985, 1990). Wimaladharma found that over 90 percent of holdings in the early 1980s were still controlled by the same families—including now adult children to whom parents had handed over management (Scudder and Wimaladharma 1990). High rates of settler turnover in Africa, Asia, and Latin America are associated with a lack of opportunity as well as with insecure tenure and unfavorable project and macro-level prices and/or price policies that deflate the returns to sustainable cropping (Cernea 1988, 1991; Chambers 1969; Christodoulou 1965; McMillan, Painter, and Scudder 1992; Salem-Murdock 1989; Saul 1988; Scudder 1981, 1984, 1985,

1991; Sorbo 1977, 1985; Van Raay and Hilhorst 1981; Weitz, Pelley, and Applebaum 1978).

These research results have implications for policy at both the national (macro) and the local (micro) levels. Based on the case study research and comparative research in Burkina [15] and in new lands settlements worldwide, we can predict that local opportunities to develop off-farm employment, as well as land quality, will influence the settlers' choice of immigration sites. In the same way we can predict that the long-term profitability of these off-farm enterprises will affect the willingness and capacity of the local inhabitants to invest in environmentally sustainable natural resource management.

In view of the importance that settlers attach to developing diversified sources of income, policy makers should concentrate, at least initially, on developing infrastructure and crop and livestock extension services in less isolated areas like Linoghin, where opportunities for diversification are greater. The principal exception to this would be isolated areas that are determined to have unusual natural resource potential, such as the land around dams (McMillan, Painter, and Scudder 1992).

Land-tenure and zoning policies should therefore strive for a balance to promote the economic interests of all of the affected groups, including hosts and immigrants, pastoralists, and agriculturalists. This planning guideline, which is often viewed solely in terms of social equity, has a number of pragmatic economic consequences. Most notably, high levels of social conflict can inhibit successful diversification and the settlers' willingness to reinvest in a region. Local pastoralists can be penalized with high fines for the destruction of farmers' crops by animals, although determining whose animals are at fault is complicated by the large number of temporary residents moving in and out of a settlement zone. Special administrative intervention may be necessary to secure pasture rights for pastoralists to accommodate the fact that there is seldom a category of either customary or modern legal codes that recognizes pasture rights (McMillan, Nana, and Savadogo 1993; McMillan, Painter, and Scudder 1992).

A final recommendation addresses the need to phase development investments in over a longer period of time. If the first generation of development planning is successful, it will no doubt attract additional new lands settlement. Doing so normally results in the creation of new markets and the expansion of markets established before settlement begins. The AVV's many futile attempts to develop project markets indicates that it is very difficult to predict where new market centers will develop. Nevertheless, government investment in roads and infrastructure designed to facilitate the development of these centers increases the probability of profitable agricultural and nonfarm enterprises. Donors might, therefore, include a second-generation set of funding plans to support the development of the market and administrative centers that emerge during the first phase of an intervention and whose success is critical to the attainment of more long-term project goals for successful, sustainable development.

7

Lessons Learned:
Policy Vision and Revision

In August 1989 the final chapter in the history of the AVV as a formal institution was closed when the agency was converted into an *office* under the Ministry of Agriculture and Livestock. Although the new agency occupies the same building and employs a small percentage of former AVV personnel, it no longer has a special mandate for settlement and development in the OCP river basins (AVV 1989a, 1989b, 1989c, 1989d, 1989e, 1990; Djigma 1989).[1] To symbolize this complete reorientation, the AVV was rechristened the Office National d'Aménagement des Territoirs, or ONAT. While these events marked the formal end of the AVV as a vehicle for follow-up planning in the OCP river basins, it did not in any way mark the end of the changes set in motion by the project. More than two decades after these changes were initiated, what lessons can be learned and, more critically, what are the implications for future policies?

Disease Control: A Partial Development Vision

The first set of planning lessons that we can extrapolate from the case study research has to do with donor investment in disease control. More specifically, the case study and comparative research on the entire project zone provide clear evidence that large-scale donor investment in river blindness control and follow-up planning did create new rural settlement and development opportunities and did contribute to an increase in the GNP of Burkina Faso. Some of the measurable indicators of this success in the Mogtedo region were sharp regional increases in total cereal and cash crop production as well as dramatic growth in the size and sales volume of area markets.

Nevertheless, the case study reminds us that a technological innovation like the OCP is only a partial development vision. The river basins may have great agricultural potential, but they are also problem-prone. Because of their historic isolation, the river basins have very little in the way of basic infrastructure, such as roads, schools, and health facilities, and onchocerciasis is never the only health hazard. Access to safe, potable water is often difficult because of deep water tables. There is also a strong propensity for land-tenure disputes due to the fact that, although many of the river basins have remained sparsely inhabited, they were never unclaimed. Land-use planning is further complicated by the fact that the river basins have traditionally been one of the most important sources of grazing and water for the Sahel's migratory livestock. Other land-use problems stem from the river basins' high concentration of protected forests and wildlife.

Neither the settlers moving into the underpopulated OCP river basins nor their national governments have the means to address these issues on their own. Nevertheless, they must be addressed *if* the resulting new lands settlement is to be sustainable as population densities increase. The latter point was confirmed by the longitudinal case study's evidence that the most important factor determining the sustainable income levels and long-term investment patterns of the V3 settlers was not the settlers' increased access to new land. Rather, it was other development investments, policies, and social factors that determined the profitability of the economic activities they engaged in. These complementary factors included the AVV programs for short- and medium-term credit, rural roads, extension services, and the settlers' access to dynamic regional and local markets.

What Types of Complementary Visions?

Based on the analysis of what did and did not happen at the AVV, I have concluded that the existing theories that have been used to guide agricultural development in sub-Saharan Africa are unlikely to be the best guides for follow-up planning in the OCP river basins.[2] The chief reason is the models' tendency to focus on increasing land and labor productivity in established cultivation zones. Often a key assumption in such development models is the potential or actual constraint on land availability. In the OCP river basins, however, the key constraints typically are labor, lack of infrastructure, and inadequate access to inputs and markets. In such a situation, the higher payoff is to farm as much land as possible with a minimum investment of labor and other expensive inputs.

If one of the goals of government and foreign donor planning in the West African Sahel is to prevent extensive exploitation of the newly cleared OCP river basins, then governments must work with the concept that it is the shortage of labor, not land, that drives the farmers' land-use decisions. Development models that impose top-down decisions regarding land use and intensive cultivation methods (like the early AVV) are unlikely to work simply because the farmers have no incentive to comply. In the absence of voluntary compliance, few government projects have either the manpower or the resources to enforce the imposed restrictions.

The case study's evidence of noncompliance with government land-use restrictions and high levels of diversification runs counter to Reyna's (1980, 1983, 1986, 1987) and Conti's (1979) argument that the AVV settlers were a powerless, disenfranchised rural proletariat. These early studies focused on the project policies that specified that (1) the settlers' land-tenure rights were state-accorded and conditional upon their adherence to the prescribed program for intensive farming and (2) most decisions concerning production costs and distribution were to be made by the AVV, even though the settlers were required to bear the direct costs (AVV 1974; McMillan 1983; Murphy and Sprey 1980; Reyna 1983, 1986, 1987). Based on an analysis of these official policies, Reyna (1986:232) concluded: "Thus their [the settlers'] control appears even riskier than that of wage laborers . . . who bear no direct production costs. AVV tenants must contribute financially to certain decisions they do not control, and are given no protection should these go awry." He went on to state that, as a result, the AVV managers enjoyed greater *de jure* control over land use than private landowners, placing the "AVV in a situation of meta-control over its tenants." Based on the same analysis of the AVV's written policies and Guissou's (1977) study of first- and second-year AVV settlers (AVV), Conti (1979) accused the AVV of exploiting women through the "capitalist organization of production through noncapitalist relations."

The case study data show, however, that rather than being oppressed by the project's (and the state's) imposed restrictions, the settlers simply ignored them or, in extreme cases, moved. Faced with massive noncompliance, the Burkinabè state had neither the resources nor the political will to enforce unpopular policies, except in the short run. In addition, despite the state's best efforts to promote a system of "unimodal," egalitarian development, certain immigrant households became noticeably more successful than others. Others were less successful, while some were successful but lost everything when a crisis befell. In sum, the AVV findings support Netting's claim (1993) that the measurable differences between rural households in terms of income and access to resources can mask a certain amount of mobility "between generations and within individual life courses both up and down the local ladder of wealth and possessions."

This economic mobility at the AVV was the result of several factors. One of the most important, and one that is extremely difficult to quantify, was management. Differing levels of management skills among the settlers were apparent in a variety of ways, including the timely performance of key production activities such as weeding, systems of rewards that served to motivate family members, and a willingness and ability to gamble on new, higher-yielding livestock and nonfarm activities. These differences in management skills confirm Matlon's (1981) observation that household endowments of land and labor had a relatively minor effect on stratification among Nigerian Hausa farming households, while off-farm enterprises contributed somewhat more. According to Matlon, the potentially critical factor in explaining differential income was resource management. Hans Ruthenberg (1968:328–329) also found that a high percentage of the variation in Tanzanian Sukumaland cotton production could be predicted by the "differing entrepreneurial qualities of the farmers." This suggests that more research is needed to determine if the necessary managerial skills can be predicted, taught, and extended.[3]

Some observers worried that Burkina's 1984 Land Tenure and Agrarian Reform Act, described in chapter 6, would create a legal means for settlers moving into the OCP river basins to amass land and create a more fixed social and economic hierarchy. In practice, the Land Tenure and Agrarian Reform Act, like the legislation that created the AVV, made very little difference in the way land was acquired (see McMillan, Nana, and Savadogo 1993) because of the state's inability to enforce the new law and the settlers' unwillingness to absorb the high social and economic costs of bypassing traditional methods of acquiring land. The key factors working against the ability of the state to enforce compliance with its policies were the traditional and persistent dependence of the farmers on extended family ties and the weak central power of the Burkinabè state. The two factors are closely related. The settlers were acutely aware that the project's ability to enforce unpopular land-management policies and to provide an integrated package of services was linked to its access to special donor funds. The settlers were reluctant, therefore, to become dependent on project aid except as a short-term intermediary solution. In the settlement areas, as throughout Burkinabè history, a strong network of social ties was believed to be the best, most reliable insurance against disaster.

These findings support Scudder's recommendation (1984:17) that "recruiting settlers from different villages within the same locale and ethnic group as opposed to different ethnic groups" is one of the main ways to improve early performance in new lands settlement and resettlement projects. Scudder notes that neighbors and co-ethnics are much more likely to form supportive self-help groups for land clearing and house building during the early insecure years of settlement. A second advantage is a reduction in the potential stress and uncertainty of adapting to new neighbors (Scudder 1984:17). The fact that a high percentage of the V3 settlers immigrated from the same home village initially did provide these advantages. As success rates began to vary, however, the high concentration of settlers from the same home village living in the case study village made it difficult for the settlers to reconcile their present social status with their previous status. The high levels of social strife that ensued precipitated accusations of sorcery, financial mismanagement, and political ambition. Under "normal" conditions of spontaneous settlement, the settlers could have adjusted to this rising strife by readjusting the settlement patterns within the village. This option did not exist at the AVV because the official settlement sites in all six villages at Mogtedo and in the seven villages at Mogtedo-Bombore were fully allocated within a five-year period. This negatively charged social atmosphere contributed to the out-migration of the most successful settlers, as described in chapter 6.

Alternative Visions

More likely to be successful would be a development model that minimizes direct government involvement in determining recruitment and settlement. This approach is similar to the concept of "assisted" or "directed" spontaneous settlement described by Scudder and others (see Goering 1978; Scudder 1981, 1984, 1985, 1992; Van Raay and Hilhorst 1981; Weitz, Pelley, and Applebaum 1978). The use of the terms *directed* and *assisted* refers to the idea of minimal government involvement to provide basic services and infrastructure to settlers immigrating on their own initiative. It is an approach that allows planners to build on the recognized strengths (entrepreneurial ability, cash resources, strong community ties, familiarity with the region or good relationships with indigenous groups) of spontaneous settlement and to avoid some of the better-documented social, ecological, and economic problems of unassisted spontaneous settlement. It is a development concept that occupies a middle ground between the two extremes of new lands settlement: completely "planned" (like the AVV) or completely "spontaneous." Priority areas for intervention include agency assistance with site selection and land-tenure rights, as well as promotion of marketing, transportation, and social services. Also important is supportive land-tenure legislation backed by an independent judiciary (see McMillan, Painter, and Scudder 1992).

Scudder (1984:4) suggests that access roads and potable water may best be provided through a "site and service" approach, as successfully implemented in a number of low-income urban communities in parts of Africa and Latin America. An attractive alternative is for governments to establish communities of sponsored settlements, similar to the AVV planned settlements, as development "beachheads" (Angel 1985:25) around which spontaneous settlers would be encouraged to take up residence (Scudder 1984:5). Implicit in the argument for mixed spontaneous and sponsored settlements is the notion that

> viable communities which attract and incorporate spontaneous settlers are not only less costly, but they are in many ways less risky and certainly more natural than communities that consist only of sponsored migrants. It does not follow, however, that these communities can flourish unsupported and unplanned. Greater support to early migrants and sound planning for those who come later will greatly improve migrant welfare and facilitate the settlement process. (Bharin 1981:141)

The extensive planning that went into the AVV-sponsored settlements shows that it is virtually impossible for even the most seasoned planner to anticipate the full range of problems and opportunities that these programs will encounter. The planning process is further complicated by the frequent lack of established cropping systems or research data on which to base extension recommendations and advice. Because the river basins have a sparse population, they often lack the basic infrastructure (roads, bridges, schools, markets, and administrative centers) that facilitates development. It is also easy to overlook other factors that may contribute to an area's remaining uninhabited, such as various human or animal diseases or unhealthy drinking water. Insecure land tenure poses further problems.

For all these reasons, it is preferable for planners to aspire to a diversified production system instead of a system like the one proposed by the AVV, which focused on the intensive production of one or two commercial crops. A development program that aspires to the development of a diversified pattern of crop, livestock, and nonfarm employment *and* minimal disruption of the settlers' preexisting social patterns offers the greatest freedom to both settlers and hosts to respond to new constraints and opportunities. The development of new enterprises and services, in turn, feeds back into sustainable farming in other important ways.

The most important has to do with retaining family labor. Household heads know that without successful noncrop enterprises that allow them to earn money for new consumer goods, young unmarried and married men are apt to seek wage labor in the cities or coastal plantations. Losing a son to foreign wage labor means losing a valuable labor resource (McMillan, Painter, and Scudder 1992). A similar argument can be made for the diversion of family labor and cash resources into the development of women's livestock and commercial activities. Without profitable sources of noncrop income, women are forced to rely on the income from private fields to fulfill personal and family needs. This private production removes labor from the larger, collectively worked family fields. Since women's earnings are likely to be spent on higher-value foods, school supplies, and clothing for themselves and their children (Baer 1991; DeWalt 1991; Gladwin and McMillan 1988; McMillan 1983, 1986, 1987a), this income affects the living standards of the entire family. Settlers with recurrent sources of income are also better able to purchase cash inputs such as fertilizer and insecticides and to pay for supplementary labor during production bottlenecks (McMillan, Painter, and Scudder 1992).

While there are many similarities between the AVV settlers' activities and the stage models described by Scudder (1981, 1985, 1991) and others (Chambers 1969; Nelson 1973; Scudder and Colson 1982), there are also major differences. One of the most important case-study findings was the rapid increase in settler income during the first five years. Scudder's sequence of four successive settlement stages (table 5.4) does not predict such an early rapid increase in income, at least among the majority. This suggests that there may be important differences between voluntary relocation (as occurred with the AVV) and the more socially and psychologically disruptive types of compulsory relocation, which were the focus of early studies and the basis for most stage models.

The same research suggests that the speed of community reorganization and income growth is likely to be very different for groups like the Mossi, who have a strong historic tradition of agricultural new lands settlement, and for groups that do not. Ethnographers argue that various Mossi social institutions have evolved in direct response to the need to facilitate new lands settlement (Finnegan 1976, 1978; Hammond 1966; S. Sawadogo 1986; Skinner 1964b, 1989). These social institutions include the Mossi people's highly flexible system of land tenure (Boutillier 1964; Saul 1988); the automatic rights of eldest sons to residence and land in their mother's village (Hammond 1966; Skinner 1964a); the exchange relationships associated with marriage alliances (Boutillier 1964; Hammond 1966; Skinner 1960a); and the flexibility with which a group is able to obtain the rights to perform traditional rituals (Finnegan 1976; Hammond 1966; Skinner 1964b) or to acquire a new chief (Skinner 1957, 1970b, 1989). In a similar way, religious conversion to Christianity or Islam has historically helped to facilitate the economic and social incorporation of Mossi labor migrants in Côte d'Ivoire and Ghana (Deniel 1967, 1970; Schildkraut 1978; Skinner 1958, 1962a). These "traditional" institutions did not cease to operate with resettlement in the AVV. Instead, the settlers used some of the same mechanisms to create new ties of social enmeshment and indebtedness to one another (see chapter 4).

The settlers in this study also differed from conventional stage models in terms of their patterns of income diversification. Much of the comparative work on new lands settlement correctly emphasizes the importance of off-farm activities, especially investment in regional centers, towns, and capitals. While this type of "urban" investment was observed among first-generation settlers at Linoghin, the settlers also invested in a new pattern of rural diversification in livestock, rural stores, and additional lands with potential for irrigation. The lack of such opportunities to diversify was, in fact, the single most important reason for the out-migration of successful AVV settlers to Kompienga.

Another difference between the case study and conventional stage models regards entrepreneurs. Scudder's discussion of entrepreneurship within the first two stages of his four-stage settlement model focuses on the need for planners to limit the access of outside entrepreneurs (often civil servants) to improved project lands. The rationale for this is that the entrepreneurs' capital may enable them to achieve economic success more quickly than the average settler by allowing them to expand their farms at the expense of less wealthy settlers. Experiences in the AVV show that this fear is genuine. Urban-based entrepreneurs and civil servants did clear large commercial plantations and "bush" farms in the OCP river basins near the national capital of Ouagadougou.

Far less attention has been focused on the new entrepreneurs who emerge as a result of their activities in the project. It was project-made entrepreneurs who spearheaded the V3 settlers' rapid transition to a more dynamic third stage of economic and social development. Unfortunately, when these highly successful entrepreneurs at Mogtedo and Rapadama departed *en masse*, they took with them both their capital and the leadership skills and vision required for Scudder's fourth settlement stage of "Handing Over and Incorporation." More research needs to be done to ensure that projects can enhance, not thwart, the highly productive energy and leadership skills of newly emerging entrepreneurs.

Evaluation: Whose Vision Counts . . . and When?

The key role played by the V3 entrepreneurs in determining the final output of donor investment in their village highlights the fact that project participants, donors, planners, and researchers all are likely to view development success in different ways. Moreover, this success is likely to be defined in different ways at different points in time.

The AVV and the OCP represent prime examples of the types of development visions that motivate foreign donors. Decisions to fund large-scale interventions like the OCP are usually based on a complex combination of political and economic priorities established by both the donors and the host countries. Complicating matters are the various agendas of the researchers who conduct the baseline studies used to design the projects. An agenda may be as abstract as the need to substantiate or refute a particular theory, or as concrete as a desire to complete a book, to pave the way toward a better job or promotion, or to develop a new, cutting-edge academic theory. The visions of foreign donors, consultants, and researchers are also influenced by contemporary cultural mores and the time frame in which they plan and execute projects.

Remember, for example, the political and economic context within which the OCP was conceived. The 1968–74 sahelian drought served to focus donor attention for the first time on the problems of chronic underdevelopment in Africa in general and on the landlocked sahelian countries in particular. In my opinion, another contributing factor was the United States government's attempts to atone for the sins of the Vietnam war. The idea that a single investment in river blindness control could yield a wide range of positive economic benefits for the drought-ridden Sahel, coupled with the prospect of achieving rapid, clearly visible, measurable results, was highly appealing in an era when many foreign interventions seemingly had failed.

Ironically, in contrast to the donors' enthusiasm, not one of the core control countries saw onchocerciasis as a major health concern prior to 1974. The sahelian governments were attracted to the control program because it was free and because the training made available through the program could be applied to other disease-control efforts. The chief attraction of the OCP for Burkina Faso was that the government perceived the project as a "carrot" to attract other types of funding to promote integrated development in the chronically underdeveloped river basins. Given Burkina's extremely high population densities in the central Mossi plateau and the existing trend of agricultural immigration from the plateau to the south, it was not difficult to elicit donor funding for complementary development.

One of the best indications of where the Burkina government's true interest in control lay is the fact that six of the twelve settlement groups created by the AVV are in the upper Nakambe (former White Volta), near Ouagadougou, an area where onchocerciasis historically has never been a serious problem. The high levels of donor funding associated with the AVV appeared to offer the Burkinabè a rare opportunity to test the idea that they could create sustainable, integrated, rain-fed agriculture if given access to sufficient donor funds. The resulting band of profitable agriculture along the river basins could then increase the GNP and reduce trade imbalances. So swift was the flood of donor aid in 1974 that the new agency (AVV) was hard pressed to spend the allocated funds within the short time frame specified by the donors (appendix B, table B-6).

In stark contrast to the original project vision of coordinated development was the settlers' quest for "new" land. As described in chapter 3, most settlers, before they immigrated, had only a vague notion of the AVV or the OCP. They viewed themselves as repeating a historic pattern of spontaneous agricultural immigration from areas of lesser to areas of greater opportunity. In the case of the AVV, they were attracted to the the project's promise of roads, credit program, subsidized inputs, food aid, and health services. They were committed to success, but that success was defined in terms of a better future for their individual families. If that commitment happened to coincide with the project's goals for intensive, sustainable agriculture, well and good; in the event it did not, they knew they could always move again.

As the OCP progressed, donors continued to be attracted by the program's low cost (estimated at U.S. $1.00 per beneficiary per year over the life of the project), its concrete measurable results, and the high economic rates of return on the initial investment (estimated at 11 to 13 percent over the life of the project and 63 percent for 1990–2023 due to the large quantity of sunk costs during the first fifteen years of investment [Benton and Skinner 1990:410–411; see also Berg et al. 1978, OCP 1986; Prost and Prescott 1984, Younger and Zongo 1989]). One result of these high returns has been a solid base of recently renewed funding through 1997, a full four years beyond the original target end date.

Maintaining the same level of committed, long-term donor support for follow-up planning in Burkina has not been easy, primarily because of costs. By 1978 the per-household cost of the AVV had soared to almost four times the original 1974 project plans estimate (U.S. $12,500 versus $3,300) (appendix B, tables B-2 and B-7). While some of the higher per-unit costs can be attributed to the smaller-than-predicted number of households that have been settled in the project villages, there were significant cost overruns, particularly for roads and mechanical field preparation. As theoretical interest in the concept of "integrated development" waned in the 1970s, the Burkina government came under donor pressure to develop a more flexible, less costly model that would be capable of handling spontaneous as well as sponsored settlements (see chapter 6; appendix B, fig. B-1). The change was also motivated by the donors' desire to focus investment on a single group of settlements that could be claimed as "theirs." The reorganization coincided with a dramatic decrease in outside donor support after 1983 (appendix B, table B-6).

At the same time, the visions of the participating villagers were changing as well. When they first came to the AVV, the settlers' initial concern was to reinstate their basic food systems. At this highly vulnerable point the project administration was very intimidating, and the settlers were further confused by the radically new methods of "democratic" social organization imposed by the project. They were particularly confused by the AVV's hostile relations with the surrounding villages. During this early, uncertain phase, described in chapters 4 and 5, the settlers were most willing to respect the project's prescribed agricultural program. This rather meek compliance can be traced to their initial insecurity as well as the early capacity of the project to enforce its edicts. Over time, as the AVV's ability to enforce its edicts lessened and as the settlers began to feel more self-assured and confident, they became freer to innovate. Unfortunately for the project planners' fixed conceptions of success, the settlers' innovations often involved a greater willingness to experiment with nonprescribed production activities. In many cases this led to their failure to comply with the project's land-use restrictions. This noncompliance coincided with a significant increase in the settlers' revenue from sources such as livestock, off-farm employment, and the produce from "illegal" bush fields.

The increase in diversification was ignored by the planners, which led them to underestimate the project's wider regional impact. For example, the AVV farm-monitoring survey focused on the "official" project fields. Based on the analysis of the survey's results for the 1978 and 1979 cropping season, Murphy and Sprey (1980) concluded that the settlers were only practicing the prescribed cropping methods on the cash crop cotton. The same survey showed that the cash value of production per capita was either stagnant or had declined after the first three years (see chapter 5). In contrast, the intensive case study of the V3 settlers revealed the extent of "nonofficial" income earned from private fields, livestock, and off-farm employment like trade and commerce. When these additional income sources were added to the income from "official" project fields, the average settler income per capita did indeed show a substantial increase over time.

These vast differences in project results raise the critical issue of timing. When is it most appropriate to evaluate project costs and benefits? Can we afford to be impatient? Also, what factors and what levels should a cost-benefit analysis consider? In 1978 the cost of resettling one family in an AVV-sponsored settlement was estimated at U.S. $12,500. This dollar amount included expenditures associated with the cost of installing basic infrastructure and operating expenses for the first five years of extension service (appendix B, table B-7; BEI-agrer 1978). Project supporters countered that it was inappropriate to evaluate cost based entirely on expenditures surrounding the original sponsored settlements because, after ten or fifteen years, these same investments would serve (and in fact were serving) a much larger number of both spontaneous and sponsored settlers. Between 1973 and 1988, for example, the cumulative outside funding for the AVV was estimated at 23,554,859,000 CFAF (U.S. $79,069,684 at 297.9 CFAF = $1.00, average exchange rate 1988, World Bank 1989), at which time the project was affecting 420,935 inhabitants in 412 villages and one industrial wood project (appendix B, tables B-5 and B-6). If these figures, averaged over the entire region, are used, then the "cost" per beneficiary for a hypothetical family of eight is U.S. $1,505 (447,664 CFAF), about one-tenth the 1978 estimate.

Focusing entirely on preconceived criteria for success can also mask creative responses to new opportunities and constraints. Project planners assumed that the highly successful cotton technology package originally developed for southwest Burkina would work as well in the lower-rainfall river basins near the country's central plateau. Consequently, they were dismayed by the settlers' stubborn refusal to use the recommended technology and to grow the recommended crop area. Later research showed that, in fact, the central river basins were marginal for cotton, except in years of average or above average rainfall. The nearby indigenous villagers and the Mossi immigrants from farther north were well aware of this. A second critical level of response that was often overlooked was the resources (such as time, cash, farm products, and energy) that the settlers invested in redeveloping and cementing social ties.

Perhaps the most striking example of the difference between the settlers' and the planners' views of success was the project's gross ignorance of settler dropout. The AVV administration considered population stability in the sponsored settlements to be a key measure of success. Because of this bias, the project planners did not attempt to ascertain why settlers dropped out until the massive exodus of 1988 occurred. Even then, the primary concern was to convince the departing settlers that they were in error (S. Sawadogo 1988a), rather than to discern their motives for leaving. This perspective overlooked the significance of the settlers' view that, in light of the limited opportunities that they had for further advancement at Mogtedo, moving to Kompienga was a rational economic decision.

It is important to remember that these local-level "revisions" only became apparent in the case study that covered the same population over a ten-year period. This long-term, longitudinal perspective has implications for the types of data needed for planning such programs, as well as for providing "feedback" to donors about the economic rates of return that they can reasonably expect within a prescribed period of time.

Conclusion

The events described in this volume remind us that not all development aid is bad. Some aid is very good. Certain types of development programs like the OCP and AVV can create new economic opportunities. These same new opportunities, however, create a host of new planning problems. Should foreign donors be held accountable for the changes caused by their interventions, and if so, for how long? The latter question has special pertinence to current plans to expand onchocerciasis control into Nigeria and central Africa and to develop a vaccine against malaria. In a similar vein, FAO and other donors are continuing to support a widespread effort to reduce the incidence of bovine trypanosomiasis. The potential environmental, economic, and social impact of these and other vector-borne disease control programs is enormous.

Unfortunately, the foreign donors who support OCP and similar types of disease-control programs have been far less interested in committing themselves to follow-up development planning to address these issues than they have been to control. The chief reason is cost. In 1986 the estimated annual cost per beneficiary for river blindness control was only U.S. $1.00. In contrast, the cost of installing even the most basic roads, bridges, and reliable wells in the isolated areas affected by control ranges from several hundred to several thousand dollars per beneficiary household. The cost of extending education and health services drives development costs up even more. Second, in contrast to follow-up planning, the results of the ocp control effort are easy to monitor, and quantitative positive results can be evident in a short period of time. A third reason for the popularity of control versus follow-up planning is that the control program's goals are highly focused and politically neutral. A development program (like the avv) is by its very nature highly political and involves juggling the political agendas of a variety of donors and national ministries as well as the goals of tens of thousands of semiautonomous households and their leaders. Finally, many donors who support the ocp are attracted by the fact that the control program appears to avoid some of the complex, messy, highly area-specific planning issues like land tenure and pastoralist grazing rights.

For all these reasons foreign donors are far more likely to be attracted to a disease-control program like the ocp than to follow-up development planning or investment for the affected regions. Nevertheless, the case study reminds us that other types of assistance are imperative for the resulting new lands settlement to be sustainable as population densities increase. Neither the settlers moving into the underpopulated ocp river basins nor their national governments have the means to address this issue on their own. The real issue today is thus not whether river blindness can or cannot be controlled but what happens when it is and who is responsible.

In light of the case study data, one could argue that foreign donors should refrain from introducing the new control technologies until funds are available for a complete package of complementary planning. One could also counterargue that donors and the national governments have a moral responsibility to control these sorts of debilitating diseases if and when a control program becomes technically and economically feasible. The case study does not begin to resolve this moral dilemma. It does illustrate, however, some of the damage that can result from a myopic focus on simple technological solutions to complex development problems. There are no simple, single, variable explanations for poverty and underdevelopment in the Sahel. Similarly, there is unlikely to be a simple technological or theoretical "cure." A new technology like the ocp is thus best construed as a necessary but only partial development "vision." The real issue is what types of complementary visions will be required to deal with the new opportunities and problems that the technology creates.

Given the complex number of variables involved in planning and implementing successful follow-up programs, it is highly unlikely that planners will "hit" on a magic program model. The most successful follow-up planning is likely to emerge from an objective assessment of what elements of earlier planning models did and did not work. This type of objective planning must be done without fear that foreign donors will withdraw support because an earlier development vision "failed." An important component of this flexible planning is periodic reality checks with program beneficiaries. In addition, planners need to realize how these assessments can be biased by their personal "visions," expectations, and assumptions.

This case study shows how the development visions and capacities of the survey farmers, the Burkinabè national government, and foreign donors who supported follow-up planning in Burkina's OCP river basins changed over a fifteen-year period. Some of these revised visions were the result of flawed theory and technology; other revisions were a response to unforeseen new opportunities and constraints. Still other changes could be traced to political exigencies in Burkina and abroad and to shifts in the researcher's own perspective. Whatever the root cause, the final local-level impact of the specific policy interventions was far more dynamic than what planners had envisioned. These and similar sorts of revised development visions need to be cultivated and enhanced rather than compared to some abstract standard of what they were supposed to have been. The chief reason is that we can never totally predict how local people will respond to development interventions. We can, however, make an honest attempt to learn from their responses and to incorporate this information into our revised visions for the future.

Appendix A: The Study Methodology

In 1978, when this study began, the AVV was just beginning to be criticized at both the national and international levels (BEI-agrer 1978; Berg et al. 1978; Madeley 1980; Reyna 1980). It was becoming increasingly difficult to justify the high costs of the project, estimated at between $12,000 and $15,000 per settled family in 1978 (see appendix B, table B-8), in a country that lacked even the most basic infrastructure and social services. Other areas of concern were the unanticipated slow rate at which planned settlement was taking place, the project's disruption of indigenous land rights, and the high rate of illegal, unassisted immigration onto project lands.

Early evaluations of the AVV (from 1974 to 1980) were based largely on administrative reports concerning the rate of settlement and total output of cash and subsistence crops (BEI-agrer 1978; Berg et al. 1978; Reyna 1980). While there had been micro-level studies on specific topics like gender issues, the FulBe herders, and illegal spontaneous settlers, these were almost all brief site reports that lacked quantitative data (Conti 1979; Nikyema 1977; Rochette 1976a, 1976b; P. Sawadogo 1975a, 1975b; Sprey and de Jong 1977a, 1977b). Principal exceptions were Guissou's research on women settlers and Ouédraogo's thesis on the AVV planned settlement Mogtedo Village 1. These studies, however, were limited by the fact that they addressed only settlers who were in their first to second year of residence in the scheme (Guissou 1977; F. Ouédraogo 1976; Sprey and de Jong 1977a, 1977b). Almost no research was available sufficient to allow policy makers to compare the local-level impact of the AVV with development programs in other parts of the country or the seven-country control zone. Within this context of growing regional and international concern and limited research data, Burkina's minister of agriculture requested that the AVV be included in a four-country survey of sahelian farming systems conducted by USAID through the Department of Agricultural Economics at Purdue University.

The main goal of Purdue's involvement was to assist the AVV's Statistical Service in improving the quality of its farm-monitoring program (see Murphy and Sprey 1980). The goal of this program was to provide information on the success or failure of specific technical innovations, as well as information on the more general effects of the agricultural program on settler income and welfare. The primary mechanism for data collection was an economic survey of a random sample of households in all of the major AVV village clusters. The unit of research was the household, defined as the residential unit that cultivated one of the 10- or 20-hectare AVV farms. The household unit was the focus of project extension policies, and it was the household that received access to one or two registered project farms. The male, recognized as the official household head, represented the family unit in all contractual dealings with the AVV (for insurance, equipment purchases, credit, commercial crop sales, and the like). Moreover, it was assumed that crops planted on the project farm would be cultivated cooperatively under the supervision of the male household head, who would also supervise the cooperative cultivation of the crops planted on the project lands.

The farm-monitoring survey included 132 households in 1978 and 313 in 1979, representing approximately 11 percent and 18 percent, respectively, of the settlers living in AVV-sponsored settlements at that time (Murphy and Sprey 1980) (table A-1). Each of the sample households was visited once a week by an enumerator with a packet of questionnaires. In the interviews the male head of household was asked questions concerning labor and nonlabor inputs (fertilizer, manure, pesticides) on the family's official project farm, which consisted of the 1- or 2-hectare homesites (depending on whether the family was classified as double or single sized), and the four 1.5-hectare (or 3.0-hectare) fields that they were authorized to farm under the official crop rotation system. Other questions focused on cash income, expense, and loss associated with noncrop production activities (trade, crafts, livestock) and the sale and nonmarket distribution of food and cash crops (Murphy and Sprey 1980). The enumerators also were required to measure the total area planted and the harvests for the sample settlers' allotted fields (Murphy and Sprey 1980). They received the same initial training as extension agents and were supervised by the central office of the AVV Statistical Service, which was also responsible for the collection and analysis of the questionnaires.

As part of the cooperative agreement, USAID funded two intensive case studies to complement the AVV's larger farm-monitoring survey research. One case study described the project's impact on an indigenous village in the Red Volta valley (see Saul 1979, 1981, 1983, 1984, 1988). The second case study, reported here, focused on the economic and social consequences of the AVV for voluntary settlers from the central plateau, one of the main areas of AVV recruitment (see McMillan 1980,

Table A-1
Farm-Monitoring Survey Sample Size, 1978–1989

	1978	1979	1983	1987	1988–1989
AVV Statistical Service Survey Total Sample[a]	132	313	—	—	60
Mogtedo and Mogtedo-Bombore	—	97	—	—	40
Linoghin	—	48	—	—	20
Bane, Kaibo-Sud, Kaibo-Nord	—	168	—	—	—
Intensive Case Study					
A. Damesma settlers at V3	—	9	26	26	20
B. Damesma settlers (first year)	—	3	—	—	—
C. Damesma settlers at Kompienga	—	—	—	—	7
D. Non-Damesma settlers at Kompienga	—	—	—	—	18
E. Settlers' home area (Kaya)—Damesma	18	12	—	—	—
F. Settlers' home area (Kaya)—other two villages	24	23	—	—	—

[a]SOURCE: Murphy and Sprey 1980:39.

1983, 1984, 1986, 1987a, 1987b). A farming systems survey was used to compare a single group of settlers who had immigrated to the same AVV project village over a three-year period from 1975 to 1977 with related households who had remained in the settlers' home area. After a pilot survey in 1977, the baseline research for the case study was conducted over two agricultural seasons from April 1978 to April 1980. In the first year, I lived in the settlers' home village, Damesma, from which more than thirty households had already immigrated to the project. In 1978 the farm-monitoring survey included forty-two households—eighteen in Damesma and twenty-four in two neighboring "traditional" villages with lower rates of immigration to the project.[1] In the second year, I was based at Mogtedo V3.

In contrast to the AVV project plan, there was no clearly defined and terminologically distinct unit in the settlers' home village that corresponded to the AVV's concept of the household with a single decision-making head. If the definition of a household in the settlers' home village was "the social unit that works together and eats together," then the majority of the home village "households" consisted of members of kin-based residential groups that worked certain fields collectively and/ or relied on the harvest of these cooperatively worked fields for basic food needs. The cooperative fields were worked by the entire household, with the produce used for the basic food and cash needs of the group. The disposition of the harvest from the collectively worked fields was under the control of the person who directed group activities. Additional fields were cultivated by individual members of these "household" units, either before or after work on the cooperatively worked fields was completed. The produce from these fields was under the control of the individual cultivator and was stored apart.[2] In 1979 the jointly worked household fields accounted for an average of 60 percent of the total area planted and 60 percent of the recorded labor hours; the remaining 40 percent represented privately worked fields.[3]

Recognition of this complex overlapping of production and consumption units in the settlers' home area led to the design of a questionnaire and interview format that recorded information on private production as well as cooperative endeavors. Each household in the sample was visited at least once a week to gather basic information on all the agricultural and nonagricultural production activities that had occurred since the previous interview. In addition to the standardized survey, a series of single interview studies of land tenure and emigration were conducted. The primary responsibility for the weekly interviews and field measurements was vested in four enumerators and myself.

After one year of living in the settlers' home village, I moved to the AVV project settlement at Mogtedo V3 with one enumerator in April 1978. In the original research plan, it was assumed that my research would merely complement the information being gathered on the Damesma households that were included in the larger 313 household farm-monitoring survey. It quickly became apparent, however, that the larger survey was unable to collect very detailed information on some of the "nonofficial" production activities that settlers were engaged in. These activities included growing investment in livestock and nonfarm employment as well as the creation of private fields for both men and women that were often outside the official project area.

For a variety of reasons that included the identification of the farm-monitoring survey's enumerators with the project staff and the fact that many of these activities were conducted by women and young unmarried men who were not being interviewed in the farm-monitoring survey (which focused on male heads of households), we determined that the case study needed to conduct the same detailed farming systems survey that we developed for the settlers' home area with twelve households from Damesma who were not included in the larger AVV farm-monitoring survey. This sample included nine V3 households and three first year settlers in another project village. During this time (May 1979–March 1980) I returned to the Damesma area for five days every month to control the data collection that continued there.

The analysis of the baseline survey, described in chapter 4, compares the results of the AVV farm-monitoring survey (n = 313) with the results of the case study re-search at Mogtedo V3 (n = 12) and in the settlers' home village (n = 35) for the 1979–1980 cropping year. Three short restudies of the settlers were conducted dur-ing the summers of 1983, 1986, and 1987.[4] The most recent restudy was conducted in 1990 as part of an eleven-country survey of settlement and development in the OCP river basins funded by UNDP and executed by the World Bank through the Institute for Development Anthropology (McMillan 1989; McMillan, Nana, and Savadogo 1993; McMillan, Painter, and Scudder 1992).

In 1983 the farming-systems survey was enlarged from ten to twenty-six house-holds. It included the ten original households from the 1979 research (one of the nine sample households containing two married brothers had split to form a separate farm in 1983), one additional household from Damesma, and fifteen households from each of the other home village groups (settlers from the area of Kaya but not from Damesma, and settlers from the Koupela region to the east of Mogtedo). Again, only households that were not included in the ongoing research efforts of the AVV Statistical Service were included. A standard form was used to gather informa-tion similar to that gathered in the 1979 survey, including field measurements and yields. The chief difference was that we were forced to rely on retrospective infor-mation on livestock and nonfarm revenues because the survey did not cover a full agricultural season. As in 1979, all members of the household were interviewed.

The same enlarged sample was surveyed again in 1987. The two sample house-holds from Koupela that left the project were replaced by the two sample households from Damesma that had subdivided. Again the same farm-management survey that had been used in 1983 was repeated with the assistance of two field assistants who had worked with me measuring fields during the 1979 and 1983 fieldwork. We also conducted a restudy of the original village census as well as a village census of mar-riages that had occurred in the project.

Between November 1988 and September 1989, I was able to conduct a more complete ten-year restudy of the settlers as part of a large eleven-country survey of settlement and development in the river basins covered by the Onchocerciasis Con-trol Programme. The survey, referred to as the OCP Land Settlement Review, was funded by UNDP and executed by the World Bank through the Institute for Devel-opment Anthropology. The project supported intensive case study research at four sites in Burkina (see McMillan, Painter, and Scudder 1992). One of the four sites included the AVV-sponsored settlements at Mogtedo, Mogtedo-Bombore, and Lin-oghin (see McMillan, Nana, and Savadogo 1993). The Burkina research was de-signed and implemented by three senior team members. Kimseyinga Savadogo, Dean of Research, School of Economics, University of Ouagadougou, was the primary person responsible for the design, testing, and analysis of the economic question-naires at all four study sites (Savadogo 1989a, 1989b, 1989c, 1989d). Jean Baptiste Nana, a sociologist, was responsible for coordinating research at the Niangoloko, Solenzo, and AVV Rapadama sites (Nana 1989a, 1989b, 1989c, 1989d, 1989e,

1989f). I was responsible for the overall coordination of research and analysis at the four sites, as well as for on-site research in the AVV planned settlements and Kompienga, the new site to which many of the most successful settlers moved after 1988.

The 1989 research included a restudy of the sample farmers who were included in the 1979 AVV farm-monitoring survey for the settlement groups at Mogtedo, Mogtedo-Bombore, and Linoghin. Ninety-seven of the 313 households in the 1979 survey were from Mogtedo and Mogtedo-Bombore; 48 were from Linoghin. Twenty-seven of the 97 households that were included in the 1979 survey at Mogtedo and Mogtedo-Bombore, and 3 of the 48 sample farmers who had been studied in 1979 at Linoghin, had left the project by 1989. A random sample of 60 of the 114 remaining households was chosen for inclusion in the farm-management survey, which was designed to be comparative with the 1979, 1983, and 1987 surveys. The chief difference was that, due to the size of the sample and the fact that we had only one research assistant to cover all 60 households, we were only able to interview the recognized male head of household and one female per family on a regular basis over the 1989 crop season.[5] A second source of information was a restudy of 20 households at V3 using the same forms that were used for the restudy of the 1979 farm-monitoring survey. By late 1988, only 18 of the 25 households we worked with in 1987 still had family members living in V3. The 1989 farming systems survey included these 18 households plus two brothers and uncles from the original households in the survey who had split off to form separate households.

A subsample of 19 of the 60 households in the Statistical Service farm-monitoring survey restudy and 14 of the 20 households in the V3 restudy were selected for a more detailed analysis of household expenditures and revenues. Each member of the family was interviewed concerning his or her crop, livestock, and nonfarm earning activities. In addition, each family member was interviewed regarding expenditures for different categories of goods and services for the preceding month and for certain large expenditures (house repairs, bicycles, and such) for the preceding year. The survey included four additional households at Mogtedo-Bombore and three additional households, with large herds, at Mogtedo V3. The four households from Mogtedo-Bombore were families that had been included in the 1979 baseline survey; the three new households from Mogtedo V3 were included to offset the bias in the farming systems and revenue/expenditure surveys that arose from the fact that the wealthiest households in the longitudinal case study left the project in 1988. The decision to expand the sample to include the one remaining very wealthy Damesma settler and two new wealthy settlers who had only immigrated the year before to replace the settlers who left was an attempt to show the crop and livestock production systems of this category of farm family.

The same farming-systems survey was conducted with a sample of twenty-five households living in the town of Kompienga. Seven of the sample farmers were families that had been living at V3 before moving in 1988 to Kompienga. The town census we conducted in August 1990 showed that fifty-five male household heads had lived in one of the AVV-sponsored settlements at Mogtedo, Mogtedo-Bombore,

Rapadama, or Mankaraga before migrating to Kompienga. As in 1979, 1983, and 1987, the farm families included in the farming-systems survey were the contact families with whom I worked most directly. These same families were also my main information source on settler versus extension agent perceptions of environmental change, immigration histories, and the special needs and concerns of female settlers.

In addition to the intensive farming systems survey, we located the present whereabouts of each of the 313 households that were included in the 1979 farm-monitoring survey. A special form was developed to gather information from settlers and extension agents on absentee family members. In the two settlement groups with the highest rate of dropout, we attempted to determine the current location and employment of each settler who had ever been authorized to farm an AVV farm in that group of villages. This information provided us with a means for assessing the rates of settler dropout from different project groups. The 1989 restudy also included a formal survey of market size and activity of the major markets most frequented by settlers living in the three contiguous blocs of Mogtedo, Mogtedo-Bombore, and Linoghin, as well as research at the adjacent gold-mining sites. Less intensive surveys of herd size, crop production, and herd and livestock expenditures were conducted with ten FulBe pastoralist households living in the agro-pastoral scheme at Gadeghin (near Mogtedo) and with ten FulBe camps surrounding Mogtedo. As with the more intensive survey, the sample was selected based on participants' willingness to be interviewed and their familiarity with me or one of my research assistants.[6]

Appendix B: Supplementary Figure and Tables

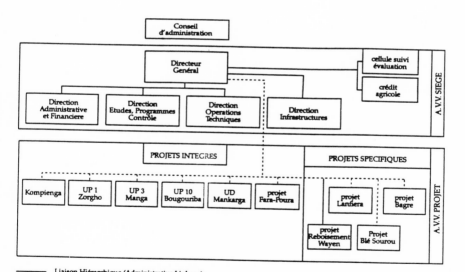

Liaison Hiérarchique (Administrative Linkage)

Conception-Coordination-Appui (conceptualization, coordination of projects, and aid in implementation)

Figure B-1. Organigram of the AVV Administrative Structure, 1982–1989. (AVV 1985c:36)

Table B-1
Anticipated Costs of the AVV Project, 1972–1996

Area	Cost (billions CFAF)[a]
Red and White Volta Valleys:	
Studies	950
Infrastructure	7,100
Administration and Personnel	2,200
Extension	1,950
Road Construction	2,300
Total	(14,500)
Black Volta Valley (Studies, infrastructure, administration, etc.):	9,500
Bagré Dam Project	18,500
Karankasso Dam Project	12,500
Tanema Dam Project	4,500
Total for All Areas	59,500

SOURCE: AVV 1974:8.

[a] When these projections were made in 1971, U.S. $1.00 = 252 CFAF.

Table B-2
Anticipated Unit Costs of the AVV Project, 1973–1996

Unit	Development Area	
	Red and White Volta Valley	Total Project Development
Projected settlement		
No. households	17,500	65,000
No. Persons	175,000	650,000
Projected area to be cleared (ha)	414,000[a]	750,000
Total cost (CFAF)[c]	14,500,000,000[b]	60,000,000,000
Cost per person (CFAF)	82,857	92,307
Cost per household (CFAF)	828,571	923,076
Cost per hectare (CFAF)	35,024	80,000
Cost per village (CFAF)	55,769,230	—

SOURCE: AVV 1974:6–8.

NOTE: There is some variation between different planning documents. The 1973 request to FAC estimated 150,000 persons in 175 villages of 500 to 550 persons each in the Red and White Volta valleys (AVV 1973d:5).

[a]414,100 ha = 450,000 ha (for agricultural development),
 − 30,000 ha (irrigated land in conjunction with the Bagré dam)
 − 6,000 ha (irrigated land in conjunction with the Tanema dam)

[b]Includes estimated costs of road construction but not the costs of dam construction or the associated irrigation projects.

[c]When these projections were made in 1971, U.S. $1.00 = 252 CFAF.

Table B-3
Anticipated Immigration to the AVV, 1973–1990

| Zones | Immigration | | |
	No. Families	No. Persons	Percent
Red and White Volta valleys	17,500	175,000	27
Black Volta Valley	11,500	115,000	18
Dam projects:			
Bagré	20,000	200,000	31
Tanema	4,000	40,000	6
Karankasso	12,000	120,000	18
Total	65,000	650,000	100

SOURCE: AVV 1974:6.

Table B-4
A Comparison of Actual and Projected Rates of Planned Settlement
at the AVV, 1973–1979

	1973	1974	1975	1976	1977	1978	1979	Total
Scheduled[a]	200	300	600	900	1,700	3,000–5,000	3,000–5,000	9,700–13,700
Actually settled	9	195	173	287	302	302	556	1,824

SOURCE: Murphy and Sprey 1980:76.

[a]According to Upper Volta Five-Year Plan, 1972–76 and 1977–81.

163

Supplementary Figures and Tables

Table B-5
Census of the AVV Areas of Intervention During 1987–1988

AVV Extension Areas	Number of Villages	Total Population	Active Population	Number of Agricultural Households
UP1-Zorgho	154	193,735	131,201	22,104
UP3-Manga	148	140,072	70,027	18,146
UP4-Tiebele	4	1,372	742	177
UP8-Bane	4	1,844	988	164
UP10-Diebougou	11	4,788	2,647	542
Sondré-Est	1	1,169	530	76
Fara-poura	22	19,305	11,041	1,933
Lanfiéra	1	4,707	2,396	465
Bagré	1	1,019	350	109
Kompienga	13	5,370	2,869	1,398
Nouhao	53	47,554	25,720	7,878
Total AVV	412	420,935	248,511	52,992

SOURCE: AVV, in McMillan, Nana, and Savadogo 1993:118; reprinted with permission of the World Book.

Table B-6
Financing of the AVV, 1972–1988 (CFAF, in Thousands)

Source of Financing	1972	1973	1974	1975	1976
BURKINA FASO					
State support	—	—	—	50,000	111,958
Treasury advance	—	—	—	—	—
Loan from state/CCCE	—	—	—	—	—
Rural development fund	—	—	—	—	—
P.T.P.-Kompienga	—	—	—	—	—
Subtotal	—	—	—	50,000	111,958
OUTSIDE SOURCES					
FAC	110,100	202,000	271,500	535,000	711,500
FED	—	—	—	—	84,130
RFA	—	—	—	—	—
USAID	—	—	—	—	—
CEAO	—	—	—	—	—
Netherlands	—	—	—	—	239,345
UNDP	—	—	87,000	174,810	115,230
World Bank	—	—	—	—	—
Italy	—	—	—	—	—
Projet UPV/80	—	—	—	—	
Subtotal	110,100	202,000	358,500	709,810	1,150,211
Total	110,100	202,000	358,500	759,810	1,262,129
Percentage	0.5	0.9	1.5	3.2	5.3

1977	1978	1979	1980	1981	1982	1983
58,500	58,000	46,350	78,000	30,000	—	10,000
200,000	—	—	20,000	—	—	—
700,000	—	—	300,000	1,100,000	1,840,000	1,050,000
—	—	—	—	—	30,000	—
—	—	—	—	—	—	—
958,500	58,000	46,350	398,000	1,130,000	1,870,000	1,060,000
520,000	530,000	618,000	530,000	510,000	390,000	775,000
5,544	519,960	—	70,723	—	1,350,000	—
—	66,000	214,500	253,096	—	—	—
126,125	84,460	—	200,640	—	—	—
—	30,960	—	44,685	—	—	—
217,791	544,174	756,000	672,000	—	—	50,000
99,725	—	—	—	—	—	—
—	—	—	—	—	—	130,000
—	—	—	—	—	—	2,244,000
—	—	51,438	—	—	—	—
969,185	1,775,554	1,639,938	1,771,144	510,000	1,740,000	3,199,000
927,685	1,833,554	1,686,288	2,169,144	1,640,000	3,610,000	4,259,000
8.2	7.8	9.0	9.2	7.0	15.3	18.0

Table B-6, continued

1984	1985	1986	1988 *	Total	%
5,000	—	—	—	447,808	1.
—	—	—	—	220,000	0.
—	—	860,000	—	5,850,000	24.
—	—	—	—	30,000	0.
—	—	—	986,547	986,547	4.
5,000	—	860,000	986,547	7,534,355	31.
475,000	165,000	—	—	6,343,100	26.
—	—	—	—	2,030,363	8.
—	—	1,285,000	—	1,818,596	7.
—	—	—	—	411,225	1.
—	—	—	—	75,645	0.
—	—	—	—	2,479,310	10.
—	—	—	—	476,765	2.
—	—	—	—	130,000	0.
—	—	—	—	2,244,000	9.
—	—	—	—	51,438	0.
475,000	165,000	1,285,000	—	16,060,442	68.
480,00	165,000	2,145,000	986,547	23,594,797	10
0.2	0.1	9.1	4.2	100	

* No new financing in 1987.

SOURCE: AVV, DEPC, 1990, in McMillan, Nana, and Savadago 1993:120; reprinted with permission of the World Bank.

Table B-7
Cost of Settling One Family, 1978

	CFAF	% of Total	Subtotals (%)
1. Preliminary studies			
Pedology 1/20,000	30,800	1.13	
(4,000 ha/year)			
Geohydrology 1/20,000	45,000	1.72	
(40,000 ha/year)			2.90
2. Settling the farmers			
Recruiting and moving	50,000	1.91	
Transportation WPF food	19,900	0.76	
Marking location of villages and fields	61,425	2.34	
Preparing master plan for bloc	2,000	0.08	
			5.09
3. Infrastructure			
Roads	557,000	21.31	
equipment and personnel	139,900	5.35	
technical assistance	45,700	1.75	
			28.41
Housing	187,600	7.18	
equipment and personnel	23,000	0.88	
			8.06
Wells	81,600	3.12	
4. Land preparation			
Land clearing (53,000 CFAF)			
Deep plowing (212,100 CFAF)	368,700	14.10	
Harrowing (103,600 CFAF)			
5. Equipment and supplies	40,700	1.56	
6. Field personnel for 3 years	138,000	5.28	
7. Update cars and furniture	34,200	1.31	
8. General expenses AVV	491,700	18.81	
9. Technical assistance			
(10 experts for 3 years)	297,000	11.36	
Total	2,614,225 (about $12,500)	100.00	

SOURCE: BEI-Agrer, Report on the AVV Program, 1978–82, cited in Murphy and Sprey, 1980:86.

Appendix B

Table B-8

Comparison of Net Crop Income in the Older AVV Planned Settlements,
1977–1988/89 (in nominal and real CFAF[a]
per Adult Labor Equivalent)

	Linoghin	Bombore	Mogtedo	Mogtedo V3
NOMINAL CFAF				
Cooperatively worked fields only[b]				
1977	55,700	—62,200—		—
1978	51,700	—50,550—		—
1979	{57,300 to 66,300}	—{56,600 to 65,000}—		—
1988	61,315	54,988	51,072	55,101
	($204)	($183)	($170)	($184)
Privately and cooperatively worked fields				
1979	—	—	—	75,566
1988	76,766	64,329	65,742	72,588
REAL CFAF, 1988 = 100				
Cooperatively worked fields only				
1979	{92,718 to 107,282}	—{91,586 to 105,178}—		—
1988	61,315	54,988	51,072	55,101
Private and cooperatively worked fields				
1979	—	—	—	122,275
1988	76,766	64,329	65,742	72,588

SOURCES: IMF 1989:256; McMillan 1983; McMillan, Nana, and Savadogo 1993; Murphy and Sprey 1980:69; Savadogo 1989a.

[a] Adjusted for inflation using IMF consumer price index for Burkina Faso (1988 = 100). Both 1979 and 1988 were good rainfall years.

[b] Figures for 1977, 1978, and 1979 are for AVV settlers in their third to fifth years of living at the project, by which time they were presumably farming the full area they were authorized to farm under the AVV system. For 1979 the first figure refers to farmers in their third year, and the second to farmers in their fourth or higher year. Net income figures for farmers in their first or second year were calculated separately in the Murphy and Sprey report (1980:69) but are not listed here.

Table B-9
Prices Used to Calculate the Gross and Net Value of Agricultural
Production, Statistical Service Survey, 1979–1980 (in CFAF)

Crop	Market Survey[a]	Official Producer Price[b]
Cotton	54	55 (first choice)
		45 (second choice)
White sorghum	62	40
Red sorghum	55	32
Millet	—	40
Maize	57	40
Cowpeas (niebe)	79	45
Peanuts (in shell)	81	37
Rice	72	
Millet	65	
Cereals (house compound)[c]	50	

[a] Murphy and Sprey 1980:58,22.

[b] Offices National des Céréales, Arrêté n°001458/MCODIM/MDR, portant fixation des prix d'achat au producteur des céréales locales pour la campagne, 1983–84. Tableau II. Evolution des Prix des Productions.

[c] Mixed white and red sorghum.

Table B-10

Price Ranges for the Major Crops at the Study Sites, 1988–1989[a] (in CFAF)

	White sorghum	Red sorghum	Millet	Maize	Cotton	Peanuts	Earth peas	Cow peas	Sesame	Rice	Tubers
Scenario I: Low prices	44	40	45	33	95	60	60	68	60	80	50
Scenario II: Medium prices	47	45	45	33	95	60	60	115	60	80	50
Scenario III: High prices	50	50	45	33	95	60	60	167	60	80	50

SOURCE: Savadogo 1989a.

Note: Gumbo and roselle were given a price of 90 CFAF/kg.

[a] There are substantial variations of prices between the high levels in the "hungry period" before harvest and the customary post-harvest price collapse. Price ranges are more relevant than either the pre- or post-harvest prices.

Table B-11
IMF Consumer Price Index, Burkina Faso

Year	1979 = 100	1988 = 100
1979	100.0	61.8
1980	112.2	69.3
1981	120.1	74.6
1982	135.1	83.4
1983	146.5	90.5
1984	153.5	94.8
1985	164.2	101.4
1986	159.9	98.8
1987	155.3	95.9
1988	161.9	100.0

SOURCES: IMF 1989; World Bank 1989:63.

Table B-12
Prices of Important Products Purchased by Farmers, 1979–1989, and Percent Change (1979 = 100) (in CFAF)

Product	1979	1989	Percent change
Plow	—	—	—
Donkey cart	40,000	95,000	137
Bicycle	29,000	50,000	72
Yamaha Dame motorcycle	—	400,000	n.a.
Mobylette CT	45,000	165,000	267
Cement (1 sack)	1,100	2,400	118
One roofing tin	1,050	2,300	119
1 pack of sugar	125	355	184
1 small soap	45	95	111
1 medium soap	75	150	100
1 large soap	150	280	87
1 small pail	600	1,800	200
1 large pail	1,250	2,600	108
1 box matches	10	15	50
1 liter gas (reg.)	80	275	244
1 liter kerosene	40	160	300
1 large metal plate	600	1,500	150
1 bicycle tire	750	1,850	147
Maggi seasoning (2 cubes)	5	10	100
1 soda	75	150	100
1 beer (nonlocal)	—	225	n.a.
1 plate cooked rice	15	50	233
1 calebasse dolo (local beer)	5	50	900
1 liter oil: peanut	200	400	100
cotton	175	350	100
Bonbons (5)	5	25	400
Rice (1 plate of white rice)	250	500	100

n.a.   Not applicable.
—   Not available.

Notes

Chapter 1. The Original Visions

1. This included the United Nation's list of twenty-five "relatively least developed" nations (with the exceptions of Senegal and Mauritania); the World Bank's list of countries "most seriously affected by the oil crisis"; and the Rome Food Conference's list of countries having the lowest per-capita and per-diem intake of calories (Berg 1975).

2. The flies become infected when they pierce the skin of an onchocerciasis sufferer and ingest microfilaria along with blood. While most of the microfilaria thus absorbed are digested, together with the blood meal, a few eventually penetrate the wall of the fly's stomach and settle in its thoracic muscles. There, after passing through three larval stages, the microfilaria become larvae capable of infecting a human host. The complete cycle requires only one week.

The probability that the larvae of any single fly will actually be transferred is low. An individual must receive repeated bites from infected flies before one or several couples of adult worms can develop. As a result, people who remain in an epidemic area for only a short time run little risk of becoming infected. After a person spends less than a year of continuous habitation in an infected zone, however, microfilaria produced by the adult worms may be found in the epidermis. A slight infection produces very mild symptoms that generally pass unnoticed. A heavy infection is acquired only after a long period of exposure to infected bites. In areas where the infection is most serious, the majority of villagers may suffer eye difficulties, and an average of 20 percent will be blind (Hamon and Kartman 1973).

3. See Angel 1985; Becker 1985; Bharin 1981; Couty et al. 1979; Dollfus 1981; Hervouet 1980; Huntings Technical Services, Ltd. 1988a; Mabogunje 1981; Mc-Millan, Painter, and Scudder 1992; OCP 1986; Raison 1979, 1981, 1985; Nicolai and Lasserre 1981; Remy 1973, 1975, 1981; Van Raay and Hilhorst 1981; Weitz, Pelley, and Applebaum 1978.

4. See Ancey 1974; Bakyono 1989; Benoit 1973a, 1973b; Conde 1978; Capron and Kohler 1975; Kohler 1968, 1972; Izard and Izard-Hertier 1958; Izard-Hertier and Izard 1958; Lahuec 1970; Lesselingue 1975; Marchal 1975; Queant and Rouville 1969; Remy 1973; Terrible 1979.

5. The Office du Niger is one of the best known of these colonial land-settlement projects. When the project started in 1932, the colonial government planned to settle 300,000 persons in association with the development of one million irrigated hectares (Remy 1973:97) located in a relatively unpopulated area of present-day Mali. The Office expected to recruit settlers from the northern Mossi province of Yatenga, 600 kilometers away (Remy 1973; de Wilde et al. 1967b:245–300). The settlers were installed in planned villages, and provided with new training and resources (fertilizer, pesticides, improved seed, marketing facilities, irrigation) that presumably would permit them to achieve much higher income levels. The colonial government assumed that the Mossi farmers would be interested in the project, given the "overpopulation, mediocre land resources, seasonal famine and high level of 'spontaneous' emigration" that characterized their traditional area (Remy 1973:97).

Over time the Office grew into a large integrated program with an ambitious variety of economic, social, and demographic goals. There was a strong belief that the project could provide "*la pepinière d'un paysannat africain modèle et modern*" (Remy 1973:98) (translation mine: a nursery for the development of a model, modern African peasant) and "*[un] pôle de développement agro-industrial majeur de l'Afrique occidentale française à la mise en valeur de la 'mer' saharienne*" (Remy 1973:96) (translation mine: a major agro-industrial development pole in West Africa for the development of the Saharan "sea"). In spite of, or in large part because of, these ambitious goals, the Office is widely regarded as one of the most long-winded examples of expensive project failure in sub-Saharan Africa (de Wilde et al. 1967; Diallo 1971; Dumont 1962; Marchal 1974, 1975, 1978; Remy 1973).

Although the Office anticipated the settlement of some 300,000 farmers, the maximum ever to reside there was 37,000 in 1967; by 1970 the number was about 30,000. The most frequently cited reasons for the project's failure are (1) the inappropriateness of the technical package and (2) an inability to attract sufficient numbers of settlers. In fact, it is virtually impossible to separate the two problems. Since the Office failed to attract enough settlers, the administration was forced to introduce labor-intensive technology, which pushed the project administration into ever greater debt. The lack of settlers has been attributed to the extremely regimented program that the Office required the settlers to follow (Hammond 1962, 1963; Zahan 1963, 1966). Many of the settlers regarded their stay at the project as a period of migrant labor in a government work camp and left the project as soon as they acquired enough cash or were ready to retire.

6. The research by the Institute of Applied Human Sciences (ISHA, or l'Institut des Sciences Humaines Appliquées) on the Vallée du Sourou is still cited as a model for planning research in areas of sponsored settlement (Remy 1973). The program included a detailed study of the area's ecology, its farming practices, and the culture of the target settler group; an ethnography of a Mossi pioneer village in the area to which the settlers would be going; an ethnography of an indigenous non-Mossi village in the area; an analysis of some of the technical problems that such a scheme would present; and a fifth study of the potential social and economic problems associated with the project (Bitard and Faffa 1958; Izard and Izard-Hertier 1958; Izard-Hertier and Izard 1958, 1959; Pehaut and Rouamba 1958). It was anticipated that the Vallée du Sourou, like the Office du Niger, would depend on immigration from the northern Mossi province of Yatenga for its settlers and that this would contribute to the *décongestion* of the settlers' overpopulated homeland. The Vallée du Sourou was eventually abandoned because of its high costs (Remy 1973:90). A new national project by the same name was recently created.

7. Until the AVV, the largest national land-settlement scheme was the Vallée du Kou, initiated in 1967. With financing from Taiwan, the project planned to irrigate 12,600 hectares and settle 1,200 families or 16,000 persons in a less populated area in the southwest near Bobo-Dioulasso (D. Ouédraogo 1979:481). Like earlier land-settlement projects in Burkina and the Office du Niger, the Vallée du Kou relied on Mossi settlers, although in this case recruitment was expanded to include areas other than Yatenga (Hartog 1979; D. Ouédraogo 1979). Unlike the earlier Gando and Sourou projects, the Vallée du Kou project carried out an active publicity campaign and provided transportation to help the settlers move. When a household enrolled in the Vallée du Kou, they received a homesite on which to construct a three-room house, an advance of 40,000 CFAF for a tin roof to be deducted from the sale of the first four harvests; supplementary rations through the first harvest; and the right to cultivate a 1-hectare irrigated plot (D. Ouédraogo 1979).

8. For U.S. $500,000.

9. For the last thirty years the French have invested heavily in technology development for cotton in Burkina's southwest through the parastatal CFDT (Compagnie Française pour le Développement des Textiles). These research and extension activities were continued by the newly created ORDs (Regional Development Organizations) in 1966. Since 1972 the ORDs and CRPAs (*Centre Regional de Promotion Agro-Pastorale*—the new name applied to the revised ORD structure) have benefited from extensive donor financing, first through the Projet Coton (1972–77) and later through the West Volta Agricultural Development Project (Projet de Développement Agricole de la Boucle du Mouhoun, or PDAOV, 1977–82) and Boucle du Mouhoun Agricultural Development Project (Projet de Développement Agricole de la Boucle du Mouhoun, or PDABM, 1982–88).

10. From the start, the AVV emphasized the need to integrate livestock into its land-use and planned-settlement program. The reasons were twofold. In the absence of fundamental changes in the national banking institutions, livestock was likely to continue to be the principal source of investment for the rural AVV settlers; livestock also augmented their income and living standards through the purchase and sale of animals and animal products like meat, milk, eggs, and hides (AVV 1973c:37). Planners also realized the critical importance of using animal manure to supplement the recommended levels of purchased mineral fertilizer. For the pastoralist populations, livestock provided a principal source of income and—to the extent that livestock or livestock services were exchanged for grain or used for meat and milk—food. Planners realized that animal manure was an essential element of any long-term strategy to develop intensive, sustainable agricultural systems in the valleys.

One set of AVV programs focused on credit and extension to promote ox-drawn traction. After the first year settlers were required to purchase a pair of oxen, a plow, and other relevant equipment on credit from the project. The annual payments were spread over a six-year period. According to plan, most settlers would sell their animals after four years, pay off their remaining medium-term credits to the project, then purchase a new pair of animals. Over time, the settlers would gradually increase the number and value of their herds, which would provide them with an ongoing fund of manure and new traction animals as well as additional cash income.

The second set of AVV livestock programs focused on the need to provide new intensive ranching opportunities for pastoralists. Prior to control, the pastoralist FulBe were one of the main groups that used the valleys for seasonal grazing. With a distinct language and culture, Burkina's seminomadic FulBe had enjoyed tight, symbiotic relations with the country's agriculturalists for centuries. Especially important was the fact that FulBe herded the agriculturalists' animals. In return the FulBe herder received the rights to the milk and a portion of the young produced by the agriculturalists' animals and, increasingly, a prenegotiated annual cash payment. During the rainy season the FulBe took their herds to more isolated areas in order to avoid animal damage to the agriculturalists' growing crops. During the dry season they typically returned to tether the animals on the agriculturalists' and their own fields. As population densities on the plateau increased in the 1960s, the FulBe pastoralists were increasingly forced to take their animals farther south in order to find isolated land with sufficient water. A result has been a steady increase in the number of pastoralists using the river basins since the 1960s (Agrotechnik 1989; AVV 1984b; Nana and Kattenberg 1979).

Several large grazing and ranching projects were designated in the original land-use plan for the Nakambe and the Nazinon rivers (formerly the White and Red Volta) (fig. 1.8). The original project plan also emphasized the following needs:

1. Research to develop new varieties of grass suitable for intensive grazing
2. Breeding programs to improve the FulBe (pastoralist) cattle stock and to create a stronger draft animal

3. Infrastructure development (mostly wells and roads) to encourage FulBe sedentarization and controlled grazing

11. Land-use plans for the Nakambe and Nazinon and specific village clusters included the delineation of large, contiguous areas as managed and protected forests. Since there were virtually no forest rangers, the AVV agricultural extension agents were asked to enforce the associated restrictions on illegal tree cutting. Agents encouraged settlers living in the AVV-sponsored settlements to gather fallen limbs and crop residues for cooking fuel. The project attempted to reinforce these efforts by distributing free eucalyptus seedlings that the settlers could plant around their fields and compounds and in small village woodlots. Other varieties of shade and fruit trees were made available for a nominal charge. Tree seedlings were grown in the AVV nursery at Ouagadougou and smaller nurseries near the settlement groups.

Chapter 2.   Damesma

1. See Finnegan (1976) and Hammond (1966) for a clear description of Mossi residential and kinship patterns. Skinner (1964b, 1989) is the best reference on the traditional Mossi political system. Hammond (1966) and Saul (1988) provide good analyses of the traditional land-tenure system. Broekhuyse (1974, 1982a, 1982b) presents the best description of residential, kinship, land-tenure, and production patterns for the settlers' traditional home area near Kaya.

2. The geographical position of a field, in particular its elevation and proximity to a seasonal lake in another village, is the most important factor that influences the potential productivity of a piece of land. Six major categories of cultivable land were identified at Damesma:

1. lowland flood recession (*kulaga, kulama*)
2. unflooded lowland or bas-fonds (*baogan, baokidiga*)
3. mid-village sandy soils (*bissiga*)
4. mid-village sandy clay soils (*bole*)
5. mid-village and highland soils near the compounds (*tempore*)
6. highland rocky soils (*rasempougua, zengadega, zimougou*)

Land types differ not only in natural soil fertility but in their vulnerability to flooding and drought, suitability for different crops, and ease of cultivation. Given the erratic rainfall, water retention is generally the most valued characteristic of a field.

3. In general, the better-quality inherited fields were reserved for the cultivation of the family's staple cereals. Cotton (which requires a high investment in cash inputs and was rightly seen as exhausting the soil) was usually planted on lower-quality land. Most cotton fields were either borrowed (44 percent) or were clan or chief fields that could not be inherited (42 percent). In 1979 more than 95 percent of the rice fields cultivated by the sample households were on borrowed land because relatively few farmers had access to the flooded lakeside land suitable for rice culti-

vation. The household fields on which corn is grown are almost never lent because of the large labor investment in composting and manuring these small plots.

Land lent for cereals and peanuts usually was not a farm family's best land but the fields they were about to leave fallow. Farmers maintained that it was easier to borrow better-quality land for cash crops than for cereals. One reason was the belief that if a farmer requested a sorghum field, he or she obviously needed it for food and would be less willing (or able) to relinquish the loan. A simple comparison of borrowed with inherited and clan fields indicated a slightly lower yield per hectare for cereals planted on borrowed land, but no marked difference in yields for cotton crops planted on borrowed versus inherited or clan land (McMillan 1983).

In 1979 the Damesma farmers were aware that continuous cultivation of a field without the addition of manure or other organic matter exhausted the soils. Farmers stated that under ideal conditions a field should be farmed for four or five years and then left fallow for ten years to rejuvenate the soil. Faced with a scarcity of good, drought-resistant land, however, the Damesma farmers had been forced into a cycle in which fields were cultivated almost continuously. By 1979, emigration from Damesma had been so great that there was no significant difference in the average land area per unit labor between Damesma and the other two villages in the baseline research (McMillan 1983). The average productivity per hectare on the overworked soils, however, was lower. Because of this, farmers were forced to sow a larger total area to meet the same level of subsistence.

Most households did have at least one terrain that they did not farm in 1979. In general, however, this land was left fallow only after it was completely exhausted, because if a farmer was not cultivating a particular field and someone asked to borrow it, he would be obligated to make the loan or risk "powerful moral and spiritual sanctions, which are taken very seriously" (Saul 1988:264). Further, if a borrowed field was allowed to lie fallow, it was considered to have reverted to the original owner. This put pressure on households to cultivate both borrowed and inherited fields as long as possible, even at very low levels of productivity.

Although a parcel may be planted continuously for a ten-year period, various sections of it may be left fallow or rotated even though the whole field may not be. A farmer can, for example, juggle the crops grown on a particular field in order to account for fertilizer usage and the crops that had been grown there before. For example, if a woman were asked what she had grown on her peanut field during the previous five years, she might respond, peanuts, peanuts, peanuts, peanuts, peanuts. This would normally mean that she had the right to a plot of peanuts on this terrain for five years—a plot that was in a slightly different location each year. Peanuts are almost never planted in the same spot two years in a row.

4. It is difficult to arrive at a precise estimate because many of the Vallée du Kou families who claimed Damesma as their village of origin had not actually lived in Damesma for several years before the move. Others who had left the village for wage labor in Côte d'Ivoire never returned to Damesma but joined relatives in the scheme. Scheme records are inaccurate because many of the registered families have

long since left the project to cultivate outside the official zone or to work as full-time merchants in Bobo-Dioulasso. Other families have begun to sharecrop for the absentee settler landlords.

Chapter 3. The AVV Project Vision

1. In actual fact, only a few settlers were ever forced to leave. When dismissal occurred, it was usually because of some antisocial behavior such as abusing a neighbor or being physically unable to operate the farm due to illness, death, or emigration of a family member.

Chapter 4. Initial Settler Adjustment

1. To make the first appointments, the extension agents used a combination of sequence of arrival, age, and first impressions about leadership ability.

2. Anyone traveling between regions in Burkina was required to present an identity card to the police. The parent's identification card and child's birth certificate were also required for enrolling students in school. The chief could facilitate the processing of both documents through the civil authorities at Kaya.

3. By 1979 livestock damage to crops was an increasing problem at the AVV. The problem became so severe that farmers in one village were forced to sleep beside their cotton fields as harvest time approached. When even this didn't stop the animals, a group of angry settlers with clubs surrounded the house of the AVV FulBe settler whom they held accountable. The angry settlers were persuaded to leave only after the extension agent promised to help them get compensation.

Another example of intervention by an extension agent involved a bitter dispute between AVV settlers and an indigenous farmer. Reportedly, the settler's dogs killed the farmer's chickens. When the AVV settlers refused either to compensate the indigenous farmer or to restrain the dogs, the local farmer poisoned one of his dead chickens. The dog ate the chicken, then spread the poison through his vomit to more than fifty chickens, dogs, and other livestock in the AVV villages. In the end, it was the AVV extension service that intervened and made the indigenous farmer submit a formal apology.

4. The two families—one from Damesma and one from a nearby Kaya village—had originally been close friends. To show the depth of their friendship, the two families exchanged aid and lavish gifts. In recent times, however, the Damesma settler had gained a reputation for great wealth and arrogant, erratic behavior. In one incident he brooded for months after accusing the next-door neighbor of stealing one of his sheep and butchering it for sale. Months later the neighbor was returning the Damesma settler's donkey, which had wandered into his fields, and made a sarcastic comment about the wealthy man's inability to control his own animals. Instead of showing gratitude, the donkey's owner emitted a torrent of verbal abuse. Later that day the neighbor's wife returned one of the gifts that the Damesma settler had given her during an earlier period when they were friends. She told him to

remember that it was a woman who gave birth to him and that his newfound wealth did not give him the right to insult people. At this point he attacked her with a hoe.

5. The other settlers were amused that this civil adjudication was being demanded by a woman. The fact that a woman instigated the action also allowed the event to pass without disrupting the social relationship between the defendant's kinsmen and the friends of the woman's husband, as it would have had the complainant been a man.

Chapter 5. Early Economic Changes and Assessment

1. Average fertilizer use on the 14 sorghum fields where fertilizer was applied was 46 kilograms per hectare (kg/ha); if the average is calculated over all 46 sorghum fields, the figure is only 15 kg/ha. Both figures were substantially below the project recommendation to apply 150 kg/ha. The principal exception to this trend was corn (64 kg/ha), a crop that was not even monitored by the Statistical Service Survey because it was not supposed to be planted in the prescribed crop rotation. Although the settlers' use of fertilizer was below the recommended levels, it was much higher than at home. In 1979 only one of the 77 sorghum and millet fields at Damesma received any fertilizer at all. Although the AVV settlers had increased their use of mineral fertilizer, they devoted less time to some of the traditional methods of preserving soil fertility, like spreading animal manure and straw, than did farmers in the home village sample.

2. The AVV uses a system of labor equivalents to determine the amount of land a household receives (table 3.1) and a similar system to determine the distribution of supplementary food aid during the first year. This potential for labor is measured by a labor index that assigns weights to persons according to sex and age. Since an adult male is considered to have the work capacity most readily transferred to a variety of tasks, this is the standard unit and is assigned a value of one. Women and children are assigned lesser values (0.75 for adult women, 0.50 for teenage boys, 0.25 for a female over 55, etc.). For purposes of comparison with projected income and production figures of the AVV, I have used the AVV system.

3. Two of the nine households in the case study survey had working boarders in 1979. At the end of the year, one boarder who lived with a case study family was given a bicycle, cash, and a portion of the grain harvest, as well as the income he earned from his own private cotton field. The other boarder was given cash, a portion of the crop, and half of the profits from the sale of the elderly settler's first pair of oxen. The terms of the relationships were seldom explicit. Cash and kind payments were construed as "gifts" and the boarder's visit portrayed as one of "checking out" the AVV. Had we coded this in-residence, boarding labor as "hired," then the total for hired labor would have been much higher than the recorded 9 percent.

4. The majority of the hired workers came from indigenous villages outside the AVV. The harvest workers were most often impoverished women and children; field clearance was performed by teenage men. The average wage rate for cotton harvests

was one sack for every six to seven harvested (approximately 100 CFAF per day) plus room and board. The wage rate was slightly higher (200 CFAF cash per day plus food and lodging) in the few cases in which laborers were hired for weeding. In 1979 settlers reported that the AVV villages were inundated by local people looking for work during low-rainfall years.

5. In 1979, Puetenga was a famous market through which black market goods entered Burkina from Togo, Niger, and Benin.

6. Distance from regional markets seems to have affected the incidence of off-farm employment in the Kaya region as well. We observed, for example, that the average income earned from secondary activities was smaller both in absolute terms and as a percent of total income in the other two Kaya villages than at Damesma. Neither of these villages was within easy walking distance to the Kaya market. Both villages also had greater opportunities for dry-season irrigated farming.

7. One family may receive eight to ten platters of meat and give an equivalent number during a two-day celebration such as the end of Ramadan or at Christmas.

8. The main difference was that large amounts of clothing and shoes were received as gifts from returning labor migrants in the settlers' home village. Except for her husband providing her with enough cotton to spin thread for a skirt, a Damesma wife was responsible for her own clothing and the clothing of her children. In contrast, the male head of the settler household purchased clothing for the entire family. New clothes were a prestige item among older unmarried children. Children at both sites used the income from their private fields to purchase manufactured cloth and clothing. In addition, young men in the home village cited the need for modern clothes (to attract girls) as one of the chief reasons behind their decision to emigrate to Côte d'Ivoire.

9. To counteract wage labor immigration, the AVV settlers gave especially generous cash gifts after harvest to their teenage and adult sons. When migrant workers returned home, they presented cash and clothing gifts to each member of their extended family. If a migrant didn't already own a bicycle or moped, he would purchase one upon his return. Few of the first-time migrants came home with any definite plans of returning abroad. They generally did return, however, once their wages were spent. By then they were usually forced to sell their newly acquired bicycles and radios. The rate of resale was so high that certain merchants in the Kaya region specialized in the purchase and resale of used consumer products sold by migrants.

10. These social problems involved the need for boys to elope with girls that they—and their parents—wanted them to marry. The boys thus relieved the girl's parents from the unsavory task of breaking a marriage alliance.

Chapter 6.   New Economic Options and Settler Choices

1. Figures do not reflect the substantial increase in immigration that accompanied the discovery of gold in late 1987. The majority of farmers attracted to the gold sites do not cultivate or plan to remain living in the area.

2. In the reorganized model, the administrative structure of the AVV was changed to reflect a separation of the functions of infrastructure development and planning (*aménagiste*) from that of project coordination (realization of particular projects within a short, defined period of time) (appendix B, fig. B-1). Central administration, planning, coordination, and support services remained at the AVV headquarters in Ouagadougou. A separate administrative structure was responsible for the administration of specific projects. Two types of projects were envisioned: (1) integrated regional development programs, and (2) special projects such as irrigation schemes, agro-pastoral zones, or industrial forests. The administrative unit for the regional development programs was the UP, or planning unit.

3. Another important tenet was the involvement of the "masses" in participatory development projects through the local Revolutionary Committee, or CR. The CRS were also given the right to allocate village lands. A third feature was the idea that future development planning be based on a sound assessment of the natural potential of different areas—for agriculture, livestock, and forestry. This potential was to be assessed by a battery of soil and hydraulic surveys.

4. During the crucial first step of the PNGTV (Programme National de Gestion des Terroirs Villageois) approach, a village elects a "land management" committee. This committee determines land allocation and deals with outside authorities. The land-management committees are supposed to represent all the major social groups living in a village, including recent immigrants, the indigenous population, and pastoralists. In step two, the land-management committee supervises the formal delineation of the village's boundaries in cooperation with the relevant regional authorities and neighboring villages. The land-management associations are supposed to be assisted in this task by government-provided aerial photos and soils surveys. Step three involves the negotiation of a contract between the village community and the state. At this stage the community agrees to respect a certain number of themes for soil and forestry preservation, improved pasturage, and suppression of bush fires. In return the state promises to help the village to realize a list of village projects. The village contract and land survey guarantees official recognition of the villagers' rights to the land and any future improvements that they might make upon it. Step four refers to the realization of the terms of the contract outlined in step three.

The PNGTV model of village land-use committees gave national-level recognition for several pilot projects to work with spontaneous settlers moving into the OCP river basins. The model was compatible with—and, indeed, heavily influenced by—the recommendations of the 1984 AVV commission on spontaneous migrants.

5. One of the first PNGTV pilot projects was initiated in the AVV planned settlements in January 1988. Both Rapadama and Linoghin, the two AVV blocs closest to Ouagadougou, experienced high rates of immigration between 1974 and 1987. Preliminary research in 1987 showed 697 agriculturalist and 55 pastoralist families within the UD of Rapadama alone (AVV 1988). Only pastoralists who cultivated the area (that is, were permanent as opposed to transhumant) were considered to have either settlement or pasture rights in the newly defined land-management zone.

During the first stage, the project planners developed a revised map of the UD's limits, then held a series of information sessions and discussions with the relevant administrative authorities (AVV 1988:15). Once the civil authorities gave their permission, the planners organized a second series of information sessions between the top civil administrator (the high commissioner) and the settlers to explain the PNGTV program. Next, more detailed information sessions and discussions were organized in each village, during which the agents described the official UD limits and the proposed delimitation process (AVV 1988:16). Then the residents' representatives worked with the extension staff and topographers and with the village's neighbors to mark the village boundaries with red paint. The boundaries were recorded on a topographic map. Parallel to these activities, two enumerators working with a sociologist conducted a census of all the spontaneous migrants living within the designated village zones (AVV 1988:18). The sociologist met with individual migrants and migrant groups to explain the proposed program. When the village sociological and boundary surveys were completed, the central AVV collaborated with the staff of the UPI.

Responsibility for land management and extension services in each newly expanded village unit was vested in a single land-management committee made up of elected members from each of the major immigrant social groups (settlers whose immigration was sponsored by the AVV, spontaneous settlers, and pastoralists farming in the region). Coordination of the different village committees was carried out by an elected regional land-management committee. Once incorporated into the new program, settler households (pastoralist as well as agriculturalist) received one or more blocs of land that were registered on a topographical map. In some cases the spontaneous settler households were allowed to keep their former fields; when fields were not located in the village area designated for crops, they were asked to move. Spontaneous settlers were allowed, in most instances, to keep their former house sites. New pumps were installed to accommodate the additional settlers—more than double the official number of settlers being served by the original AVV-created infrastructure and extension services.

6. As we did not measure all the fields, we were unable to determine the levels of input use per unit land for the entire area. Interviews with extension agents and settlers, however, suggest that average fertilizer use on cotton fields was substantially below the recommended 150 kilograms per hectare.

7. In the past, the price has descended to as low as 25 CFAF per kilogram in December and January, the holiday period when farmers need the most cash.

8. Average prices used to calculate the value of agricultural production in the Statistical Service Survey research in 1979 were based on a two-year study of local markets (see Murphy and Sprey 1980; McMillan 1983; appendix B, table B-9). The prices used for the 1988–89 restudy were based on the median prices that farmers received for their products based on the reported crop sales over one calendar year (see McMillan, Nana, and Savadogo 1993; appendix B, table B-10). Both 1979 and 1988 were considered good agricultural years.

9. The figures used to adjust income appear in appendix B, table B-11. These figures were developed by Burkina's national statistical service based on the purchases of a typical non-wage-earning urban household. We attempted to develop our own inflation indicators by comparing prices on key products purchased in 1979 and 1989 (appendix B, table B-12).

10. Savadogo (1989c) calculated the settlers' net returns to animal husbandry in two ways: (1) a "low" return scenario that considered all feed costs by imputing a value to nonpurchased food and to full losses due to death and theft and (2) a "high" return scenario that did not consider imputed costs or losses but only the cash operating costs. The rate of loss was an important factor in a farmer's investment strategy.

11. If farmers had fewer than five cattle, the cattle were generally kept on-farm. The major cash expense was veterinary care, with some payment for dietary supplements such as salt. Larger herds were boarded with the pastoralist FulBe. The actual cash and kind costs of boarding cattle were difficult to estimate because many of the costs were conceived as a "gift" exchange between herder and boarder. Pastoralists also had the right to a certain percentage of the herd, estimated at one young cow every two to four years. When taken together (including the price of the calf divided over three years), the cash and kind costs of herding livestock could run over 100,000 CFAF per year for farmers with large herds of more than 40 cattle.

12. In 1989 the two high incomes that were recorded for the animal trade and butchering at Mogtedo-Bombore were actually the same person—the older married son of a prosperous sedentarized FulBe with large cattle herds. The two highest incomes for off-farm employment recorded at V3 were those of a woman engaged in rice trade and the marabout.

13. Because of the danger that we might be perceived as government spies, we were unable to explore the issue of gold revenues in great detail. Settlers were reluctant to tell exactly how much they had earned when we interviewed them in the economic survey. We conducted more detailed interviews with fifteen gold miners. The miners who were interviewed by another settler, a person they knew, were guaranteed complete anonymity, including age and sex.

14. Linoghin was the only one of the three blocs where the stone dikes were adopted widely during the first two seasons of promoting the new technology. Even here the first dikes were built on the more accessible fields around the settlers' houses, not in the bush fields where cotton was traditionally grown.

15. See Gabre-Madhin and Reardon 1989; Reardon and Delgado 1989, 1990; Reardon and Islam 1989; Reardon and Matlon 1989; Reardon, Delgado and Matlon 1992.

Chapter 7. Lessons Learned

1. Being in the administrative category of an office under the Ministry of Agriculture and Livestock, ONAT can consult within its own and other ministries in the design and implementation of special projects. If ONAT retains the AVV's base of

construction equipment, it may also be asked to intervene in the realization of particular types of infrastructure. Many of these projects will undoubtedly continue to be in the ocp river basins.

2. Eicher and Staatz 1986; Gladwin 1991; Johnston and Kilby 1975; Lele 1984; Matlon and Spencer 1984; Mellor 1966; Mellor, Delgado, and Blackie 1987; Poats and Fresco 1986; Poats, Schmink, and Spring 1988; Schultz 1964; Shaner, Philipp, and Schmehl 1982.

3. Netting (1993) observes that the increased economic mobility and inequality linked to differential achievement are especially pronounced where recent settlement of an arable area with the potential for intensive production occurs along with an expanding market. He cites Eder's (1982) longitudinal study of migrant farmers from Cuyo Island who moved to Palawan in the Philippines in the 1930s and 1940s. Although the pioneer men and women farmers did not differ significantly from one another in age, education, previous occupation, or start-up capital, by the 1970s pronounced variations were observed among the three groups in terms of property ownership, land, livestock, bank savings, and houses. This marked economic inequality was attributed to differences in competence, personality, and motivation (Eder 1982:4). Netting argues that the "traditional" system of corporate land ownership and intrahousehold labor exchange in these areas of new lands settlement militated against a more fixed social and economic hierarchy.

Netting also notes that a fixed pattern of stratification or polarization is more often seen on large estates and haciendas where settlement is recent, population densities lower, and where indigenous rights are not clearly established. He cites the example of the Philippines, where the expanding demand for sugar, tobacco, and indigo in the nineteenth century, combined with an official land registry established by the Spanish colonial and American governments, made it both profitable and legally possible for elites to claim large private holdings, often appropriating the land of smallholders (Hyami and Kikuchi 1982:71–74). Hacienda owners monopolized the most productive areas, extracting high rents and paying fixed daily wages, while protecting their property with police and private armies. Where peasant communities have not been broken up or dispossessed by an external elite operating with state support, the tendency has been for smallholders to accumulate land and become entrepreneurs using machinery and wage laborers (Netting 1993:233).

Appendix A.   Study Methodology

1. Based on an initial population and land census, each of the three Kaya villages was divided into four groups of households representing the major economic and social groups. Three to five households were chosen from each of the four clusters. In 1978 sixteen households were chosen from Damesma. For political reasons the 1978 sample also included the households of four nonrandomly chosen village leaders (the chief and three neighborhood chiefs), for a total sample size of twenty. The four nonrandomly chosen households were dropped from the sample in 1979.

In early 1979 one household in the 1978 sample immigrated to the Vallée du Kou and two immigrated to the AVV. Another household was dropped because of their lack of interest in the survey. The Damesma sample included twelve households during the 1979 agricultural season, for a total sample of eighteen households in Damesma and twelve households in each of the neighboring two villages with lower immigration rates. During the second agricultural season (1979), the sample was reduced to twelve households in Damesma and twenty-three in the other two villages, for a total sample of thirty-five.

2. Several cases were documented of women relying on grain from their private fields once food stores from the cooperatively worked family fields were exhausted. In other households women used their private grain to provide an extra meal for themselves and their children. Some individuals sold part of their private harvest and used the cash for personal needs or, in the case of women, for the needs of their children. Some cash was usually used to purchase livestock and goods for commerce and petty manufactures.

3. The amount of time an individual allocated to the cultivation of the household's cooperatively worked fields versus his or her own privately worked fields varied enormously in response to different factors, including the total size of the household and the individual's relationship to the group. For example, other things (technology, the crop package, nonfarm wage labor) being equal, the amount of time a married woman could devote to her private production activities was related to her childbearing responsibilities, age, and health, as well as to the number, sex, and age of her older children working with the group. Her position was also affected by the presence and relative status of any co-wives.

The ideal for most Mossi men was to accumulate as large a household as possible. To retain family members, a household had to be able to adjust to the changing opportunities and constraints of individual family members. For example, when a man died, his sons might cease to farm the same cooperative field, although they usually continued to live in the same residential compound and often lent equipment and helped one another out during peak labor periods. Just as households divided (as in the death of a father), so they might also combine in response to the death of a family member, a new profitable crop package, immigration, or illness. For the purposes of the case study, it was the residential unit to which a particular group was bonded for collective labor and/or basic food needs that was considered to be a household.

4. The 1983 restudy was funded by a grant from USAID through the South-East Consortium for International Development (SECID), Office of Women in Development. The 1987 restudy was funded by a grant from the Graduate School, Office of Research, University of Kentucky, and the National Institutes of Health, Biomedical Small Grants Program, University of Kentucky.

5. The majority of interviews for the farming-systems survey were conducted during the dry-season months, February through May 1989, with cross-checking and coding being carried out during June. The first step involved interviewing the male

household head and other members of the family about changes in household composition. We then gathered retrospective information on each family member's private crop production activities. In step three we interviewed the male household head about the family's collective crop production activities in 1987 and 1988, as well as any private crop, livestock, or off-farm employment income he had earned. One female head was interviewed concerning her crop production levels during 1987 and 1988 and her recollected use of mineral fertilizer, manure, seed, insecticides, and family and nonfamily labor on each of the fields she planted in 1988. In a separate series of interviews over several months, we elicited the number and size of current livestock, the sale and purchase of animals during the preceding years, and the loss of animals due to death or theft during the preceding five years. Grain sales were evaluated for three periods: July–September 1988 (just before the 1988 harvest), October–December 1988 (during the 1988 harvests), and January–June 1989. We also gathered retrospective information on the male household head's income earned from off-farm employment sources, including purchase and resale of consumer goods, trade in livestock and agricultural products, beer making, basket weaving, and processed food. Each male and female family head was interviewed three to five times. From June through August 1989 we conducted more detailed interviews with individual family members in thirty-three AVV households and five former AVV households now at Kompienga concerning their total revenues and expenditures during the preceding year.

6. My research at Mogtedo V3 during the 1989 crop season was assisted by Fatou Kabore, an animatrice with the Ministry of the Environment, and Salifo Boena, now a researcher with the national agricultural research institute, INERA, who was the original enumerator for the case study research in the settlers' home village in 1978 and V3 in 1979. Tinga Ouédraogo, a high school student and son of a successful AVV settler, and several other of the AVV schoolchildren conducted various studies on rural markets, village services, and the pastoralist households living near V3. Sommaila Sawadogo supervised the research on settler dropout from Mogtedo and Mogtedo-Bombore. Frédéric Guira, who was the research coordinator for the AVV farm-monitoring survey, was responsible for all interviews with the sixty households in the 1979 restudy of that survey as well as various special substudies on the Linoghin market and village extension groups. Professors Kimseyinga Savadogo and John Sanders were the primary persons responsible for the design and analysis of the farm-monitoring survey. During my research at Kompienga, I was assisted by Moustapha Ouédraogo, the son of one of the Damesma settlers at V3 who had immigrated to Kompienga in 1988. He was also responsible for the research on the pastoralist households living in the Gadeghin agro-pastoral zone and gold mining.

Bibliography

Agrotechnik

1988   Etude de développement régional dans le bassin versant de la Kompienga: Rapport diagnostic. Frankfurt: Agrotechnik.

1989   Etude de développement régional dans le bassin versant de la Kompienga: Rapport final. Référence N°:84.70.049. Frankfurt: Agrotechnik.

Akwabi-Ameyaw, K.

1990   OCP Land Settlement Review, Country Case Study: Ghana. Binghamton, N.Y.: Institute for Development Anthropology.

Amin, S.

1974   Modern Migrations in Western Africa. In Modern Migrations in Western Africa, edited by Samir Amin, pp. 64–124. London: Oxford University Press.

Ancey, G.

1974   Facteurs et systèmes de production dans la société mossi d'aujourd'hui: Migrations, travail, terre et capital. In Enquête sur les mouvements de population à partir du pays Mossi 2. Ouagadougou: ORSTOM.

Angel, S.

1985   Spontaneous Land Settlement on Rural Frontiers: An Agenda for a Global Approach. Paper presented at the International Seminar on Planning for Settlements in Rural Regions: The Case of Spontaneous Settlements. Nairobi, Kenya, November 11–20. Mimeo.

Apthorpe, R., ed.
1968   *Land Settlement and Rural Development in Eastern Africa*. Nkanga Publication Series, No. 3. Kampala: Transition Books.

Apthorpe, R., and J. MacArthur
1968   Land Settlement Policies in Kenya. In *Land Settlement and Rural Development in Eastern Africa*. Nkanga Publication Series, No. 3. Kampala: Transition Books.

Autorité des Aménagements des Vallées des Volta (AVV)
1973a   *Programme d'infrastructures, 1974–1975*. Ouagadougou: AVV.
1973b   *Programme de mise en valeur 1974*. Ouagadougou: AVV.
1973c   *Propositions d'actions en vue de l'amélioration de l'élevage*. Ouagadougou: AVV.
1973d   *Demande de financement au fonds d'aide et de coopération*. Ouagadougou: AVV.
1973e   *Bilan des activités, année 1973—Programme 1974*. Ouagadougou: AVV.
1974   *La Mise en valeur des Vallées des Volta: Principes d'aménagement et perspectives*. Ouagadougou: AVV.
1981a   *Nouvelles méthodes d'intervention de l'AVV*. Vol. 1: *Principes généraux*. Ouagadougou: AVV.
1981b   *Nouvelles méthodes d'intervention de l'AVV*. Vol. 1 (Annex): *Annexes*. Ouagadougou: AVV.
1983   *Programme de développement de l'AVV, 1983–1986*. Ouagadougou: AVV.
1984a   *Etude de factibilité: Unité de Planification 1*. 3 vols. Ouagadougou: AVV.
1984b   Etude agropastorale dans l'unité de planification No. 1 (UPI). Ouagadougou: AVV, UPI.
1984c   La production vivrière des périmètres aménagés de l'AVV au cours de la campagne agricole, 1983–1984. Ouagadougou: AVV, Cellule de Suivi-Evaluation.
1985a   Plan quinquennal AVV, 1986–1990: Synthèse. Draft. Ouagadougou: AVV.
1985b   *Rapport d'évaluation: Unité de Planification 1, Zorgho, Burkina Faso*. Ouagadougou and Zorgho: AVV.
1985c   *L'Impact socio-économique du programme de lutte contre l'onchocercose au Burkina (1974–1984)*. Ouagadougou: AVV.
1985d   Annexe I: Textes fondamentaux relatif à la réorganisation foncière et agraire au Burkina Faso. Ouagadougou: AVV, Direction des Etudes, Programmes et du Controle (DEPC).
1988   *Programme réforme agraire et gestion de l'espace UPI-Zorgho (UD de Linoghin; UD de Rapadama): Rapport général*. Ouagadougou: AVV, DEPC.
1989a   Mission d'évaluation de l'AVV: Mise en place d'une nouvelle structure (aide memoire). Ouagadougou. December 3–20. Mimeo.
1989b   *Document de transfert de la zone pastorale de Gadeghin/ UPI au CRPA du Centre*. Ouagadougou: AVV.

1989c   *Document de transfert de la zone pastorale de la Nouhao au CRPA du Centre Est.* Ouagadougou: AVV.

1989d   *Rapport: Transfert du projet reboisement industriel de Wayen au Ministère de l'Environnement et du Tourisme.* Ouagadougou: AVV.

1989e   *Rapport des activités de l'AVV: Campagne 1988/89.* Ouagadougou: AVV.

1990   *Rapport annuel: Projet transfert des populations de la Kompienga.* Ouagadougou: AVV.

Autorité des Aménagements des Vallées des Volta, Unité de Planification No. 1 (AVV-UPI)

1986   Rapport annuel, 1986: Cellule Production Animale et Végétale. Zorgho: AVV, UPI. Mimeo.

1987   Rapport d'activités. Zorgho: AVV, UPI, Cellule Production Animale et Végétale. Mimeo.

1988   Rapport d'activités: Premier semestre 1988. Zorgho: AVV, UPI, Cellule Production Animale et Végétale. Mimeo.

1989a   Rapport d'activités, février−mai 1989: Opération cordons pierreux. Zorgho: AVV, UP, Cellule Production Animale et Végétale. Mimeo.

1989b   Etude sur l'occupation de l'espace dans l'UD de Mogtedo II. Zorgho: AVV, UPI, Cellule Organisation Monde Rural et Formation (COMRF).

1990   Rapport sur la gestion des terroirs villageois de l'UD de Linoghin. Zorgho: AVV, UPI, COMRF.

Baer, R.

1991   Inter and Intrahousehold Income Allocation: Implications for Third World Food Policy. In *Anthropology and Food Policy*, edited by D. McMillan, pp. 112−25. Athens: University of Georgia Press.

Bakyono, A.-M.

1989   Etude des migrations: Burkina Faso. Ouagadougou: ORSTOM. Mimeo.

Balesi, C. J.

1979   *From Adversaries to Comrades-in-Arms: West Africans and the French Military, 1885−1918.* Waltham, Mass.: Crossroads Press.

Baris, P., P. Bonnal, and M. Pescay

1983   Mission d'Evaluation: Aménagement des Vallées des Volta. Ouagadougou: AVV. November. Mimeo.

Barnett, T.

1977   Evaluating the Gezira Scheme: Black Box or Pandora's Box. In *Rural Development in Tropical Africa*, edited by J. Heyer, P. Roberts, and G. Williams, pp. 306−24. New York: St. Martin's Press.

Barrett, V., G. Lassiter, D. Wilcock, D. Baker, and E. Crawford

1981   *Animal Traction in Eastern Upper Volta: A Technical, Economic and Institutional Analysis.* East Lansing: Michigan State University, Department of Agricultural Economics.

Becker, B. K.

1985   Spontaneous/Induced Rural Settlements in Brazilian Amazonia. Paper presented at the International Seminar on Planning for Settlements in Rural Regions: The Case of Spontaneous Settlements. Nairobi, Kenya, November 11–20.

BEI-agrer

1978   *Programme Global d'Etudes et d'Investissements de l'Autorité des Aménagements des Vallées des Volta (1978–1982).* 6 vols. Brussels: Bureau Courtoy.

Benoit, M.

1973a   *Espaces agraires mossi en pays Bwa.* 2 vols. Ouagadougou: ORSTOM.

1973b   Le champ spatial mossi dans les pays du Voun-Hou et de la Volta Noire (Cercle de Nouna, Haute-Volta). *Cahiers des Sciences Humaines* 10 (2):115–37.

Benoit, M., and J. P. Lahuec

1975   L'insertion des éléments du champ migratoire mossi dans les différents contextes régionaux: Essai d'une Cartographie du Synthèse. In *Enquête sur les mouvements de population à partir du pays mossi* 1 (2):169–212. Ouagadougou: ORSTOM.

Benton, B., and E. Skinner

1990   Cost Benefits of Onchocerciasis Control. ACTA Leidensia 59 (1–2): 405–11.

Berg, E. J.

1975   *The Recent Economic Evolution of the Sahel.* East Lansing: University of Michigan, Center for Research on Economic Development.

Berg, E. J., J. Bisilliat, M. Burer, H. Graetz, R. Melville, V. Volyvan, J. Park, R. C. Sawadogo, H. Sederlof, and K. van der Meer

1978   OCP Economic Review Mission. Ouagadougou: Onchocerciasis Control Programme.

Bharin, T. S.

1981   Review and Evaluation of Attempts to Direct Migrants to Frontier Areas Through Land Colonization Schemes. In *Population Distribution Policies in Development Planning.* Population Studies 75:141–3. New York: United Nations, Department of International Economic and Social Affairs.

Bitard, J. P., and J. C. Faffa

1958   *Di: monographie d'un village Marka de la vallée du Sourou.* Ouagadougou: Service de l'hydraulique de Haute Volta for ISHA (Institut des Sciences Appliquées de l'Université de Bordeaux).

Boutillier, J. L.

1964   Les structures foncières en Haute-Volta. *Etudes Voltaïques* 5:84–94.

Broekhuyse, J. T.

1974   *Développement du nord du plateau mossi.* 4 vols. Amsterdam: Institut royal des régions tropiques, Département des recherches sociales.

1982a   *Production et productivité agricoles dans la savanne sèche.* Amsterdam: Institut royal des régions tropicales, Département des recherches sociales.

1982b   *Restructuration des institutions rurales.* Amsterdam: Institut royal des régions tropicales, Département des recherches sociales.

Brokensha, D., and T. Scudder
1968   Resettlement. In *Dams in Africa*, edited by N. Rubin and W. M. Warren, 20–62. London: Frank Cass.

Butcher, D.A.P.
1971   *An Organizational Manual for Resettlement: A Systematic Approach to the Resettlement Problem Created by Man-made Lakes, with Special Reference to West Africa*. Rome: Food and Agriculture Organization of the United Nations.

Buursink, J., with T. Painter
1990   *Land Settlement Review, A Review of Settlement Experiences in: Benin, Côte d'Ivoire, Guinea, Guinea-Bissau, Niger, Senegal, and Sierra Leone (Seven Country Review)*. Binghamton, N.Y.: Institute for Development Anthropology.

Caldwell, J. C.
1975   *The Sahelian Drought and Its Demographic Implications*. Overseas Liaison Committee, Paper No. 8. Washington, D.C.: American Council on Education.

Capron, J., and J. M. Kohler
1975   Environnement sociologique des migrations agricoles. In *Enquête sur les mouvements de population à partir du pays mossi 1*. Ouagadougou: ORSTOM.

Catrice, P.
1931   L'emploi des troupes indigènes et leur séjour en France. *Revue catholique de l'intérêt général* 20: 388–409.

Cernea, M.
1988   *Involuntary Resettlement in Development Projects: Policy Guidelines in World Bank Financed Projects*. World Bank Technical Paper No. 80. Washington, D.C.: The World Bank.
1991   Involuntary Resettlement: Social Research, Policy and Planning. In *Putting People First: Sociological Variables in Rural Development*, 2nd ed., edited by M. Cernea, 340–94. New York: Oxford University Press for The World Bank.

Chambers, R.
1969   *Settlement Schemes in Tropical Africa: A Study of Organizations and Development*. New York: Praeger.

Clanet, J. C.
1983   Rapport sur le repeuplement des vallées libérées de l'onchocercose dans l'ouest voltaïque (secteurs de la Comoe, de la Leraba, de Samandeni et de St. Pierre). Ouagadougou: Université de Ouagadougou. November 20. Mimeo.

Christensen, C., A. Dommen, N. Horenstein, S. Pryor, P. Riley, S. Shapouri, and H. Steiner
1981   *Food Problems and Prospects in Sub-Saharan Africa: The Decade of the 1980s*. Foreign Agricultural Economic Report No. 166. Washington,

D.C.: U.S. Department of Agriculture, Africa and Middle East Branch, International Economics Division, Economic Research Services.

Christodoulou, D.

1965 Land Settlement. Some Oft-neglected Issues. *Monthly Bulletin of Agricultural Economics and Statistics* 14 (10):1–6.

Colson, E.

1971 *The Social Consequences of Resettlement: The Impact of the Kariba Resettlement upon the Gwembe Tonga.* Kariba Studies, IV. Manchester: University of Manchester Press.

Conde, J.

1978 *Migration in Upper Volta.* Washington, D.C.: The World Bank, Development Economics Department.

Conti, A.

1979 Capitalist Organization of Production through Non-capitalist Relations: Women's Role in a Pilot Resettlement in Upper Volta. *Review of African Political Economy* 15/16:75–92.

Coulibaly, S., J. Gregory, and V. Piche

1980 *Importance et ambivalence de la migration voltaïque. Les migrations voltaïques.* Vol. 1. Ouagadougou: Institut national de la statistique et de la demographie.

Couty, P., J. Y. Marchal, P. Pélissier, M. Poussi, G. Savonnet, and A. Schwartz, eds.

1979 *Maîtrise de l'Espace Agraire et Développement en Afrique Tropicale: Logique Paysanne et Rationalité Technique.* Paris: ORSTOM.

Davis, S.

1934 *Reservoirs of Men.* Geneva: Librarie Kundig.

Delavignette, R. L.

1970 French Colonial Policy in Black Africa, 1945–1960. In *Colonialism in Africa, 1870–1960,* edited by P. Duignan and L. H. Gann, 2:251–85. Cambridge: Cambridge University Press.

Delgado, C. L.

1979 *Livestock versus Foodgrain Production in Southeast Upper Volta: A Resource Allocation Analysis. Livestock Production and Marketing in the Entente States of West Africa.* Vol. 1. East Lansing: University of Michigan, Center for Research on Economic Development.

Deniel, R.

1967 *De la savanne à la ville.* Aix-en-Provence: Centre Africain des Sciences Humaines Appliquées.

1970 Croyances religieuses et vie quotidienne. Islam et christianisme à Ouagadougou. *Recherches voltaiques* 14. Paris: Laboratoire d'Etudes Sociologies et Géographiques Africaines. Ecole Practique des Hautes Etudes-Centre National de la Recherche Scientifique (EPHE-CNRS).

Deuson, R., and J. H. Sanders

1990   Cereal Technology Development in the Sahel: Burkina Faso and Niger
        (Viewpoint). *Land Use Policy* 7 (3):195–7.

DeWalt, K.

1991   Integrating Nutritional Concerns into Adaptive Small Farm Research
        Programs. In *Anthropology and Food Policy*, edited by D. McMillan,
        126–44. Athens: University of Georgia Press.

de Wilde, J. C., P.F.M. McLoughlin, A. Guinard, T. Scudder, and R. Maubouche

1967   *Experiences with Agricultural Development in Tropical Africa.* 2 vols. Balti-
        more: Johns Hopkins University Press for The World Bank.

Diallo, Y.

1971   *Les aménagements hydro-agricoles en Afrique au Sud du Sahara. Enquête au
        Mali à l'Office du Niger.* Paris: Laboratoire d'Etudes Sociologiques et Géo-
        graphiques Africaines, Ecole Practique des Hautes Etudes (EPHE-CNRS)

Dim Delobsom, A. A.

1932   *L'empire du Mogho-Naba: Coutumes des Mossi de la Haute Volta.* Paris:
        Domat Montchrestien. Institut de droit comparé, Etudes de sociologie et
        d'ethnologie juridiques, 2. Paris: Les Editions Domat-Montchrestien.

Djigma, A.

1989   Memorandum: Participation à la définition et à la mise en place d'une
        nouvelle structure suite à la restructuration de l'AVV. October 5. Mimeo.

Dollfus, O.

1981   Phénomènes pionniers et problèmes de frontières: Quelques remarques en
        guise de conclusion. In *Les Phénomènes de "Frontière" dans les pays tropi-
        caux. Travaux et Mémoires de l'Institut des Hautes Etudes de l'Amérique La-
        tine* 32:445–8.

Dr.-ing., Walter International

1987   *Etude d'élaboration d'un programme de déplacement des populations de la zone
        d'inondation du barrage hydro-électrique de la Kompienga.* Wittenbergstrasse,
        République Federale d'Allemagne: DIWI (Dr.-ing. Walter International).

Dumont, R.

1962   *L'Afrique Noire est Mal Partie.* Paris: Editorial du Seuil. Economic Com-
        mission for Africa.

Echenberg, M. J.

1975   Paying the Blood Tax: Military Conscription in West Africa, 1914–1929.
        Canadian Journal of African Studies 9:171–92.

Eder, J.

1982   *Who Shall Succeed: Agricultural Development and Social Inequality on a Phil-
        ippine Frontier.* New York: Cambridge University Press.

Eicher, C., and J. Staatz

1986   Agricultural Development Ideas in Historical Perspective. In *Food in Af-
        rica*, edited by A. Hansen and D. McMillan, 43–63. Boulder: Lynne
        Rienner Publishers.

Fage, J. D.
1964   Reflections on the Early History of the Mossi-Dagomba Group of States.
        In *The Historian in Tropical Africa*, edited by J. Vansina, R. Mauny and
        L. V. Thomas, 177–91. London: Oxford University Press.

Finnegan, G.
1976   Population Movement, Labor Migration and Social Structure in a Mossi
        Village. Ph.D. diss., Brandeis University.
1980   Employment Opportunity and Migration among the Mossi of Upper
        Volta. In *Research in Economic Anthropology*, Vol. 3, edited by G. Dalton,
        291–322. Greenwich, Conn.: JAI Press, Inc.
1984   The Mossi. In *Muslim Peoples: A World Ethnographic Survey*, edited by
        R. V. Weekes, 546–52. Westport, Conn.: Greenwood Press.

Finnegan, G., and G. Delgado
1980   Cachez la Vache: Mossi Cattle, FulBe Keepers, and the Maintenance of
        Ethnicity. In *Image and Reality in African Interethnic Relations: The FulBe
        and Their Neighbors*, edited by E. A. Schultz. Studies in Third World
        Studies 11:31–50.

Fortes, M.
1971   Some Aspects of Migration and Mobility in Ghana. *Journal of Asian and
        African Studies* 6 (1):1–20.

Gaitskill, A.
1959   *Gezira, A Story of Development in the Sudan*. London: Faber and Faber.

Giri, J.
1983   *Le Sahel demain: catastrophe ou renaissance?* Paris: Editions Karthala.

Gladwin, C., ed.
1991   *Structural Adjustment and African Women Farmers*. Gainesville: University
        of Florida Press.

Gladwin, C., and D. McMillan
1988   Is a Turnaround in African Agriculture Possible Without Helping Women
        Farmers? *Economic Development and Cultural Change* 37:345–69.

Glantz, M., ed.
1976   *The Politics of Natural Disaster*. New York: Praeger.

Goering, T. J.
1978   *Agricultural Land Settlement*. Washington, D.C.: The World Bank.

Gregory, J.
1974a   Development and In-Migration in Upper Volta. In *Modern Migrations in
        West Africa*, edited by Samir Amin, pp. 304–20. London: Oxford Uni-
        versity Press.
1974b   Underdevelopment, Dependency and Migration in Upper Volta. Ph.D.
        diss., Cornell University.

Guira, A.
1989   Compte rendu de réunion de la Commission Interministérielle de Concer-
        tation sur le Schéma directeur du bassin versant de la Kompienga.

June 14. Ouagadougou: Direction Générale de la Maîtrise d'Ouvrage de la Kompienga. Mimeo.

Guira, F.

1989 Groupement Structures and Village Markets: Linoghin, Mogtedo and Mogtedo Bombore. Field report (handwritten).

Guissou, J.

1977 *Etude sur les besoins des femmes dans les villages de l'AVV et proposition d'un programme d'intervention.* Ouagadougou: Societé Africaine d'Etudes et de Développement.

Guyon, G.

1986 *Rapport d'évaluation de la phase préparatoire d'un programme de gestion des terroirs villageois Burkina Faso.* Ouagadougou: Caisse Centrale de Coopération Economique.

Hammond, P.

1959a Economic Change and Mossi Acculturation. In *Continuity and Change in African Cultures,* edited by W. R. Bascom and M. J. Herskovits, pp. 238–56. Chicago: University of Chicago Press.

1959b The Functions of Indirection. In *Comparative Studies in Administration,* pp. 183–94. Pittsburgh: University of Pittsburgh, Administrative Science Center.

1962 Technological Change and Mossi Acculturation. Ph.D. diss., Northwestern University.

1963 The Niger Project: Some Cultural Sources of Conflict. In *Emerging Africa,* edited by W. H. Lewis, 12–28. Washington, D.C.: Public Affairs Press.

1964 Mossi Joking. *Ethnology* 3:259–67.

1966 *Yatenga: Technology in the Culture of a West African Kingdom.* New York: The Free Press.

Hamon, J., and L. Kartman

1973 Onchocerciasis: Poverty and Blindness. *World Health* (October), pp. 3–9.

Hansen, A., and A. Oliver-Smith, eds.

1982 *Involuntary Migration and Resettlement. The Problems and Responses of Dislocated Peoples.* Boulder: Westview Press.

Hartog, T.

1979 La Vallée du Kou: Un exemple d'intervention planifiée et d'encadrement paysan dans l'ouest voltaïque. In *Maîtrise de l'espace agraire et développement en Afrique tropicale,* edited by P. Couty et al., pp. 481–90. Paris: ORSTOM.

Hervouet, J. P.

1977 *Peuplement et mouvements de population dans les vallées des Volta blanche et rouge.* Ouagadougou: ORSTOM.

1978 La mise en valeur des vallées des Volta blanche et rouge: Un Accident historique. *Cahiers ORSTOM: Série sciences humaines* 15(1):81–7.

1980   *Du Faidherbia à la Brousse: Modifications culturales et dégradation sanitaire.* Ouagadougou: ORSTOM.

1983   Bilan de l'occupation des terres des vallées libérées de l'onchocercose après 10 ans de lutte antisimuldienne (Haute Volta-Mali). Ouagadougou. Mimeo.

1990   Le mythe des vallées dépeuplée par l'onchocercose. Montpellier: *Cahiers GEOS* (Atelier de géographie de la santé, Université Paul Valery).

Hervouet, J. P., J. C. Clanet, F. Paris, and H. Some

1984   Settlement of the Valleys Protected from Onchocerciasis after Ten Years of Vector Control in Burkina. OCP/GVA/ 84.5. Ouagadougou: OCP. Mimeo.

Hilton, T. E.

1960   Frafra resettlement and the population problem in Zuarungu. *Bulletin de l'IFAN* 22 (3–4):426–42.

Hirschman, A.

1958   *The Strategy of Economic Development.* New Haven: Yale University Press.

Hunting Technical Services, Ltd.

1988a *Final Report: Socioeconomic Development Studies in the Onchocerciasis Control Programme Area. Vol. 1: Main Report.* Hemel Hempstead, Herts, England: Hunting Technical Services, Ltd.

1988b *Socioeconomic Development Studies in the Onchocerciasis Control Programme Area. Vol. 2: National Oncho Zone Development Studies and Development Proposals.* Hemel Hempstead, Herts, England: Hunting Technical Services, Ltd.

1988c *Socioeconomic Development Studies in the Onchocerciasis Control Programme Area. Vol. 3: National Oncho Zone Development Studies and Development Proposals.* Hemel Hempstead, Herts, England: Hunting Technical Services, Ltd.

1988d *Socioeconomic Development Studies in the Onchocerciasis Control Programme Area. Vol. 4: Bibliography.* Hemel Hempstead, Herts, England: Hunting Technical Services, Ltd.

Hyami, Y., and M. Kikuchi

1982   *Asian Village Economy at the Crossroads: An Economic Approach to Institutional Change.* Tokyo: University of Tokyo Press.

International Monetary Fund (IMF)

1989   Burkina Faso. *International Financial Statistics Yearbook, 1989.* Washington, D.C.: IMF.

Izard, M.

1965   Traditions historiques des villages du Yatenga, Cercle de Gourcy. *Recherches Voltaïques* 1.

1970   Introduction à l'histoire des royaumes mossi. *Recherches Voltaïques* 12–13.

1971   Les Yarse et le commerce dans le Yatenga pré-colonial. In *The Develop-*

ment of Indigenous Trade and Markets in West Africa, pp. 214–27. London: Oxford University Press for the International African Institute.

Izard, M., and F. Izard-Hertier

1958   *Bouna: Monographie d'un village Pana de la vallée du Sourou (Haute-Volta)*. Ouagadougou: Service de l'hydraulique de Haute Volta pour l'ISHA.

Izard-Hertier, F., and M. Izard

1958   *Aspects humains de l'aménagement hydro-agricole de la Vallée du Sourou*. Ouagadougou: Service de l'hydraulique de Haute Volta pour l'ISHA.

1959   *Les Mossi du Yatenga: Etude de la vie économique et sociale*. Bordeaux: ISHA.

Jaeger, W. K.

1983   *Agricultural Mechanization: The Economics of Animal Draft Power in Africa*. Boulder: Westview Press.

Jayne, T., J. C. Day, and H. E. Dregne

1989   *Technology and Agricultural Productivity in the Sahel*. USDA, Economic Research Service, Agricultural Economic Report No. 612. Washington, D.C.: United States Department of Agriculture.

Johnston, B., and P. Kilby

1975   *Agriculture and Structural Transformations: Economic Strategies in Late Developing Countries*. London: Oxford University Press.

Kabore, B. R., A. Brilleau, and G. Badolo

1985   *Etudes démographiques UPI, Zorgho: Zone des Plateaux*. Ouagadougou: AVV.

Kabore, F., and J. Guigma

1990   Enquête Marché. August. (Handwritten).

Kafondo, T.

1989   Rapport de stage: La Gestion des terroirs villageois: Cadre d'application de la réorganisation agraire et foncière en milieu rural au Burkina Faso. Cas de Rapadama UPI/AVV. October. Maître de Stage: Some Jules Marie. Ouagadougou: AVV.

Koenig, D.

1990   *OCP Land Settlement Review, Country Case Study: Mali*. Binghamton, N.Y.: Institute for Development Anthropology.

Kohler, J. M.

1968   *Activités agricoles et transformation socio-économique de l'ouest du plateau Mossi*. Paris: ORSTOM.

1972   *Les migrations des Mossi de l'ouest*. Paris: ORSTOM.

Lahuec, J.-P.

1970   Une communauté évolutive Mossi Zaonghe (Haute Volta). *Etudes Rurales*:37–9.

Lele, U.

1984   Rural Africa: Modernization, Equity, and Long-Term Development. In *Agricultural Development in the Third World*, edited by C. Eicher and J. Staatz, pp. 436–52. Baltimore and London: Johns Hopkins University Press.

Lesselingue, P.

1975 Migrations internes—Aspects psycho-sociologiques. In *Enquête sur les mouvements de population à partir du pays Mossi* 2 (3):1–30. Ouagadougou: ORSTOM.

Liese, B., J. Wilson, B. Benton, and D. Marr

1991 *The Onchocerciasis Control Programme in West Africa.* PRE Working Paper. No. 740. Washington, D.C.: The World Bank.

Mabogunje, A. L.

1981 Objectives and Rationales for Regional Population Redistribution in Developing Countries. In *Population Distribution Policies in Development Planning.* Population Studies, 75:19–29. New York: United Nations, Department of International Economic and Social Affairs.

Madeley, J.

1980 Resettlement Scheme in Trouble. *West Africa* (November 17) 3304: 2303–5.

Marchal, J.-Y.

1974 Office du Niger: Ilôt de prospérité paysanne au pôle de production agricole. *Revue Canadienne des études africaines* 8 (1):73–90.

1975 Géographie des aires d'émigration en pays mossi. In *Enquête sur les mouvements de population à partir du pays mossi* 2 (3):310–71. Ouagadougou: ORSTOM.

1978 L'Onchocercose et les faits de peuplement dans le bassin des Volta. *Journal des africanistes* 48 (2):9–30.

Martin, P. M., and P. O'Meara, eds.

1986 *Africa.* Bloomington: Indiana University Press.

Matlon, P. J.

1981 The Structure of Production and Rural Incomes in Northern Nigeria: Results of Three Village Case Studies. In *The Political Economy in Income Distribution in Nigeria,* edited by H. Bienen and V. P. Diejomaon, pp. 323–72. New York: Holmes and Meier.

Matlon, P. J., and D. Spencer

1984 Increasing Food Production in Sub-Saharan Africa: Environmental Problems and Inadequate Technological Solutions. *American Journal of Agricultural Economics* 56:671–6.

McMillan, D.

1980 *Land Rights and Resettlement.* Purdue University: Department of Agricultural Economics.

1983 A Resettlement Project in Upper Volta. Ph.D. diss., Northwestern University.

1984 *Changing Patterns of Grain Production in a Resettlement Scheme in Upper Volta.* Washington, D.C.: Center for Women in Development, South-East Consortium for International Development (SECID).

1986 Distribution of Resources and Products in Mossi Households. In *Food in*

Sub-Saharan Africa, edited by A. Hansen and D. E. McMillan, pp. 260–73. Boulder: Westview Press.

1987a   Monitoring the Evolution of Household Economic Systems over Time in Farming Systems Research. *Development and Change* 18:295–314.

1987b   The Social Impacts of Planned Settlements in Burkina Faso. In *Drought and Hunger in Africa: Denying Famine a Future*, edited by M. Glantz, pp. 297–322. Cambridge: Cambridge University Press.

1989   *Draft Country Case Study: Burkina Faso* (Analysis of Material from Site Reports and Other Research at avv-upi, Kompienga, Solenzo, and Niangoloko). December. Binghamton, N.Y.: Institute for Development Anthropology.

1989   Seasonality, Planned Settlement and River Blindness Control. *MASCA Research Papers in Science and Archaeology* 5: 96–120.

1992   Adaptation of rap to Monitoring Settlement Trends in Areas Covered by Successful Disease Control Programs. In *Rapid Assessment Procedures: Qualitative Methodologies for Planning and Evaluation of Health Related Programmes*, edited by N. S. Scrimshaw and G. R. Gleason, pp. 147–66. Boston: International Nutrition Foundation for Developing Countries (INFDC).

1993   Diversification and Successful Settlement in the River Blindness Control Zone of West Africa. *Human Organization* 52 (3):269–82.

McMillan, D., J.-B. Nana, and K. Savadogo

1990   *Onchocerciasis Control Programme. Land Settlement Review Case Study: Burkina Faso*. Binghamton, N.Y.: Institute for Development Anthropology.

1993   Settlement and Development in the River Blindness Control Zone. Case Study: Burkina Faso. World Bank Technical Paper No. 200. Series on River Blindness Control in West Africa. Washington, D.C.: The World Bank.

McMillan, D., T. Painter, and T. Scudder

1990   Onchocerciasis Control Programme, Final Report of the Land Settlement Review: The Experience with Land Settlement in the ocp River Basins and Strategies for Their Development. Binghamton, N.Y.: Institute for Development Anthropology.

1992   *Settlement and Development in the River Blindness Control Zone*. World Bank Technical Paper Number 192. Series on River Blindness Control in West Africa. Washington, D.C.: The World Bank.

Mellor, J.

1966   *The Economics of Agricultural Development*. Ithaca: Cornell University Press.

J. Mellor, C. Delgado, and M. J. Blackie

1987   *Accelerating Food Production in Sub-Saharan Africa*. Baltimore: Johns Hopkins University Press for the International Food Policy Institute.

Murphy, J., and L. Sprey
1980   The Volta Valley Authority: Socio-economic Evaluation of a Resettle-
        ment Project in Upper Volta. West Lafayette, Ind.: Department of Agri-
        cultural Economics, Purdue University.

Nagy, J., J. Sanders, and O. Ohm
1988   Cereal Technology Interventions for the West African Semi-Arid Trop-
        ics. *Agricultural Economics* 2:179–208.

Nana, J. B.
1989a   Rapport sur le site de la zone de sous-secteur de Niangoloko et de la forêt
        classée de Toumousseni. Binghamton, N.Y.: Institute for Development
        Anthropology.
1989b   Rapport sur le site. Programme PNGTV Rapadama. Binghamton, N.Y.: In-
        stitute for Development Anthropology.
1989c   Rapport sur le site de sous-secteur de Solenzo. Binghamton, N.Y.: Insti-
        tute for Development Anthropology.
1989d   Enquête Ressources Naturelles de la Zone de Niangoloko. Binghamton,
        N.Y.: Institute for Development Anthropology.
1989e   Enquête Ressources Naturelles dans le sous-secteur de Solenzo. Bingham-
        ton, N.Y.: Institute for Development Anthropology.
1989f   Enquête sur les groupements. Ouagadougou: Caisse Centrale.

Nana, J. P., and D. Kattenberg
1979   *Etude préliminaire de la question des migrants spontanés.* Ouagadougou: AVV,
        DEPC, Section Sociologie.

Nelson, M.
1973   *The Development of Tropical Lands: Policy Issues in Latin America.* Balti-
        more: Johns Hopkins University Press for Resources for the Future.

Netting, R.
1993   *Smallholders, Householders: Farm Families and the Ecology of Intensive, Sus-
        tainable Agriculture.* Stanford: Stanford University Press.

Nicholson, S.
1986   Climate, Drought and Famine in Africa. In *Food in Sub-Saharan Africa*,
        edited by A. Hansen and D. McMillan, pp. 107–28, Boulder: Lynne
        Rienner Publishers.

Nicolai, H., and G. Lasserre
1981   Les systémes de cultures traditionnels et les phénomènes pionniers en Af-
        rique tropicale. In *Les Phénomenes de "Frontière" dans les pays tropicaux.
        Travaux et mémoires de l'Institut des Hautes Etudes de l'Amérique Latine*
        32:95–115.

Nikyema, J. J.
1977   Mémoire de fin d'études: Migration organisée de population (AVV). Oua-
        gadougou: AVV.

Bibliography

Onchocerciasis Control Programme (OCP)

1985   *Ten Years of Onchocerciasis Control.* OCP/GVA/85.1B. Geneva: World Health Organization.

1986   *Report on the Evaluation of the Socioeconomic Impact of the Onchocerciasis Control Programme.* Report No. JPC7.3 (OCP/86.7), Onchocerciasis Control Programme in West Africa, Joint Programme Committee, Seventh Session, Accra, Ghana, December 9–12.

1989   Onchocerciasis Control Programme in West Africa: Report, Joint Programme Committee. Tenth Session, The Hague, Netherlands, December 4–7, 1989.

1990   Onchocerciasis Control Programme in West Africa. Progress Report of the World Health Organization for 1990 (September 1, 1989–August 31, 1990). Eleventh session. Joint Programme Committee, Conakry, December 3–6, 1990. JPC11.2 (OCP/PR/90).

Ouédraogo, D.

1979   La Vallée du Kou (Haute Volta): Un sous-espace aliéné. In *Maitrise de l'espace agraire et développement en Afrique Tropicale,* edited by P. Couty et al. 481–90. Paris: ORSTOM.

Ouédraogo, F.

1976   *L'aménagement du bloc de Mogtedo dans le cadre de la mise en valeur des vallées des Volta.* Bordeaux: Université de Bordeaux III, Institut de Géographie Tropicale et d'Etudes Régionales.

Painter, T.

1990   *OCP Land Settlement Review, Country Case Study: Togo.* Binghamton, N.Y.: Institute for Development Anthropology.

Paris, F.

1980   *Etude géographique d'une zone d'endémie onchocerquienne (Bourgouriba et de la Volta Noire): Dynamique des cultures et d'habitat depuis 1974.* Ouagadougou: OCP and ORSTOM.

1983   L'Occupation des vallées de la Bougouriba et de la Volta Noire. Dynamique des cultures et de l'habitat depuis 1974. Ouagadougou: OCP et ORSTOM. Mimeo.

Pehaut, Y., and P. Rouamba

1958   *Vallée du Sourou: Problèmes humains (rapport préliminaire).* Bordeaux: ISHA.

Poats, S., M. Schmink, and A. Spring, eds.

1988   *Gender Issues in Farming Systems Research and Extension.* Boulder: Westview Press.

Preparatory Assistance Mission to the Governments of Dahomey, Ghana, Ivory Coast, Mali, Niger, Togo, Upper Volta (PAG)

1973   *Onchocerciasis Control in the Volta River Basin Area.* OCP/73.1. Geneva: World Health Organization.

Programme National de Gestion des Terroirs Villageois (PNGTV)

1989a   *Rapport de synthèse et d'analyse des expériences pilotes de gestion des terroirs villageois*. Ouagadougou: Ministère du Plan et de la Coopération, Secrétariat Général, PNGTV. Mai.

1989b   Le Programme National de Gestion des Terroirs Villageois: Orientations, aperçu du programme et propositions d'implantation durant sa 1ère phase. Ouagadougou: Ministère du Plan et de la Coopération, PNGTV. November.

Prost, A., and N. Prescott

1984   Cost-effectiveness of blindness prevention by the Onchocerciasis Control Programme in Upper Volta. *Bulletin of the World Health Organization* 62 (5):795–802.

Queant, T., and C. de Rouville

1969   *Etudes humaines sur la région du Gondo Sourou: Agriculteurs et éleveurs de la région du Gondo-Sourou*. Ouagadougou: Travaux de CVRS, n°. 1.

Raison, J.-P.

1979   Les Modèles d'intervention et leurs objectifs. In *Maîtrise de l'espace agraire et Développement en Afrique Tropicale: Logique Paysanne et Rationalité Technique*, edited by P. Couty, J. Y. Marchal, P. Pélissier, M. Poussi, G. Savonnet, and A. Schwartz, pp. 281–86. Paris: ORSTOM.

1981   La colonisation des terres neuves en Afrique Tropicale: réflexions sur quelques travaux récente. In *Les Prénoménes de "Frontière" dans les pays tropicaux. Travaux et Memoires de l'Institut des Hautes Etudes de l'Amerique Latine* 32:59–76.

1985   Les mouvements spontanés de migration en milieu rural dans les pays africains francophones: évaluation et propositions. Paper presented at the International Seminar on Planning for Settlements in Rural Areas: The Case of Spontaneous Settlements. Nairobi, Kenya. November 11–20.

Reardon, T., and C. Delgado

1989   Income Diversification of Rural Households in Burkina Faso. Washington, D.C.: The World Bank, Environment Department, Human Resources Development Division. Mimeo.

1990   Income Diversification of Rural Households in Burkina Faso. In *Professional Development Workshop on Dryland Management*, edited by J. Trolldalen, pp. 71–8. Washington, D.C.: The World Bank, Environmental Department.

Reardon, T., C. Delgado, and P. Matlon

1992   Determinants and Effects of Income Diversification Amongst Farm Households in Burkina Faso. *Journal of Developing Studies* 28:264–96.

Reardon, T., and N. Islam

1989   Issues of Sustainability in Agricultural Research in Africa. In *Proceedings of the Symposium on the Sustainability of Production Systems in Sub-Saharan Africa*, edited by S. W. Bie, pp. 43–68. As, Norway: NORAGRIC, Agricultural University of Norway (September 4–7).

Reardon, T., and P. Matlon
1989   Seasonal Food Insecurity and Vulnerability in Drought-Affected Regions of Burkina Faso. In *Seasonable Variability in Third World Agriculture: The Consequences for Food Security*, edited by D. Sahn, pp. 118–36. Baltimore: Johns Hopkins University Press.

Reardon, T., P. Matlon, and C. Delgado
1988   Coping with Household-level Food Insecurity in Drought-affected Areas of Burkina Faso. *World Development* 16:1065–74.

Remme, J., and J. B. Zongo
1989   Demographic Aspects of the Epidemiology and Control of Onchocerciasis in West Africa. In *Demography and Vector Bourne Diseases*, edited by M. Service, pp. 367–86. Boca Raton: CRC Press.

Remy, G.
1968   Les mouvements de population sur la rive gauche de la Volta Rouge region de Nobere (region de Nobere). *Cahiers ORSTOM: Série science humaine* 5 (2):45–66.
1973   *Les migrations de travail et les mouvements de colonisation Mossi.* Travaux et Documents 20. Paris: ORSTOM.
1975   Les migrations vers les "Terres Neuves": Un nouveau courant migratoire. In *Enquête sur les mouvements de population à partir du pays mossi* 1 (2): 331–454. Ouagadougou: ORSTOM.
1981   Les Mossi à la rencontre de la grande brousse (région de Dédougou, Haute-Volta). In *Les Phénomènes de "Frontière" dans les pays tropicaux. Travaux et Mémoires de l'Institut des Hautes Etudes de l'Amérique Latine* 32:117–31.

Rey, C.
1980   Analyse de la situation agro-pastorale dans l'ORD du Centre-Nord, Kaya (janvier 1980). RHV: Service Départementale de Planification du Département du Centre-Nord. Mimeo.

Reyna, S.
1980   Impact of Autorité des Aménagements des Vallées des Volta. Abidjan: REDSO/WA.AID.
1983   Dual Class Formation and Agrarian Underdevelopment: An Analysis of the Articulation of Production Relations in Upper Volta. *Canadian Journal of African Studies* 2 (17):221–34.
1986   Donor Investment Preference, Class Formation, and Existential Development: Articulation of Production Relations in Burkina Faso. In *Anthropology and Rural Development in West Africa*, edited by M. Horowitz and T. Painter, pp. 221–48. Boulder: Westview Press.
1987   The Emergence of Land Concentration in the West African Savanna. *American Ethnologist* 14 (3):523–41.

Rochette, R.
1976a   Notes sur les défrichements spontanés dans les blocs de Mogtedo,

Mogtedo-Bombore, Rapadama, Rapadama Sud and Wayen. Ouagadougou: AVV, Service Sociologie. Mimeo.

1976b   Les éleveurs Peuls pendant l'hivernage 1976 dans les blocs AVV de Wayen, Rapadama, Rapadama Sud, Mogtedo, et Mogtedo-Bombore (Rive Gauche de la Volta Blanche). Ouagadougou: AVV, Service Sociologie. Mimeo.

Ruthenberg, H.

1968   Some Characteristics of Smallholder Farming in Tanzania. In *Smallholder Farming and Smallholder Development in Tanzania*, edited by H. Ruthenberg, pp. 325–55. *Afrika-Studien* no. 14. Munich: Weltforum Verlag.

Salem-Murdock, M.

1989   *Arabs and Nubians in New Halfa: A Study of Settlement and Irrigation.* Salt Lake City: University of Utah Press.

Sanders, J.

1989a   Developing New Agricultural Technologies for the Sahelian Countries: The Burkina Faso Case. Mimeo.

1989b   Agricultural Research and Cereal Technology Introduction in Burkina Faso and Niger. *Agricultural Systems* 30:139–54.

1990   Resource Depletion and Policy Reform in the Sahel. West Lafayette, Ind.: Department of Agricultural Economics, Purdue University. May 29.

Sanders, J., J. Nagy and S. Ramaswamy.

1990   Developing New Agricultural Technologies for the Sahelian Countries: The Burkina Faso Case. *Economic Development and Cultural Change* 39(1):1–22.

Sanou, Saidou

1986   Land Tenure Structures in Agricultural Sector of Hounde, Burkina: A Study in Rural Social Change and Development. Ph.D. diss., Michigan State University.

Saul, M.

1979   Notes on the History and Demography of Bentenga. West Lafayette, Ind.: Department of Agricultural Economics. Mimeo.

1981   Beer, Sorghum and Women: Production for the Market in Rural Upper Volta. *Africa* 51(3):746–64.

1983   Work Parties, Wages and Accumulation in a Voltaic Village. *American Ethnologist* 10(1):77–96.

1984   The Quaranic School Farm and Child Labour in Upper Volta. *Africa* 54(2):71–87.

1988   Money and Land Tenure as Factors in Farm Size Differentiation in Burkina Faso. In *Land and Society in Contemporary Africa*, edited by R. Downs and S. Reyna, pp. 243–79. Hanover, N.H.: University Press of New England.

Savadogo, K.

1989a   Analysis of Off-Farm Income. Land Settlement Review Draft Site Report. Binghamton, N.Y.: Institute for Development Anthropology. Mimeo.

1989b   Land Tenure Systems. Land Settlement Review Draft Site Report. Binghamton, N.Y.: Institute for Development Anthropology. Mimeo.

1989c   Livestock in the Farming System. Land Settlement Review Draft Site Report. Binghamton, N.Y.: Institute for Development Anthropology. Mimeo.

1989d   Factors Explaining Household Food Production Systems. Land Settlement Review Draft Site Report. Binghamton, N.Y.: Institute for Development Anthropology. Mimeo.

Savadogo, K., and C. Wetta

1991   The Impact of Self-imposed Adjustment: The Case of Burkina Faso. *Innocenti Occasional Papers.* No. 15, Special Subseries: Structural Adjustment in Sub-Saharan Africa. April. UNICEF.

Savadogo, K., J. Sanders, and D. McMillan

1989   Farm and Female Incomes and Productivities in the River Blindness Settlement Programs of Burkina Faso. Land Settlement Review Draft Site Report. Binghamton, N.Y.: Institute for Development Anthropology.

Sawadogo, P.

1975a   Enquête socio-économique par entretien non-dirigé avec les exploitants dans les parcelles de Tiebele. Ouagadougou: AVV.

1975b   Etude des potentialités des différentes zones de Haute Volta en migrants suceptibles de s'installer sur les vallées des Volta. Ouagadougou: AVV, Service Sociologie.

Sawadogo, S.

1986   Du pays Mossi aux zones d'aménagement des vallées du Burkina: migration et mutation sociale au Burkina Faso. Thèse de doctorat de 3me cycle. Université de Toulouse le Mirail, Institut des Sciences Sociales.

1988a   Départ des migrants vers la Kompienga. Zorgho: Unité de Planification (UP) N° 1, Cellule Organisation du Monde Rural et Formation. March. Mimeo.

1988b   Etude de l'occupation de l'espace dans l'UD de la Bombore. Zorgho: UPI. December. Mimeo.

1989   Rapport Préliminaire—Départs de Mogtedo et Mogtedo-Bombore. Binghamton, N.Y.: Institute for Development Anthropology, Land Settlement Review Draft Site Report. Mimeo.

Schildkraut, E.

1978   *People of the Zongo: The Transformation of Ethnic Identities in Ghana.* Cambridge Studies in Social Anthropology, No. 20. Cambridge: Cambridge University Press.

Schildkraut, E., and G. Finnegan

1974   Themes and Variations in Mossi Ethnography. Unpublished manuscript.

Schultz, T.

1964   *Transforming Traditional Agriculture.* New Haven: Yale University Press.

Scudder, T.

1962   *The Ecology of the Gwembe Tonga.* Kariba Studies, II. Manchester: University of Manchester Press.

1968   Social Anthropology, Man-made Lakes, and Population Relocation in Africa. *Anthropological Quarterly* 41(3):168–76.

1969   Relocation, Agricultural Intensification and Anthropological Research. In *The Anthropology of Development in Sub-Saharan Africa.* Monographs for the Society of Applied Anthropology, 10.

1981   *The Development Potential of New Lands Settlement in the Tropics and Subtropics: A Global State-of-the-Art Evaluation with Specific Emphasis on Policy Implications.* Binghamton, N.Y.: Institute for Development Anthropology.

1984   *The Development Potential of New Lands Settlement in the Tropics and Subtropics: A Global State of the Art Evaluation with Specific Emphasis on Policy Implications.* AID Program Evaluation Discussion Paper No. 21. September. Washington, D.C.: United States Agency for International Development.

1985   *The Experience of the World Bank with Government-Sponsored Land Settlement.* Report No. 5625, Operations Evaluation Department. Washington, D.C.: The World Bank.

1991   Sociological Framework for the Analysis of New Lands Settlements. In *Putting People First: Sociological Variables in Rural Development,* 2nd ed., edited by M. Cernea, pp. 148–87. N.Y.: Oxford University Press.

Scudder, T., and E. Colson

1982   From Welfare to Development: A Conceptual Framework for the Analysis of Dislocated People. In *Involuntary Migration and Resettlement,* edited by A. Hansen and A. Oliver-Smith, pp. 267–88. Boulder: Westview Press.

Scudder, T., and K.P. Wimaladharma

1985   *The Accelerated Mahaweli (Sri Lanka) Programme and Dry Zone Development, Report No. 6.* Binghamton, N.Y.: Institute for Development Anthropology.

1990   *The Accelerated Mahaweli (Sri Lanka) Programme and Dry Zone Development, Report No. 7.* Binghamton, N.Y.: Institute for Development Anthropology.

Shaner, W., P. Philipp, and W. Schmehl

1982   *Farming Systems Research and Development: Guidelines for Developing Countries.* Boulder: Westview Press.

Singh, R.

1988   *Economics of the Family and Farming Systems in Sub-Saharan Africa.* Boulder: Westview Press.

Bibliography

Skinner, E. P.

1957　An Analysis of the Political System of the Mossi. *Transactions of the New York Academy of Science*, June, pp. 740–50.

1958　Christianity and Islam among the Mossi. *American Anthropologist* 60: 1102–19.

1960a　The Mossi Pogsioure. *Man* 60:20–23.

1960b　Traditional and Modern Patterns of Succession to Political Office among the Mossi of the Voltaic Republic. *The Journal of Human Relations* 8:394–406.

1962a　The Diffusion of Islam in an African Society. *Annals of the NY Academy of Science* 106:661–68.

1962b　Trade and Markets among the Mossi People. In *Markets in Africa*, edited by P. Bohannon and G. Dalton, pp. 237–78. Evanston: Northwestern University Press.

1964a　The Effect of Co-residence of Sister's Son on African Corporate Patrilineal Descent Groups. *Cahiers d'Etudes Africaines* 4(16):467–78.

1964b　*The Mossi of Upper Volta: The Political Development of a Sudanese People.* Stanford: Stanford University Press.

1965　Labor Migration Among the Mossi of Upper Volta. In *Urbanization and Migration in West Africa*, edited by H. Kuper, pp. 60–84. Berkeley: University of California Press.

1970a　The Changing Status of the "Emperor of the Mossi" Under Colonial Rule and Since Independence. In *West African Chiefs: Their Changing Status Under Colonial Rule and Independence*, edited by M. Crowder and O. Ikime, pp. 98–123. N.Y.: African Publishing Company.

1970b　Processes of Political Incorporation in Mossi Society. In *From Tribe to Nation in Africa*, edited by R. Cohen and J. Middleton, pp. 175–200. Scranton: Chandler Publishing.

1989　*The Mossi of Burkina Faso: Chiefs, politicians and soldiers.* Prospect Heights, Ill.: Waveland Press.

Société Africaine d'Etudes et de Développement (SAED)

1976　*Etude d'un programme régional de développement intègré.* 2 vols. Ouagadougou: SAED.

1980　*Aménagement hydroélectrique de la Kompienga. Etude socio-économique de la zone d'inondation.* Ouagadougou: SAED.

Société d'Etudes de Projets d'Investissement en Afrique (SEPIA)

1990　Etude Demographique: Projections de la population Burkinabè pour les années 1990, 1995 et 2000. Ouagadougou: SEPIA.

Songre, A.

1973　Mossi Emigration from Upper Volta: The Facts and Implications. In *Employment in Africa: Some Critical Issues*, pp. 199–255. Geneva: International Labour Office.

Sorbo, G.M.

1976   *Scheme and Off-Scheme Interests: A Study of Nubian Resettlement in the Sudan.* Norway: University of Bergen.

1985   *Tenants and Nomades in Eastern Sudan: A Study of Economic Adaptations in the New Halfa Scheme.* Trenton: The Red Sea Press.

Sowers, F.

1986   Moving On: Migration and Agropastoral Production Among the Fulbe in Southern Burkina Faso (Mossiland). Ph.D. diss., University of California, Berkeley.

Sprey, L., and C. de Jong

1977a   Agricultural Development in Upper Volta: The AVV Settlement Projects. In *Annual Report 1976,* pp. 31–6. Wageningen, Netherlands: International Institute for Land Reclamation and Improvement.

1977b   Aspects de Développement Agricole dans le projet de colonisation de l'Autorité des Aménagements des Vallées des Volta (AVV). Wageningen, Netherlands: International Institute for Land Reclamation and Improvement.

Tabsoba, E. K.

1973   Rural Development in Upper Volta. Paper presented at the Develop from Below Field Trip/Workshop, October 12–20, 1973. Addis Ababa, Ethiopia.

Terrible, M.

1979   *Occupation du sol en Haute-Volta: Son évolution entre 1952–56 et 1975.* Ouagadougou: Centre Régional de Télédétection de Ouagadoguou.

Thompson, V., and R. Adloff

1975   French Economic Policy in Tropical Africa. In *Colonialism in Africa 1970–1960,* Vol. 4, edited by P. Duignan and L. Gann, pp. 127–64. Cambridge: Cambridge University Press.

Van Raay, G., and J. Hilhorst

1981   Land Settlement and Regional Development in the Tropics: Results, Prospects and Options. Draft Discussion Paper. The Hague: Institute for Social Studies Advisory Board.

Vayssie, J.

1982   L'Evaluation du bloc de Mogtedo. Ouagadougou: AVV.

Weitz, R., D. Pelley, and L. Applebaum

1978   Employment and Income Generation in New Settlement Projects. World Employment Paper 10, Working Papers 3. Geneva: International Labour Office 10/WP 3.

Williams, J.

1974   Scourge of Sahel Rivers. *The Geographical Magazine,* November, pp. 78–9.

The World Bank

1989   *Burkina Faso Economic Memorandum.* 2 vols. Report No. 7594-BUR. Washington, D.C.: The World Bank.

Bibliography

World Health Organization (WHO)

1980   Onchocerciasis Control in the Volta River Basin Area: Information Paper. OCP/74.1. Rev. 4, May.

Yanogo, A.-F.

1988   Contribution de l'AVV—Expérience Mogtedo-Bombore. Zorgho: AVV-UPI.

Younger, S., and J.-B. Zongo

1989   West Africa: The Onchocerciasis Control Programme. In *Successful Development in Africa: Case Studies of Projects, Programs and Policies*, edited by R. Bheenick, pp. 27–56. Washington, D.C.: The World Bank.

Zahan, D.

1963   Problèmes sociaux posés par la transplantation des Mossi sur les terres irriguées de l'Office du Niger. In *African Agrarian Systems*, edited by D. Biebuyck, pp. 392–403. London: Oxford University Press.

1966   Immigrant Communities of Office du Niger. In *Social Implications of Industrialisation and Urbanisation in Africa South of the Sahara*, edited by International Africa Institute, pp. 99–101. Paris: UNESCO.

1967   The Mossi Kingdoms. In *West African Kingdoms in the Nineteenth Century*, edited by D. Forde and P. Kaberry, pp. 152–78. London: Oxford University Press.

Index

adult labor equivalent (ALE): impact on farm size, 45–46; net income per unit, 117–18; production expenses of, 116–17

agriculture: income from, in home villages, 74–75; income from, in V3, 71, 72, 74–75; innovations in, 72–73; net income from, 117, 168; net value of production, 169; rain-fed, 7, 12, 16; subsistence, 12; sustainable, 22

ALE. *See* adult labor equivalent

ancestor veneration, 30

animal husbandry: development planning for, 7, 16, 176; expenses for, 116, 184; FulBe people and, 82, 184; income opportunities from, 80, 82, 118–19, 176; livestock damage to crops, 119, 179; manure used in farming, 176; net returns on, 184; number of animals in AVV settlements, 118–19; role in household economy, 80; women's dependence on, 79, 82

animal traction: introduction of, 12, 45; as part of project cultivation package, 45; profits from sale of animals, 74–75; repurchase of animals, 74–75

animists: in Damesma, 59–60; in Mossi population, 30; in V3, 59–60

Autorité des Aménagements des Vallées des Volta (AVV). *See* Volta Valley Authority

AVV. *See* Volta Valley Authority

bicycles, 85

Bissa communities, 12

Bittou, 21

Black Volta. *See* Mouhoun River basin

blindness. *See* onchocerciasis

Bombore River, 48, 50

boodkasma. *See* elders

boodoos. *See* clans

Mouhoun River basin: cotton growing in, 12, 16; Dagara villages in, 12

Murphy, Josette, xv, 152

Muslim population: in Damesma, 59–60; in V3, 59–60

nabas. See village chiefs

Nakambe River basin: Bissa villages on, 12; forest management in, 177; FulBe livestock grazing in, 103, 176; grazing and ranching projects for, 176–77; land use categories of, 16 (map 8); planned settlement of, 15, 22, 47–48; refugee villages during colonial period, 14

Nana, Jean Baptiste, 155

Nazinon River basin: land use categories of, 16 (map 8); planned settlement of, 15

neighborhoods in Damesma, 23, 26

Netherlands' financial support of AVV, 18

Netting, R., 185

new lands settlement models, 136–40, 149; alternatives to AVV model, 139–43; basic infrastructures and, 140; constraints to success, 136–37; difficulties in contingency planning, 140; diversified production systems in, 140; existing social patterns of settlers, 140–41; four stage (Scudder), xvi, 96–98, 141, 142; indicators for success of, 139–41; minimal government involvement in policies, 139; population density and, 9, 39. *See also* settlement of new lands

new lands settlement projects: Office du Niger, 174–75; Vallée du Kou, 175; Vallée du Sourou, 175. *See also* Volta Valley Authority

ni kiema. See elders

noncrop production activities, economic impact of, 86

nonfarm employment opportunities, 132, 184

occupations, nonfarm, 82–86, 119–23

OCP. *See* Onchocerciasis Control Programme

Office du Niger project, 174–75

Office National d'Aménagement des Territoirs, 135, 184–85. *See also* Volta Valley Authority

ONAT. *See* Office National d'Aménagement des Territoirs

onchocerciasis: blindness and, 1–2, 7–8, 173; control zone for, 1; deterrent to new lands settlement, 14–15, 135–36; economic impact of, 1–2; incidence of, 7, 8; incidence rates and population density, 12; infection process in, 173; treatment of, 8; vector of, 8

Onchocerciasis Control Programme (OCP), xix, 2; assessment studies, 9; in Burkina Faso, 12, 15, 143–44; control zone, xxi (map 1), 8; cost effectiveness of, 9; costs of, 9, 144, 147; development planning and, 136, 147–48; Economic Unit, 8–9; foreign donor interest in, xix, 143–44, 147–48; goal of, 10; impact on new lands settlement, 135–36; insecticide treatments of control zone, 8; socioeconomic impact of, 9; takeover by African nationals, 8; vector control as major activity, 10

Ouagadougou (Burkina Faso), 7

Ouédraogo, Moustapha, 187

Ouédraogo, Tinga, xvii, 187

Ouédraogo (clan name), 28–29

oxen. *See* animal traction

PAM (Programme Alimentaire Mondial), 45

pastoralists. *See* FulBe people

PDAOV (Projet de Développement Agricole de la Boucle du Mouhoun), 175
People of the Zongo (Schildkraut), 40
Piiktenga market, 106, 180
planned settlements: cost recovery from, 16; costs per household, 16; Nakambe River basin, 15, 47–48; Nazinon River basin, 15; recommendations for success of, 130–33. *See also* new lands settlement projects
PNGTV (Programme National de Gestion des Terroirs Villageois), 111–12, 182–83
Poebila settlers in V3, 56
Poedogo clan immigrants to V3, 56, 57; religious affiliation of, 59
population density: effects on new lands settlement, 9, 39; in relation to river basins, 12, 13 (map 7); relationship to onchocerciasis incidence, 12
poverty: in central plateau region, 12; in Sahel region, 4, 12
private domain lands, 42
Programme Alimentaire Mondial (PAM), 45
Programme National de Gestion des Terroirs Villageois (PNGTV), 111–12, 182–83
Projet Coton, 175
public domain lands, 42
Purdue University (Department of Agricultural Economics), 152

rainfall: average in West Africa, 3 (map 3); mean normalized, 6 (fig. 1.1)
ranching projects in land use planning, 176–77
Rapadama (village), sponsored settlements at, 102, 103, 112, 130
Red Volta River. *See* Nazinon River basin

research methodology, xix–xxvi, 86–87, 151–57
resource management skills of settlers, 138
Révolution Démocratique et Populaire, 111
Reyna, S., 137
rice growing, 4, 177–78
rituals, celebratory, 64–65
river basins of Burkina Faso, 10–15; agroclimatic zones of, 11 (map 6); foreign donor development interest, 143–44; forests of, 10, 12; government's motivation for development, 144; irrigation potential of, 12; lack of settlement in valleys, 14; problems in development of, 135–36, 143–44; state proprietorship of, 42; use by FulBe people, 176
river blindness. *See* onchocerciasis
Rome Food Conference, 4

saghse. *See* neighborhoods
Sahel region: agroclimatic zones, 3 (map 3); definition of, 2; drought years 1968–73, 3–7, 143; economic conditions of, 4; economic history of, 2; foreign aid disbursements, 6 (fig. 1.2); map of, 2; poverty of, 4
Sanders, John, 187
Sankara, Thomas, xxiv, 111
Saul, Mehir, 30–31, 177
Savadogo, Kimseyinga, 155, 187
Sawadogo clan, 28–29
Sawadogo, Sommaila, 187
Scudder, Thayer, xvi, 96–98, 141, 142
settlement of new lands: census in AVV project areas, 163; cycles of, 9; rate in AVV project, 162; spontaneous, 9, 102–3. *See also* new lands settlement models
settlers in AVV villages: animal hus-

bandry expenses, 116, 184; contracts of, 42–43; crop production expenses, 116; cultivation techniques promoted for use, 44, 54, 72–73; dismissal from project of, 179; economic mobility of, 138; eligibility requirements of, 44; farm sizes, 43; governance of, 46–47; income growth of, 130, 141, 146; nonfarm income sources, 119–23; per family costs, 167; relationships with FulBe people, 109–10; relationships with indigenous people, 109–10; resource management skills of, 138; responsibilities of, 44–45; social traditions undercut by policies, 68–70; views of, 147

settlers in V3: bond friendships among, 58; community building between, 53–54; compliance with planning restrictions, 145; conflict resolution between, 66–68; cotton strike of, 98; demand for machine-made goods, 86; differential incomes among, 139; dropout of, 101–2; economic diversification of, 71–72, 79–82; entrepreneurial success of, 142–43; factors influencing success of, 136; fictive relationships between, 58; hostility between, 55–56, 179–80; income from crop production, 71, 72, 74–75, 146; indigenous population and, 63–64; joking relationships between, 58; labor migration of, 90–91; leaders of, 54–55; livestock as investment of, 80, 82; migration to Kompienga region, 101, 147; nonagricultural expenditures, 89 (table 5.3); noncrop production activities of, 86; nonfarm employment of, 82–86; outmigration of, 127–30, 139, 142, 147; predictions

of economic success for, 97–98; relationship with home villages, 64–66; reliance upon extension services, 54; religious affiliations of, 59–60; responses to government restrictions, 137, 145–46; secondary occupations of, 82–86, 119; social tension among, 139; unofficial cropping activities of, 86, 145–46; women's economic role as, 93–95

Skinner, Elliott, 25, 177
social institutions in planned settlements, 57–58, 68–70, 140–41
social traditions of settlers: growth of new mechanisms in, 68–69; impact of AVV policies on, 68–70
soils, condition of, 1, 7, 12, 113
sorghum production. *See* food grain production
sosoga. *See* work parties
spontaneous settlement of new lands, 9, 102–3
standard of living: projected impact on, by settlement project, 19
state laws and land tenure, 41–42, 110, 138
Statistical Service (of Volta Valley Authority): farm income analysis by, 87; farm-monitoring survey by, 72–73; farm-monitoring survey program, 152
subsistence agriculture, 12
sustainable agriculture, 22

Taptoin village, 49–50
tenga naba. *See* village chiefs
terrains: organization for cultivation, 78; size of, 36
Togo as part of Voltaic Culture Area, 27
transportation options, 85
trees in settlements areas, illegal cutting of, 177
trypanosomiasis epidemics, 14

About the Author

DELLA E. MCMILLAN began her research on follow-up planning in Burkina Faso's river basins affected by control as a graduate student at Northwestern University in 1977. Since then she has returned for numerous restudies. Between 1981 and 1988, McMillan served on the faculty of the University of Florida and the University of Kentucky. From November 1988 to September 1990 she was the deputy director of an eleven-country review of settlement and development in the onchocerciasis control zone of West Africa that was conducted by the Institute for Development Anthropology. Since 1990 she has worked as an independent consultant with the United States Agency for International Development, the United Nations Development Program, and the World Bank. She also serves as a research affiliate of the Department of Anthropology and the Center for African Studies at the University of Florida and as a Senior Research Associate with Tropical Research and Development in Gainesville, Florida. She has edited *Anthropology and Food Policy: Human Dimensions of Food Policy* and *Food in Sub-Saharan Africa* (with Art Hansen) and co-authored a two-volume series on river blindness as part of the World Bank Technical Paper Series (numbers 192 and 200), as well as numerous articles and chapters in books.